The primary requisite for writing about food is a good appetite.

—A. J. LIEBLING

THE SPLENDID TABLE'S®
HOW TO EAT WEEKENDS

THE SPLENDID TABLE'S®
HOW TO EAT WEEKENDS

New recipes, stories & opinions FROM PUBLIC RADIO'S AWARD-WINNING FOOD SHOW

LYNNE ROSSETTO KASPER AND SALLY SWIFT

Clarkson Potter/Publishers
NEW YORK

ALSO BY LYNNE ROSSETTO KASPER

The Splendid Table

The Italian Country Table

ALSO BY LYNNE ROSSETTO KASPER AND SALLY SWIFT

The Splendid Table's How to Eat Supper

Copyright © 2011 by Minnesota Public Radio
Photographs copyright © 2011 by Ellen Silverman

Published in the United States by Clarkson Potter/Publishers, an imprint of the Crown Publishing Group,
a division of Random House, Inc., New York.
www.crownpublishing.com
www.clarksonpotter.com

CLARKSON POTTER is a trademark and POTTER with colophon is a
registered trademark of Random House, Inc.

Library of Congress Cataloging-in-Publication Data
Kasper, Lynne Rossetto.
  The splendid table's, how to eat weekends / Lynne Rossetto Kasper and Sally Swift. — 1st ed.
    p. cm.
  Includes index.
  (alk. paper)
  1. Cooking. 2. International cooking. I. Swift, Sally. II. Splendid table (Radio program) III. Title.
IV. Title: How to eat weekends.
  TX714.K3677 2011
  641.5—dc22   2010052630

ISBN 978-0-307-59055-8
eISBN 978-0-307-95332-2

Printed in China

Design by Wayne Wolf/Blue Cup Creative
Jacket design by Wayne Wolf/Blue Cup Creative
Jacket photographs by Ellen Silverman

10 9 8 7 6 5 4 3 2 1

First Edition

DEDICATION

Once again this book is for Frank, **the man I love,** and for Jenny Luebke and Jen Russell, who have made the show fly for all these years, no matter what.
LRK

For my love Michael, and our hungry pack of wolves—Oliver, Lucy, and Mackenzie.
SS

Contents

I

INTRODUCTION

We may not have known it at the time, but the minute we put pen to paper for our last book, *The Splendid Table's How to Eat Supper,* we started writing this one, too. That book was about weeknight cooking, and though quick, seat-of-the-pants suppers are a staple in both of our lives, there was a lot we had to leave by the side of the road, like a bunch of our favorite dishes. We decided those dishes meant for the other two days of the week needed a book of their own.

What is eating weekends? We think of it as the luxury and the pleasure of taking the time to make things from scratch because they taste better than anything found on a supermarket shelf. It's about spending a lazy afternoon in a new neighborhood where maybe we don't speak the language, but can find new markets and restaurants. It's about the excitement of weaving ourselves into other cultures, and bringing them to our tables with our own hands.

One thing that separates Americans from the rest of the world is that ultimately at our origins most of us are immigrants, a gift for food lovers and opportunity to learn more about each other.

More people are finding their way to the stove today than in half a century. As a nation, we're rediscovering that cooking is the balm for much of what ails us: it's a way to save on food costs, a way to unwind from the stresses of the day, a way to reconnect with those we care about, a way to ensure that the foods we eat nourish us, and it's a way to escape without the expensive plane ticket.

By the time you're reading this, our radio show, *The Splendid Table®*, will have been on the air for nearly twenty years. You know the saying about having a front row seat at the revolution? That's what we feel like.

We have seen how far America's relationship with food has evolved. We Americans know more about food than ever before. Given the option, we're no longer content to eat whatever supermarkets and chain restaurants offer. We've become demanding and are changing the marketplace. We want authentic flavors, sound ingredients, and foods that feed our minds as well as our bellies.

Cooks and noncooks alike have become more aware and curious about the dimensions of food that aren't obvious. We want to know where our food comes from, how it's grown, who grows it, under what conditions, and how it arrives in our markets. We're now compelled to debate the hard topics like school lunch reform, how government food dollars are spent, and how to be certain that our food is healthily raised and accessible, no matter where we are on the economic scale. Terms like *local, organic,* and *sustainable* have a permanent place in our vocabulary. A long-overdue revolution is taking place on American plates—in both what we eat and why.

Our American palates have changed as well. As we were working on several of the more traditional recipes for this book, we noticed a flatness in some. We're used to such rock-'em-sock-'em flavors today that many of those older recipes didn't make the cut. But some did.

We debated for weeks about whether to include Renaissance Lasagne (page 145). It's a recipe about which we're both very sentimental, and it's based on the sensuous and little-known tastes of the Renaissance. Lynne devoted years to researching and studying that period in Italy. In fact, she is on a first-name basis with Lucrezia Borgia (the infamous yet beloved Duchess of Ferrara of the sixteenth century). That research resulted in her masterful (Sally's word) first book, *The Splendid Table.* It was that book and, in fact, that recipe, that drove Sally to call Lynne all those years ago to make a radio program. So you see the attachment, right?

Our dilemma was that the lasagne is a far cry from the tomato-and-cheese-sauced version most of us know. This lasagne is a subtle blend of cinnamon-scented meat ragù and cream, and delicate sheets of pasta. It should be served simply—alone, as a separate course. We wondered, will it be too quiet for you? Will you like it?

This book brought us back to a love of quiet dishes. We realized that simplicity can be just as satisfying as the constant pursuit of exotic flavors and cutting-edge technique. That said, not everything in this book is easy. Some of these recipes are projects that require time, commitment, and patience. We promise you, though, that every one of the monumental ones here is worth the time. They will pay you back tenfold for the effort you invest, and we will be there to help with the tricky parts. Remember that there is a reason these dishes are special. There's no reason to waste time, money, and energy on anything less than extraordinary. We figure you feel the same way.

And then there's reality—share the work if you can; lighten the load. Look for the camaraderie of four or six hands together at the stove and in the sink. Make a trip to the Indian market a weekend family outing rather than a last-minute, solo, end-of-the-day scramble. Slow down, take two days to prepare a meal, invite friends, and revel. It's the weekend: let loose.

One of the reasons we've worked so happily together for so many years is that both of us look for the intersections between food and life. We're always looking to understand how what goes into our mouths transcends taste. It's the driving force behind the radio show and has brought about interviews with a fascinating mix of people from every imaginable dimension of this force we call *food*.

With their stories and our own, we take you inside the bigger picture behind many of our recipes, including how, when, and why these dishes are eaten on their home turf. You'll find history, lore, serving and shopping guides, and menus celebrating the cuisines we Americans have come to yearn for.

Here's hoping that what you find on the following pages will make you hungry, and bring new ideas and possibilities for new adventures. But mostly, we hope it will inspire you to rediscover the simple joys of cooking. The two of us take so much pleasure in it. And nothing would make us happier than for the recipes we've assembled here to help you do the same.

Lynne and Sally

We asked wine writer Michael Franz, editor and co-creator of *Wine Review Online* (and Sally's husband), if he might come up with the proper wines to set off some of these dishes. In a moment of uninformed generosity, Michael accepted. Now, after eighteen months of tasting every dish in these pages, sometimes twice, and dealing with our penchant for acidic flavors, spices, and chiles of all sorts (all usually wine's dire enemies), Michael offered us this introduction. And that was before he got our profound thanks.

UNDERSTANDING THE WINES IN THIS BOOK

Testing wine pairings for the dishes in this book was an interesting process—and also a bit of a workout. Many trips to the basement for additional bottles were required after encountering flavors that made me wonder whether my intuitive picks could be bested by other wines.

You'll find a lot of complex dishes in these pages, including a fair number with tart, sweet, or spicy elements that will stretch your palate while also providing plenty of surprises on the wine side of the equation. For example, Chardonnay has become the whipping-boy wine for many foodies in recent years, and yet it matched beautifully with far more of these dishes than I would have guessed.

Since the spirit of Lynne and Sally's book is all about culinary adventure and discovery, I've tried to leave room for you to experiment by offering wine advice in general stylistic terms, though I've often provided a specific wine as an example for those seeking more precise guidance.

Cheers,
Michael Franz

A SHOPPER'S *Manifesto*

It's no longer about just us. Buy food today and you might as well have dropped a pebble in a pond—that purchase reverberates in the world.

Some of us believe we're healthier for eating from local, organic, and sustainable farmers and producers. Hopefully that's true, but eating today touches the environment, the ethical treatment of people and animals, the vitality of communities and their lands, and the value of the small and unique. And yes, how we eat directly touches the people we care about.

These days we're all doing the best with what we have, but if at all possible, please try to prepare these dishes with organic ingredients. That USDA "Certified Organic" sticker isn't the perfect solution. But for now, though, it is a better option than most.

In the best of all possible worlds, shop as close to the source as possible. When we can, we get a lift from handing our money over to the farmer who actually grew the lettuce.

MENUS, BACKSTORIES, AND GAME PLANS

It doesn't matter where you get your appetite, so long as you eat it at home.

—ANONYMOUS

Korean tacos?

Mexican chile in your sushi?

Wonton skins for your mozzarella—

curried lamb ravioli? That's us. Americans. For us, the big jumbled mix of our immigrant cuisines reigns supreme. So does our unique, open-minded curiosity about other cultures' foods. We've got a chance to eat and cook in ways that would stand Fannie Farmer's hair on end.

Weekend cooking is a chance to venture into new territory, be it checking out the markets and hole-in-the-wall eateries where English isn't a first language, or taking home a culture in your grocery sack.

These menus are some favorites—a Mexican *comida,* a Vietnamese home-style Sunday lunch, a scaled-down Italian feast from the Renaissance, Indian party food, and a real Chinese celebration. Each menu has its own backstory—how the meal is eaten on its home turf, why the dishes are what they are, information on key techniques to take into your kitchen, and, perhaps most important, where to go to learn more. Each menu that follows lays out a game plan so you can get to the table with some semblance of sanity and enjoy your company.

Consider these menus introductions. Several lifetimes are needed to truly know each of these cuisines. In short, we know what we don't know and urge you to dive deeper by looking into the works of some of the masters of these cuisines, which are listed at the end of each menu.

Wine pairing suggestions and storage instructions are included in the individual recipes.

A Mexican COMIDA

THE MENU

Tomatillo Salsa with Fresh Cheese from El Cardenal
in Mexico City (PAGE 52)

Jicama & Mango Sticks in Chile & Lime (PAGE 40)

Yucatán Pork in Banana Leaves (*Cochinita Pibil*) (PAGE 223)

Simple Black Beans & Rice

Corn Tortillas

Chile-Spiked Mexican Wedding Cakes (PAGE 302)

Watermelon Water (*Agua de Sandia*) (PAGE 229)

The burritos and tacos, the guacamole and chips we eat barely touch the astonishing tastes waiting in each of Mexico's regions. There, each cook, village, and valley shows off its own dishes. Mexican food could never be summed up by one type of tamal, taco, or, for that matter, one kind of bean. It is incredibly simple food, and at the same time deeply sophisticated, with unexpected flavors and ways of combining ingredients.

Surprisingly, many of Mexico's dishes aren't spicy hot. Here is a guide to cooking a Mexican meal full of authentic flavors, pretty extraordinary ones at that.

How to Eat a Mexican Meal

The most important meal of the day is the *comida*, which is eaten between 2:00 and 4:00 p.m. That is after a full *desayuno* (breakfast), a midday *antojo* (craving), but luckily before the *cena* (light dinner). It sounds daunting, but portions are appropriate—tacos, for instance, are the size of a small child's hand, not its head, as they are in the United States.

The *comida* usually starts with a small snack or soup, then a main course of meat or fish served with rice and beans, and a dessert. Salsa and corn tortillas are always on the table. Beer, wine, and Mexico's delicious freshly flavored waters—*agua frescas*—made from fruits and flowers are served throughout the meal.

PULLING IT OFF

Two Days Prior:

Marinate the Yucatán Pork in its spice paste.

Bake the Chile-Spiked Mexican Wedding Cakes.

One Day Prior:

Roast the Yucatán Pork in Banana Leaves.

Day of the Comida:

Make the Tomatillo Salsa with Fresh Cheese, the Jicama & Mango Sticks in Chile & Lime, the black beans and rice, and the Watermelon Water.

Reheat the Yucatán Pork in Banana Leaves.

Simple Black Beans

Jicama & Mango Sticks in Chili & Lime

Watermelon Water (Agua de Sandía)

A Mexican Comida

Pickled Onions

DRIP DROP ROAS

No 8

Yucatán Pork in Banana Leaves (Cochinita Pibil)

Tomatillo Salsa with Fresh Cheese

The MEXICAN PANTRY and KITCHEN

HELPFUL CULINARY TOOLS:
- A citrus squeezer for juicing citrus fruits
- A blender (a Mexican cook's best friend) for salsas, seasoning pastes, and drinks
- A *molcajete*, a volcanic rock mortar and pestle, the traditional tool for grinding spices and making sauces

UNIQUE CULINARY TECHNIQUES:

Roasting over an Open Flame or on a Hot Griddle:
This is one of the most distinctive techniques in cooking authentic Mexican. Chiles, tomatillos, garlic, onions, and masa are all routinely roasted, toasted, and charred over high heat, often just an open flame. The technique gives the food an intensity and earthiness hard to duplicate elsewhere. See the directions for the spice paste in our Yucatán Pork in Banana Leaves (page 223) for an example.

Frying of the Sauce:
This is a technique that is shared with Indian, Southeast Asian, and ancient Spice Islands cuisines. Isn't it interesting that it's common with cultures that favor intricate spicing? In Mexico, a sauce (it could be salsa, a complicated mole, or simple tomato sauce) is puréed and then sautéed in hot fat until the sauce "breaks," or separates with pools of oil on the surface. Just as in flame roasting, this additional frying deepens and concentrates the flavors and builds a sauce with more structure.

SHOPPING A MEXICAN MARKET—ESSENTIAL FOODS AND FLAVORS

Jars, Bottles, and Cans: chipotles in adobo sauce, salsas, hot sauces, membrillo (sweet quince paste), cajeta (Mexico's goat milk), dulce de leche

Frozen Foods: tamales, banana leaves, fruit purées, huitlacoche (corn mushrooms)

Spices and Aromatics: dried whole and ground chiles, achiote (annatto) seed, canela (cinnamon sticks), avocado leaves, epazote, Mexican oregano

Dry Goods: beans, rice, hominy, masa harina, tortillas

Fresh Produce: chiles, tomatillos, avocados, limes, plantains, jicama, fresh epazote

Cured and Cooked Products: crema, Queso Fresco, Queso Añejo, chorizo sausage

Some Brands We Like: Goya, La Morena, San Marcos, Herdez, La Costeña, Orale, Badia, La Flor

A word
ABOUT SHOPPING ETHNIC MARKETS

These are the places where quality and selection can be plentiful while prices are lower than at specialty food shops. **Check the ingredients lists for anything that doesn't sound like you'd want it in your kitchen,** but please don't limit yourself to our shopping lists. There's an entire world of new foods out there to discover.

BUILDING THE **LIBRARY** **MEXICO**

Rick Bayless, *Authentic Mexican,* HarperCollins, 1987, and *Rick Bayless's Mexican Kitchen,* Scribner, 1996 **Diana Kennedy,** *The Essential Cuisines of Mexico,* Clarkson Potter, 2009, and *From My Mexican Kitchen: Techniques and Ingredients,* Clarkson Potter, 2003 **Ricardo Muñoz,** *Stuffed Chiles of Mexico: An Anthology of Recipes,* UNAM, 2009 (bilingual), and *Los Clásicos de la Cocina Mexicana,* Larousse, 2009 (in Spanish) **Patricia Quintana,** *The Taste of Mexico,* Stewart, Tabori & Chang, 1986, and *Cuisine of the Water Gods,* Simon & Schuster, 1994 **Susannah Trilling,** *Seasons of My Heart: A Culinary Journey Through Oaxaca,* Ballantine, 1999 **Maria Dolores Torres Yzabel,** *The Mexican Gourmet,* Thunder Bay Press, 1995

The Power of Light

Architect Sarah Susanka, creator of The Not So Big House franchise (www.notsobighouse.com), believes that eating under pools of light that are centered on the table brings on instant intimacy. That one thing, a pool of light in the right place, makes the meal, the table, and we who gather around it the focal point of the room.

The ideal situation in Sarah's eyes is a pendant hanging directly over the table, and it is the height of that fixture that is most important. Sarah explains that many people make the mistake of hanging their lights too high. They should hang low over the table, just above eye level, for the most dramatic and comfortable effect.

It is side lighting that makes things cozy. Place wall sconces or table lamps on dimmers elsewhere in the room so they can be easily adjusted. Dimmers also can give you a dining room where there isn't one. Leave your table area dark. When you want everyone to sit down, bring up the dining area lights and dim the lights in the living area. Theatrical and very effective.

If you're saddled with glaring overhead fluorescents, turn them off and go for candle-light. Never underestimate the festivity of a nice big candelabra and a collection of votives on the table—everyone (and every dish) looks better in candlelight.

On the Perfect
Dining Room Table

Is there a table that can draw out the shy, push back the bossy, and make the food more delicious? The definitive answer came from a surprising source—writer, director, and hostess extraordinaire Nora Ephron. Nora campaigns for round tables because of their perfect flexibility. Three can eat as easily as eight; you can see *and* hear everyone else, which means lively talk across the table is practically ensured; yet you are still able to tuck quietly into a conversation with the person seated next to you.

Additional seats can always be sneaked in because no table legs or corners get in the way, and food is easily passed and shared, both around and across. And when you need even more space, adding leaves turns a round table into an oval—Lynne's personal favorite for its space-saving qualities.

A
HOME-STYLE
Vietnamese
SUNDAY LUNCH

THE MENU

Rice Paper Rolls of Herbs & Shrimp (PAGE 42)

Cucumber & Melon Salad with Mint (PAGE 80)

Vietnamese Green Mango Noodle Salad
with Grilled Pork (PAGE 128)

Caramelized Catfish Sand Pot (PAGE 141)

Simple White Rice

Ginger Syrup for All Seasons (PAGE 321) with Asian Pears

Vietnamese Coffee*

* **In a glass, mix a strong shot of espresso with
sweetened condensed milk to taste.
Add additional regular milk to taste.
Pour over ice or drink lukewarm.**

No other Asian cuisine plays the contrasts of fresh herbs, fruits, and vegetables against vivid, sometimes forceful flavorings quite the way Vietnamese cooking does. Each part of Asia has its identifying mix of fresh and fermented ingredients (the two foundations of all Asian flavors), but Vietnam's versions are unsurpassed. This collection of dishes starts you off with a basic idea of what this amazing cuisine embraces.

How to Eat a Vietnamese Meal

In Vietnam, the food is usually served all at once, a free-for-all family style. You use chopsticks, and each person is responsible for a nearby dish and must be ready to pass it on demand. Most Vietnamese foods are best eaten from a rice bowl. Scoop a small portion of rice into the bowl, and top it with small pieces of the dish. For dishes that don't fit in bowls, such as our Rice Paper Rolls of Herbs & Shrimp (page 42), pass a stack of small salad plates, and place individual bowls of dipping sauce alongside. Condiments are constants on the table: pickles, fried shallots, sprigs of fresh herbs, sliced scallions, and those ubiquitous dipping sauces. Everyone seasons and eats as they wish.

PULLING IT OFF

Two Days Prior:

Make the Caramelized Catfish Sand Pot and the Ginger Syrup for All Seasons.

Make the Nuoc Cham Dipping Sauce for the Rice Paper Rolls.

One Day Prior:

Prep the ingredients for the Vietnamese Green Mango Noodle Salad with Grilled Pork and the Rice Paper Rolls of Herbs & Shrimp.

Day of the Lunch:

Assemble the Rice Paper Rolls of Herbs & Shrimp, the Vietnamese Green Mango Noodle Salad with Grilled Pork, and the Ginger Syrup for All Seasons with Asian Pears.

Make the white rice and the Cucumber & Melon Salad with Mint.

Reheat the Caramelized Catfish Sand Pot.

Make the Vietnamese Coffee.

A Home-Style Vietnamese Sunday Lunch

Caramelized Catfish Sand Pot

Cucumber & Melon Salad with Mint

Rice Paper Rolls of Herbs & Shrimp

Simple White Rice

Vietnamese Green Mango Noodle Salad with Grilled Pork

The VIETNAMESE PANTRY and KITCHEN

HELPFUL CULINARY TOOLS:
- Sand pot clay cookware (see page 139) for casseroles and soups
- Bamboo skewers for grilling and serving

UNIQUE CULINARY TECHNIQUES:

A quick lesson in Vietnamese flavorings and techniques is embodied in these traditional seasonings. Each one is like a small blueprint of how to construct Vietnam's unique tastes.

Dipping Sauce (Nuoc Cham):
Take a bite of a freshly wrapped spring roll dipped in Vietnam's classic nuoc cham and you will begin your culinary education in how Vietnam balances flavors. That dipping sauce works together fermented, sweet, sour, and the intensity of accent seasonings—here they are garlic and chile. Other sauces, of course, figure in the cuisine, but this is the hallmark sauce of Vietnam.

Caramel Sauce (page 142):
Vietnamese cooks use caramel sauce made from sugar and water to give stews and even grilled meats and tofu beautiful color and a surprisingly nutty sweetness.

The Table Salad:
Table salad platters are set out along with grilled foods, soups, and stir-fries (especially ones from South Vietnam) and are heaped with fresh greens, lime wedges, sliced chiles, and herbs such as mint, coriander, saw leaf, and holy basil. Tear them into your soup, over your rice, or into a salad, or wrap them into rice paper rolls. Once you get into table salads, you'll wonder why American cooks see fresh herbs only as accents.

SHOPPING A VIETNAMESE MARKET—ESSENTIAL FOODS AND FLAVORS

Jars, Bottles, and Cans: fish sauce, soy sauce, anchovy sauce, hoisin, ground chili paste, bean sauce, coconut milk, sesame oil, tamarind paste, rice vinegar, preserved bean curd

Frozen Foods: dumplings, noodles, frozen seafood, Vietnamese sausages, hard-to-find fruits and vegetables

Dry Goods: rice, rice noodles and rice paper rounds (Elephant is a reliable brand), rice flours, tapioca starch and tapioca pearls

Fresh Produce: bird's eye and Thai chiles, ginger, galangal, holy basil (*rau que*), cilantro (*rau mui*), lemongrass, lime leaves, Vietnamese coriander (*rau ram*), saw leaf (*ngo gai*), sugarcane

Some Brands We Like: Viet Huong, Three Crabs, Flying Fish, Koon Chun, Pearl River Bridge, Elephant, Two Ladies

On Being
the Perfect Host

Journalist Sally Quinn, one of Washington, D.C.'s ultimate hostesses, summed it up: **"If you've invited someone to dinner, remember that it's about them, not you."** A liberating thought when you think about it.

Binh Duong and Marcia Kiesel, *Simple Art of Vietnamese Cooking*, Prentice Hall, 1991 **Bach Ngo and Gloria Zimmerman,** *The Classic Cuisine of Vietnam*, Plume, 1986 **Andrea Nguyen,** *Into the Vietnamese Kitchen*, Ten Speed Press, 2006 **Mai Pham,** *Pleasures of the Vietnamese Table*, HarperCollins, 2001 **Nicole Routhier,** *The Foods of Vietnam*, Stewart, Tabori & Chang, 1989 **Charmaine Solomon,** *Encyclopedia of Asian Food*, Periplus Editions, 1996

An
Italian
RENAISSANCE SUPPER

THE MENU

Farmer's Aperitivo*

Olives

Roasted Almonds

Salami in Small Dice, Speared on Skewers

An Unusual Italian Salad (PAGE 101)

Renaissance Lasagne (PAGE 145)

Venetian Iced Raspberry Cream (PAGE 313)

*** For Farmer's Aperitivo,
stir a shot of red wine into a cup of hot Master Broth** (PAGE 58) **or
Cheater's Broth** (PAGE 62) **and serve in mugs.**

The cuisine everyone loves and claims as their own still has secrets to tell, even after all the borrowing and improvising Italian food has inspired.

Believe it or not, many "new" foods in Italy are inspired by the most glamorous era of its past, so we are taking you back to the lavish banquet halls of the Italian Renaissance with a menu that tastes amazingly modern.

Italy's innovative chefs plunder the cookbooks of the period, and once you taste these dishes you will know why. One caveat: if we were sitting down to a banquet in sixteenth-century Italy, we'd eat our way through some sixty dishes in five courses (there would have been thirty pairs of hands busy in the kitchen). This is your guide to making a simpler version happen. Keep your eyes open as you cook, because at every turn are flavor combinations and techniques to carry over to everyday cooking.

How to Eat an Italian Meal

Savoring the individual dish is everything in Italy. A meal comes in courses, just as in the United States, but in the Italian spirit the courses are often small plates of what we'd eat as a side dish. For instance, a mix of roasted vegetables might be offered alone as a first course.

Italians ease into a gathering, with light tastes of dishes meant to provoke appetite, but never satisfy it. Called *antipasti*, meaning "outside the meal," these should be simple things. In this menu they are practically primal: olives, nuts, and small bites of salami.

PULLING IT OFF

Up to One Month Prior:

Make the Venetian Iced Raspberry Cream and the candied lemon peel for An Unusual Italian Salad.

Two Days Prior:

Make the Baroque Ragù for the Renaissance Lasagne and the balsamic syrup for An Unusual Italian Salad.

One Day Prior:

Make the pasta for the Renaissance Lasagne.

Prep the greens for An Unusual Italian Salad and the cheese for the Renaissance Lasagne.

Day of the Supper:

Make the Farmer's Aperitivo.

Assemble the Renaissance Lasagne and arrange the olives, almonds, and salami into an antipasti platter.

The ITALIAN PANTRY and KITCHEN

HELPFUL CULINARY TOOLS:
- A heavy rolling pin for pasta or a pasta machine
- An oversized colander for draining pasta
- A flat-ended wooden spatula for stirring sauces

UNIQUE CULINARY TECHNIQUES:

Using Premium Olive Oils as Seasoning:

Italians are the kings of "anointing" finished dishes with a drizzle of olive oil with distinctive flavor. If you are going to go for broke and buy an oil for flavoring rather than cooking, you want an extra-virgin oil with a press date on it. Olive oil fades after a year, so don't buy it unless you know when it was pressed.

Pasta Water:

A half cup of pasta water thickens, seasons, and brings more flavorful quantity to light sauces and vegetable sautés. That water, scooped out just before the pasta is drained, turns seemingly scant and dry sautés into generous sauces, a trick Italians call "lengthening" or *allungamento*.

Pasta plus Cheese and then Sauce:

Tossing pasta first with grated cheese, then saucing, is an unusual technique that gives you a rougher and earthier version of a pasta— entirely different from grating cheese over a sauced pasta.

Count to Ten:

Before putting your money down for cured meats and cheeses, taste and then count to ten after swallowing. You want to see if there are any "off" aftertastes. You'll be surprised at what you don't taste in that first bite. Unpleasant aftertastes come from poor quality or poor storage. Either way, if it doesn't taste good, don't buy it.

SHOPPING AN ITALIAN MARKET—ESSENTIAL FOODS AND FLAVORS

Jars, Bottles, and Cans: extra-virgin olive oils, canned whole tomatoes, tomato paste, olives, salted capers, tuna, anchovies

Dry Goods: pastas, ground cornmeal, dried porcini mushrooms, cannellini beans, borlotti beans, peeled fava beans, farro, Arborio or carnaroli rice, panettone Christmas bread and panforte from Siena

Cured and Cooked Products: Italian artisan cheeses, cured fatback (*lardo*), pancetta, prosciutto, salami

Some Brands We Like: DeCecco, Del Natura, Rustichella, Latini, Cipriani, Malpighi, Muir Glen, La Quercia, Salume, Biellese, Molinari, Kirkland Toscano, Laudemio, Olio Verde, McEvoy Ranch, Moustere Groves

Pasta never shows up as a side dish. It's too engaging and demands too much craft to be shuffled off to play second fiddle. It's always a first course, or the most important one. "Main" dishes as we think of them really don't exist in Italy. That classic second course—meat, fish, or poultry—is merely easing toward the finish of the meal.

Eating in Italy is about human engagement. For your sanity and your own pleasure, let the meal progress at a leisurely pace, giving plenty of time between courses, and serve the coffee after the dessert. If you'd like, this is when liqueurs, nuts for cracking, and fruits could be set out. Lingering at the table is the most Italian custom of all.

Mario Batali, *The Babbo Cookbook,* Clarkson Potter, 2002, and *Molto Italiano,* Ecco, 2005 **Nancy Harmon Jenkins,** *Flavors of Puglia,* Broadway Books, 1997 **Fred Plotkin,** *Italy for the Gourmet Traveler,* Kyle Books, 2010, and *La Terra Fortunata: The Splendid Food and Wine of Friuli Venezia-Giulia, Italy's Great Undiscovered Region,* Broadway Books, 2001 **Mary Taylor Simeti,** *Pomp and Sustenance: Twenty-Five Centuries of Sicilian Food,* Knopf, 1989 **Oretta Zanini de Vita,** *Encyclopedia of Pasta,* University of California Press, 2009

A FESTIVE Indian DINNER

THE MENU

Papadums*

Assorted Pickles*

Wedding Lamb Biriyani (PAGE 245)

Yogurt Raita (PAGE 250)

Ginger Syrup for All Seasons (PAGE 321)
with Mangoes and Pistachios

* Buy ready-made pappadums and pickles in Indian markets or the
ethnic section of larger grocery stores.

India's food isn't just a can of curry powder and a jar of chutney (although a lot can be done with that pair); it is ancient and deeply regional, with a stunning collection of eating possibilities. Imagine a country where a spice might be roasted, fried, soaked, used whole or freshly ground, and that often all of those variations will be in the same dish.

Combine that attention to detail with innumerable and very separate regions and religions, and a caste system—each dictating different ways of eating—and you begin to get an idea of the possibilities India possesses. We hope this menu gives you a taste of what the cuisine embraces, and we also hope you find cooking methods you'll use constantly, no matter what you're making.

How to Eat an Indian Meal

In a typical Indian meal everything is served at the same time, including the dessert. The meal is placed on a giant platter called a *thali*, or in the center of the table where everyone helps themselves. It is, however, *eaten* in courses, appetizers first with pickles or relish, then the main dish with bread or rice and the additional vegetable, and then a dessert, usually fruit, at the end. Rice or bread is always on the table, as are small amounts of highly flavored condiments to complement the other dishes—things like yogurt, chutneys, and sweet or pungent pickles.

Water and fruit juices are drunk with the meal, though in some parts of India a meal can end with yogurt or buttermilk, which is believed to help digestion.

PULLING IT OFF

One to Two Days Prior:

Make the lamb for the Wedding Lamb Biriyani and the Ginger Syrup for All Seasons.

Day of the Dinner:

Assemble and bake the Wedding Lamb Biriyani.

Make the Yogurt Raita.

Assemble the Ginger Syrup for All Seasons with mangoes and pistachios.

Toast the papadums and set out the pickles.

The INDIAN PANTRY and KITCHEN

HELPFUL CULINARY TOOLS:
- A spice grinder or coffee grinder to grind whole spices for maximum flavor
- A food processor to make purées and sauces
- A spice box, which is a round stainless steel tin with a lid and individual compartments for the spices most often used in your household

UNIQUE CULINARY TECHNIQUES:

Roasting on a Hot Griddle:
Spices are toasted for maximum flavor before using, breads are cooked and rewarmed, and papadums come to life when toasted over a hot griddle.

Spice Pastes:
Indian cooks often blend spices with fresh ginger or chiles, tomatoes, or just water into a paste, which is then fried in fat much the same way Mexican cooks fry their moles. The difference in taste between a raw spice paste and a cooked one is quite stunning. The first step in the recipe for Wedding Lamb Biriyani (page 245) walks you through the process.

Reducing Yogurt as You Would Broth:
In the same way that Western cooks create a layer of intense flavor by simmering broth or wine into a sauté of meat or vegetables so it reduces down to its essence with barely any liquid left, in the Indian kitchen you can do the same thing with yogurt. The yogurt makes a dish deliciously tangy and creamy. Whole-milk yogurt lends a rich-tasting layering; with low-fat yogurt there's more tang.

Finishing Sautés:
Cooked dishes get a last fresh-cooked seasoning. Sautéed onion, ginger, or garlic with whole spices such as mustard seeds, cumin, fennel, or coriander is used to finish many Indian recipes. Raisins and nuts could be in the pan, too. These hot seasonings top finished dishes just as Americans might add a pat of butter.

SHOPPING AN INDIAN MARKET—ESSENTIAL FOODS AND FLAVORS

Jars, Bottles, and Cans: sauces, tamarind concentrate, curry pastes, chutneys (use for marinating, saucing, and sautéing and for dressings)

Frozen Foods: Breads such as roti, naan, parantha, and chapati; stuffed fritters, such as samosas and croquettes; vegetables and frozen fruit purées

Spices and Aromatics: Indian spice blends are usually quite pure. Check out chaat masala, garam masala, chana masala, biriyani blends, and kofta mixes.

Dry Goods: basmati rice, dried lentils, beans, teas and chais

Fresh Produce: curry leaf, kaffir lime leaves, galangal, fresh turmeric, greens of all sorts

Cured, Cooked, and Dairy Products: yogurt, lassis, and cheeses such as paneer; check refrigerated cases for freshly made chutneys

Snacks: Indians are über-snackers. Try chakali (deep-fried rings of spicy chickpea and lentil batter) made by Vijaya Foods

Some Brands We Like: Deep, MDH, Shan, SWAD, Maya, Patek

Eating with the fingers is tradition in much of the country, though that is beginning to change in urban areas. Pieces of bread scoop up morsels of food, and saucy dishes top beds of rice for easier handling. Only the right hand is used for eating, as the left is considered "unclean" and is reserved for handling a glass or spooning food onto a plate.

Our Indian menu is not an example of an everyday meal in India. Biriyani is a dish of celebration, usually a meal in itself accompanied by something simple to contrast its richness. Here it's a raita, a fresh, cooling relish of yogurt, cucumber, garlic, and chile.

Yamuna Devi, *The Art of Indian Vegetarian Cooking*, Bala Books, 1987 **Raghavan Iyer,** *660 Curries*, Workman, 2008, and *The Turmeric Trail*, St. Martin's Press, 2002 **Madhur Jaffrey,** *Madhur Jaffrey's Flavors of India*, Clarkson Potter, 1995, and *An Invitation to Indian Cooking*, Ecco, 1999 **Maya Kaimal,** *Savoring the Spice Coast of India*, HarperCollins, 2000 **Julie Sahni,** *Classic Indian Cooking*, Morrow, 1980, and *Classic Indian Vegetarian Cookery*, Grub Street, 2003

A Chinese
CELEBRATION

THE MENU

Sichuan-Inspired Pickled Vegetables (PAGE 55)

Simple White Rice

Chicken in Chinese Master Sauce (PAGE 183)

Growing Fortune Salad (PAGE 93)

Chinese Hot & Sour Soup (PAGE 68)

Ginger Shrimp Stir-Fry with Snow Peas, Chinese Mushrooms
& Baby Corn (PAGE 209)

Long-Life Noodles of Chinese Broccoli & Garlic Pork (PAGE 126)

Lychee Nuts & Orange Wedges*

* Buy fresh or canned lychee nuts in Asian markets, shell them,
and combine with bite-sized pieces of peeled oranges.

Here is the thing about Chinese food: there is so much to taste and know. Three thousand years of one of the planet's most enlightened cultures make this cuisine. You could eat a different Chinese dish at each meal for the rest of your life and never taste them all. China's food traditions are as vast as the country's geography. Sadly, authentic Chinese flavors rarely show up at our local take-out places, but if you cook, you get to enjoy those dishes you don't find in restaurants. And that is what this special menu is about.

How to Eat a Chinese Meal

You could set out the entire meal at once, but for a celebration, present the menu in the order outlined here. The idea is to guide your guests' palates, leading them through an arc of tastes and nuances and contrasts, ending with noodles as the dinner's finale to wish your guests a long life.

Set each place with a bowl for rice, a small plate, a small soup bowl, chopsticks (set a fork, too, for comfort's sake), and a soup spoon (ideally porcelain). As the host, you'll sit with your back to the door (to be nearest the kitchen) with your guest of honor facing you. First tastes of dishes, especially stir-fries fresh from the wok, and the choicest bits are offered to the guest of honor or to the eldest at the table.

Soup isn't eaten first; instead, it is sipped throughout the meal, or in the middle of it. Bites of rice are eaten in between dishes. Etiquette demands that you never stand your chopsticks in your rice, as this symbolizes death; instead, place them flat on top of your bowl or alongside it, and never eat every bit on your plate. This signals your host that there wasn't enough food.

PULLING IT OFF

Up to a Month Prior:

Make the broth for the Chinese Hot & Sour Soup.

Two Days Prior:

Make the pickled vegetables for the Sichuan-Inspired Pickled Vegetables and the dipping sauces for Chicken in Chinese Master Sauce.

One Day Prior:

Make the Chicken in Chinese Master Sauce.

Prep the salad greens and dressing for the Growing Fortune Salad, and prep the ingredients for the Chinese Hot & Sour Soup.

Day of the Celebration:

Prep the Ginger Shrimp Stir-Fry with Snow Peas, Chinese Mushrooms & Baby Corn, and Long Life Noodles.

Assemble the lychee nuts and orange wedges and the Growing Fortune Salad.

Make the white rice.

Heat the soup.

Stir-fry the Ginger Shrimp Stir-Fry with Snow Peas, Chinese Mushrooms & Baby Corn.

Stir-fry Long-Life Noodles.

The CHINESE PANTRY and KITCHEN

HELPFUL CULINARY TOOLS:

- A wok, ideally rolled steel or iron (never nonstick or enameled), 14 to 16 inches in diameter, flat-bottomed, with a long wooden handle
- A long-handled metal spatula or wok shovel for stir-frying
- A large stainless steel mesh strainer with a long bamboo handle
- A cleaver (excellent quality for the money and used to cut everything)

UNIQUE CULINARY TECHNIQUES:

The Stir-Fry:

A proper stir-fry always begins with the technique of "hot wok, cold oil." Heat the empty wok to smoking hot, then add the oil, and finally add your ingredients. Following this order will ensure no sticking.

Cutting Ingredients into Precise Shapes:

There are reasons Chinese recipes demand specific shapes. The cut and shape determine a dish's look, tastes, and textures. Small pieces need only quick bursts of high heat; this is important in a country where fuel has been in short supply since the days of Attila the Hun.

Marrying Flavors with Sugar:

Often tiny amounts of sugar go into a dish not for their sweetness, but because some cooks believe the sugar helps flavors come together.

SHOPPING A CHINESE MARKET—ESSENTIAL FOODS AND FLAVORS

Jars, Bottles, and Cans: hoisin sauce, chili paste, soy sauce, oyster sauce, plum sauce, bean sauces (hot, brown, red, or fermented), chile garlic sauce

Frozen Foods: dim sum, fresh noodles, scallion pancakes, Peking doilies, wonton skins, egg roll skins, hard-to-find fruits

Spices and Aromatics: Sichuan peppercorns, star anise, five-spice powder, dried chiles, salted and fermented black beans, black vinegar from Zhejiang or Guangdong, Shao Xing cooking wine, Asian sesame oil

Dry Goods: mushrooms of all kinds (especially shiitake), tiger lily buds, cellophane or bean thread noodles, egg and wheat noodles, rice noodles, dried red dates, long-grain rice

Produce: water chestnuts, bamboo shoots and other Asian vegetables, seafood, ginger, fresh herbs, tofu

Cured and Cooked Products: Chinese sausages, bacon, preserved ducks, roasted pork, duck, and chicken

Some Brands We Like: Koon Chun, Mee Chun, Lee Kum Kee, Pearl River Bridge, Twin Pagoda, Kikkoman (yes, the Japanese soy sauce)

Balancing Flavors

In a Chinese menu you want a play of flavors—sweet, tart, sour, spiced, and a dish that quietly tastes only of its main ingredients, such as our Ginger Shrimp Stir-Fry with Snow Peas, Chinese Mushrooms & Baby Corn (page 209). The same is true of textures. We don't know of another cuisine where the sensations you feel as you eat count for so much, as in the crunch of a crisp pickle or the melting quality of master sauce chicken.

Each of these menu elements exists for a reason. They evolved out of three thousand years of complicated history, with food constantly playing a central role. That famous yin-yang design, with its swirls of dark and light, reveals the Chinese philosophy of food, health, and life—all of life is balance. You eat to balance your innate nature, your health, the seasons, your pleasure, and your spirit, and you eat beliefs, as in lettuce for the New Year, because its name in Cantonese—*saang choy*—sounds like the Cantonese expression for "growing or producing fortune."

BUILDING THE LIBRARY CHINA

Eileen Yin-Fei Lo, *Mastering the Art of Chinese Cooking,* Chronicle Books, 2009 **Grace Young,** *The Wisdom of the Chinese Kitchen,* Simon & Schuster, 1999 **Grace Young** and **Alan Richardson,** *The Breath of a Wok,* Simon & Schuster, 2004 **Nina Simonds,** *A Spoonful of Ginger,* Alfred A. Knopf, 1999 **Ken Hom,** *Easy Family Recipes from a Chinese-American Childhood,* Knopf, 1997 **Nicole Mones,** *The Last Chinese Chef,* Houghton Mifflin, 2008 **Barbara Tropp,** *The Modern Art of Chinese Cooking,* Morrow, 1982

Sit on It:
The Dining Chair

A chair can torture or cosset; it's all in how it was designed, and how each of our bodies takes to it. Yet we rarely think twice about putting a matched set together.

Antiques authority Judith Miller, author of *Chairs* (Conran, 2009), says if you look back to the thirteenth and fourteenth centuries, there was only one chair in a given room, and the person of highest status would get it. It's where our word *chairman* originates.

Judith is set against the dining set; she backs a far more playful approach. **Think about putting together a collection of different chairs for your dining table.** Interesting aesthetically, possibly economical, and definitely practical; a variety ensures that you will have a chair for both the six-year-old and the six-footer.

You will feel hungry in an hour.

—CHINESE FORTUNE COOKIE MESSAGE

A TRIO OF WINTER FEASTS *Two goals drive these menus:* First, the food has to be a standout and easy to pull off. Second, you, the host, should be able to sit happily at the table in absolute control, as opposed to slumped against a kitchen cabinet, whisk in hand, muttering unpleasant observations about guests and certain cookbook authors. Wine pairings are found in individual recipes.

A
Winter Holiday
DINNER

THE MENU

Pickled Herring*

Slow-Roasted Pork with Glazed Orange Slices (PAGE 232)

Gingered Purée of Winter Roots (PAGE 274)

Broccoli with Lemon

Mustard-Glazed Red Cabbage with Apple (PAGE 284)

Double Pear Pudding Cake with
Warm Caramel-Cognac Sauce (PAGE 296)

* **Buy ready-made in the refrigerated section of your grocery store.**

In spite of our shared Mediterranean heritage, oddly Scandinavian tastes lure us in as winter descends. Celebrate anything with this menu. It could be Christmas, the New Year, a stellar report card, or a new puppy.

Let us love winter, for it is the spring of genius.

—PIETRO ARETINO

PULLING IT OFF

Three Days Prior:

Season the pork.

Make the pears for the Double Pear Pudding Cake and the Warm Caramel-Cognac Sauce.

One Day Prior:

Bake the Double Pear Pudding Cake.

Make the Gingered Purée of Winter Roots and the Mustard-Glazed Red Cabbage with Apple.

Day of the Dinner:

Put out the pickled herring.

Roast the Slow-Roasted Pork with Glazed Orange Slices.

Make the broccoli with lemon.

Reheat the Gingered Purée of Winter Roots, the Mustard-Glazed Red Cabbage with Apple, and the Caramel-Cognac Sauce.

A
Potluck
THANKSGIVING

THE MENU

Wild Mushroom & Walnut Pâté (PAGE 50)

Crisp Roast Turkey with Garlic, Apple & Basil (PAGE 200)

Apple Brandy Pan Gravy (PAGE 203)

Cornbread Pudding with Rough Country Greens (PAGE 134)

Gingered Purée of Winter Roots (PAGE 274)

West Indies Green Beans (PAGE 276)

Butternut "Pumpkin" Pie (PAGE 318)

Five-Nut Caramel Tart (PAGE 305)

Please note the word *potluck*. Feel free to assign dishes.

PULLING IT OFF

Three Days Prior:

Make the Wild Mushroom &
Walnut Pâté, the West Indies
Spice Blend (page 175) for the
West Indies Green Beans, and
the piecrusts for the Butternut
"Pumpkin" Pie and the
Five-Nut Caramel Tart.

Bake the cornbread for the
Cornbread Pudding with
Rough Country Greens.

Two Days Prior:

Cook the greens for the
Cornbread Pudding with
Rough Country Greens.

Roast the squash for the
Butternut "Pumpkin" Pie.

One Day Prior:

Brine the turkey.

Make the broth for the Apple
Brandy Pan Gravy.

Bake the Five-Nut Caramel
Tart and the Cornbread
Pudding with Rough Country
Greens.

Bake the Butternut
"Pumpkin" Pie.

Make the Gingered Purée of
Winter Roots and the green
beans for the West Indies
Green Beans.

Thanksgiving Day:

Roast the Crisp Roast Turkey
with Garlic, Apple & Basil.

Make the Apple Brandy Pan
Gravy.

Reheat the Cornbread
Pudding with Rough Country
Greens, the Gingered Purée
of Winter Roots, and the West
Indies Green Beans.

A
Vegan
THANKSGIVING

THE MENU

Dried Figs, Apricots & Pistachios

Timbale of Sweet Peppers, Greens & Hominy (PAGE 172)

Orange Onion Salad with Warmed Coriander Oil (PAGE 77)

West Indies Green Beans (PAGE 276)

Fruit Sorbets* with Ginger Syrup for All Seasons (PAGE 321)

* Serve store-bought sorbets such as pumpkin, apple, and pear.

For all who have politely survived on creamed onions and cranberry sauce year after year, this is for you.

An optimist is a person who starts a diet on Thanksgiving Day.

—IRV KUPCINETT

Two Days Prior:

Make the Pepper-Tomato Sofritto for the Timbale of Sweet Peppers, Greens & Hominy; the West Indies Spice Blend (page 175) for the West Indies Green Beans; and the Ginger Syrup for All Seasons.

One Day Prior:

Assemble the Timbale of Sweet Peppers, Greens & Hominy.

Cook the green beans for the West Indies Green Beans.

Thanksgiving Day:

Set out dried fruit and pistachios.

Assemble the Orange Onion Salad with Warmed Coriander Oil.

Bake the Timbale of Sweet Peppers, Greens & Hominy.

Make the West Indies Green Beans.

Serve the sorbet.

STARTERS, SNACKS, AND SMALL PLATES

Jicama & Mango Sticks in Chile & Lime

| *Serves 4 to 6* | *10 minutes prep time* | *These are best cut no more than 6 hours ahead and refrigerated (put the jicama in water to keep it from browning). Season them shortly before serving.*

Beguiling as a French fry, but with so much more charisma (mango, lime, and chile deserve nomination as a hallowed culinary trinity), these sticks are what you want to have on hand when time is short and snacks are essential. With some *agua fresca* (page 228), maybe tequila, and a big pot of Yucatán Pork in Banana Leaves (page 223) waiting on the stove, you have a full-blown party wrapped up (page 4).

1 medium **jicama** (about 1 pound), peeled and cut into
 ½-inch × 3-inch sticks
2 medium firm ripe **mangoes** (about 1½ pounds), peeled
 and cut into ½-inch × 3-inch sticks
Juice of 1 medium **lime**
Generous pinch of **salt**
About 1 teaspoon ground pure **chile**, medium to hot
 depending on your taste

1. Spread out the jicama and mango sticks and sprinkle with the lime juice. Then dust them with a little salt and the chile, turning the pieces so each side gets a bit of seasoning.
2. Serve them clustered in paper cones or small glasses.

WORK NIGHT ENCORE

Finishing Touches: Cut into small dice, the jicama and mango pieces are excellent as a garnish for High Summer Tomato-Melon Soup (page 74). Diced small and tossed together, they could top grilled fish, meats, or vegetables.

MUSIC TO CLEAN UP BY

We take the time to consider what music to play with dinner when we entertain, right? Well, it may be a better use of your time to spend some energy on the music you're going to need to get through the cleanup. We went to our resident music expert TOM MOON, author of *1000 Recordings to Hear Before You Die* (Workman, 2008),

for a short list of motivating, whip-cracking recordings to get us through that pile of dishes.

First things first, to get people out the door, Tom suggests the first movement of Symphony no. 38 from *The Late Symphonies* by the Vienna Philharmonic, with Karl Bohm conducting. This Mozart practically levitates you out of your chair. Moon's understatement: "It signals that the mood has changed." When the house is clear, take your pick of the following: Bob Marley and the Wailers: "Three Little Birds" from *Exodus* •

Ernest Ranglin: "King Tubby Meets the Rockers" from *Below the Bassline* • Tal Farlow: "You Stepped out of a Dream" from *The Swinging Guitar of Tal Farlow* • Cal Tjader: "Gringo City" from *Primo* • Cecilia Bartoli: "Sventurata Navicella" from *The Vivaldi Album* • Aretha Franklin: "Do Right Woman," from *I Never Loved a Man the Way I Love You* • Chet Baker: "But Not for Me" from *Let's Get Lost: The Best of Chet Baker Sings* • Schubert: B-flat Piano Sonata, Clifford Curzon, piano

Too much good taste can be boring.

—DIANA VREELAND

Rice Paper Rolls of Herbs & Shrimp

Makes 16 spring rolls; | *60 minutes prep time;* | *You could do these early in the day, cover*
serves 4 to 8; halves or | *20 minutes assembly* | *with a lightly dampened towel, and*
doubles easily | *time* | *refrigerate until serving time. Serve as*
| | *part of a Vietnamese menu (page 12).*

These fresh roll-ups have an impudent edge. Whereas most Vietnamese rolls
depend on a dipping sauce for spark, here the sparks are flying inside the roll—with
garlic shrimp, hoisin noodles, mint, basil, lime, and crisp marinated vegetables.

NUOC CHAM DIPPING SAUCE

4 large **garlic cloves**, minced
¼ cup fresh **lime juice** (2 to 3 limes)
½ cup **rice vinegar**
⅓ cup **Asian fish sauce** (nuoc nam)
1 to 3 small fresh **red Thai chiles**, thinly sliced, to taste
1 to 3 tablespoons **sugar**, or to taste

SHRIMP

¾ pound raw large **shrimp**, shelled, each shrimp
    cut into 4 small pieces
2 large **garlic cloves**, minced
1 teaspoon **Asian fish sauce**
2 teaspoons fresh **lime juice**
2 teaspoons **sugar**
1 tablespoon expeller-pressed **canola** or
    safflower oil

CARROT-DAIKON SALAD

2 large **carrots**, cut into ¹⁄₁₆-inch julienne (if organic,
    do not peel)
6-inch piece **daikon radish**, peeled and cut into
    ¹⁄₁₆-inch julienne

**Communal cooking is
the way to go. Line up
the ingredients and let
friends roll their own.
Each step of the recipe
could be done several
hours ahead and
refrigerated. At will,
substitute green
papaya or underripe
avocado for the carrot
and daikon.**

WINE These rolls pair
beautifully with McClaren
Valley Unwooded
Chardonnay.

4 teaspoons **sugar**
2 tablespoons **rice vinegar**
¼ teaspoon **salt**
1 small fresh **red Thai chile**, thinly sliced

NOODLES

6 ounces thin **rice noodles**

ASSEMBLY

16 8-inch rounds of **rice paper** (*banh trang*)
8 **Bibb lettuce leaves**, halved and ribs removed
⅓ cup **hoisin sauce**
Juice of 1 medium **lime**
1½ to 2 loosely packed cups fresh **mint leaves**,
   washed and dried
1½ to 2 loosely packed cups fresh **cilantro leaves**,
   washed and dried

1. Make the Nuoc Cham Dipping Sauce: In a small bowl, mix the garlic, lime juice, rice vinegar, fish sauce, chiles, and sugar, starting with 1 chile and 1 tablespoon of the sugar and increasing to taste. Let the sauce rest at room temperature for 30 minutes to 1 hour. The sauce can be refrigerated for several days.

2. Make the shrimp: In a large bowl, combine the shrimp with the garlic, fish sauce, lime juice, and sugar. Let stand for 10 minutes. Heat a 10-inch skillet over high heat, swirl in the oil, and stir-fry the shrimp for 30 seconds to 1 minute, or until barely firm. Immediately turn out onto a plate and cool.

3. Make the Carrot-Daikon Salad: In a medium bowl, toss the carrots, daikon, sugar, rice vinegar, salt, and chile. Let stand for 15 minutes, then drain and pat dry.

4. Make the noodles: Soak the noodles in a deep bowl covered with very hot tap water for 5 to 8 minutes, or until tender. Drain and rinse with cold water, then drain again thoroughly. Spread the noodles out on a towel and pat dry before using.

5. Assemble the spring rolls: Moisten both sides of a rice paper round with hot running water. Spread it out on your work surface. In a few moments it will soften. Pat away any excess water.

6. At the top third of the round, put a small piece of lettuce that covers it by two thirds. Daub the lettuce with about ¼ teaspoon of the hoisin sauce. On top of that, spread a shallow pile of noodles, then several pieces of shrimp.

(recipe continues)

7. Squeeze about ½ teaspoon of the lime juice over the shrimp. Top with a generous tablespoon or two of the Carrot-Daikon Salad and 3 big mint leaves.

8. Roll up by one third, tightly packing the filling as you go. Place 3 cilantro leaves and 3 smaller mint leaves atop the roll, fold in the sides over the herbs, and tightly roll up the cylinder all the way. Spread them out on a platter as you make more. If holding for more than 30 minutes, refrigerate, covered.

9. Serve the spring rolls by cutting each in half on the diagonal if you wish. Stand up the pieces on a platter accompanied by small bowls of room-temperature Nuoc Cham Dipping Sauce.

WORK NIGHT ENCORES

Chicken Rice Noodle Soup: Prep extra noodles, fresh herbs, lettuce, and dipping sauce for a work night main-dish soup.

Heat chicken broth, then add ¼ cup dipping sauce, half a thinly sliced onion, a minced garlic clove, and 1 teaspoon minced fresh ginger for every 2 cups broth. Simmer for 10 minutes.

Stir thinly sliced boneless chicken breast and rice noodles into the broth and heat for about 2 minutes, or until the chicken is cooked through.

Ladle into soup bowls, scattering the soup with torn lettuce and lots of mint and basil. Season with fresh lime juice to taste.

To the alchemy that turns groceries into meals.

—ANONYMOUS

Jumble Cheese

| *Makes about 1 cup* | *10 minutes prep time* | *Keeps refrigerated several weeks*

This simple and distinctive recipe, born of wartime thrift and ecology, came to us via an interview with master chef Jacques Pépin. Here you use those typically disdained ends and bits of leftover cheeses. Worked into a blend of crushed garlic, black pepper, and, of course, having a French heritage, a little wine, the cheese becomes an astonishingly fine spread.

Stored in the fridge for as long as it lasts, it ripens as the days go by.

2 **garlic cloves**
½ pound **mixed cheeses**, rinds removed and cut into 1½- to 2-inch chunks
¼ to ½ cup dry **wine**
Freshly ground **black pepper**

1. With the food processor running, drop in the garlic to mince. After a few seconds, turn off the machine and scrape down the sides of the bowl. Then add the cheeses, wine, and pepper to taste. Process for 30 seconds, or until the mixture is creamy, but not too soft.

2. Pack the spread into small jars or crocks, cover, and refrigerate. Bring to room temperature before serving.

Remember, this is a recipe of remainders, so a few spoonfuls of brandy, port, or other flavorful alcohol could easily stand in for the wine or be added with it. Nearly any cheese combination flies in Jumble Cheese, but for starters, think about balancing the sharp, pungent, and deliciously funky with the mild, creamy, and fresh.

WINE Some foods demand a specific wine, but this spread works well with almost anything, white or red, but preferably dry.

What Makes
Elsie
PUT OUT?

According to a study done in the United Kingdom with some five hundred dairy farmers, **cows that are addressed by name gave an average of 454 more pints of milk a year.** This is not news to farmers who have known all along what scientists had to dig for. Cows are intelligent and emotional creatures that respond to individual appreciation. The last thing they want is to be considered one of the herd. Sound familiar?

Mahogany-Glazed Chicken Wings

Serves 4 to 6 | *10 minutes prep time; 12 to 48 hours refrigeration in marinade; 2 hours oven time* | *The wings reheat well in a 350°F. oven for 15 to 20 minutes.*

Kids wolf down these chicken wings, and although grown-ups try to be more urbane, they rarely succeed. Wonderfully sticky, sweet, sour, and addicting, the wings are pure family party food. Think play-offs, Super Bowls, or movie nights—pull out the TV trays, slip in the DVD, and pile up the napkins.

½ cup **hoisin sauce**
½ cup **soy sauce**
¼ cup **honey**
¼ cup **Chinese plum sauce**
¼ cup dry **sherry**
¼ cup **cider vinegar**
6 large **garlic cloves**
3¼ to 4 pounds **chicken wings**, rinsed and pierced in several places with a paring knife

1. In a blender or food processor, purée the hoisin sauce, soy sauce, honey, plum sauce, sherry, cider vinegar, and garlic. Reserve ¼ cup of the marinade for basting the wings. Combine the remaining mixture with the chicken wings in large plastic bags and refrigerate for 12 to 48 hours.

2. Preheat the oven to 325°F. Line a large shallow baking pan (a half-sheet pan is ideal) with foil. Set a large cake rack inside the pan. Arrange the wings on the rack, trying not to stack them so they can all caramelize evenly.

This marinade takes to ribs, slow-roasted whole chickens, vegetables, and grilled fish and burgers. A fresh batch of marinade becomes a dipping sauce for grills, roasts, seafood, and most vegetables, but especially yams.

WINE Look for a warmer-climate, southern Italian red like Nero d'Avila, or a Primitivo or Salice Salentino from Puglia.

3. Roast the chicken for 1¼ to 1½ hours, turning the wings often and basting them with the reserved marinade until the last 30 minutes of cooking. Halfway through the roasting, pierce each wing several times with a knife to release some of its fat and help it crisp. The wings are cooked when they are easily pierced with a knife. If in doubt, roast longer.

4. Give the wings a final crisping by raising the heat to 450°F. for 15 to 20 minutes, turning them so they are a rich red-brown on all sides. Pile the wings on a platter and serve warm or at room temperature.

SIX THINGS TO DO WHEN THE OVEN IS HOT

1. Roast beets and apples in their skins and toss them in a salad.

2. Freshen up stale crackers, cookies, and nuts.

3. Slow-roast tomatoes by cutting them in half; sprinkling with sugar, pepper, salt, and olive oil; and roasting until shriveled.

4. Make croutons, garlicky crostini, and homemade bread crumbs.

5. Make homemade stock by piling leftover bones and vegetable trimmings in a big pot; cover with water and let cook overnight in a 300°F. oven.

6. Make cheese crisps by grating cheese, tossing with flour and cayenne, and spreading the mixture thinly on a sheet pan and baking until melted and golden brown. Break into pieces when cool.

It's so beautifully arranged on the plate, you know someone's fingers have been all over it.

—JULIA CHILD

Wild Mushroom & Walnut Pâté

| *Serves 15 to 20; halves easily* | *1 hour prep time; 75 minutes cook time; 6 hours refrigeration* | *Keeps refrigerated 3 to 5 days. This terrine works best in a long narrow 6- to 8-cup terrine or a 9 × 5 × 3-inch bread pan.* |

Elegantly rich, this is the perfect bit of luxury for a houseful of enthusiastic eaters. Silky-smooth mushroom cream tenderly holding pieces of both fresh and dried mushrooms and walnuts is why this pâté has been a mainstay at Sally's parties for years. This is a recipe from one of Sally's favorite food writers, Deborah Madison. Much like its original author, this is a generous dish, in both taste and spirit.

1 ounce dried **porcini mushrooms** (about 1 cup)
6 tablespoons **unsalted butter**, plus more for the pan
2 medium **leeks** (white parts only), chopped
3 large **garlic cloves**, minced
½ cup **walnuts**
Salt
1 pound **white mushrooms**, thinly sliced
2½ teaspoons chopped fresh **thyme**
¼ to ½ pound fresh **shiitake** or **cremini mushrooms**, thinly sliced
3 large **eggs**
1 cup **heavy cream**
¼ cup dried **bread crumbs**
1½ tablespoons fresh **lemon juice**
Freshly ground **black pepper**

WINE Since this is a starter course and part of a meal, it makes sense to start with a lighter wine. Try a Semillon from Washington State or Australia, or a light red like a Cabernet Franc from the Loire Valley, such as Chinon or Bourgueil.

1. In a medium bowl, cover the dried porcini with 1½ cups warm water and set aside to soak for 30 minutes. Butter the pan for the pâté, then line it, including the ends, with parchment or wax paper and butter again. Preheat the oven to 350°F. Lift the porcini from the water with a slotted spoon, gently squeeze them dry, and chop them into small pieces.

Carefully decant the mushroom liquid into a small saucepan, taking care not to pour in the gritty sediment from the bottom, and bring the liquid to a boil. Reduce until 2 tablespoons remain. Set aside.

2. In a wide skillet, over medium-high heat, melt 2 tablespoons of the butter until foamy. Add the leeks, garlic, and walnuts; reduce the heat to medium, and cook, stirring occasionally, for about 6 minutes, until the leeks are tender. Season with salt and transfer to a blender.

3. In the same skillet over medium-high heat, melt 2 tablespoons of the butter. When the butter foams, add three quarters of the white mushrooms and a pinch of the thyme. Sauté until they begin to color. Add them to the blender.

4. Melt the remaining 2 tablespoons butter and continue the process with the remaining white mushrooms, shiitake, and chopped porcini, plus more pinches of the thyme. Set the batches of cooked mushrooms aside together in a large bowl.

5. Add the eggs and cream to the blender and purée until the mixture is completely smooth. Pour the mixture into the large bowl with the reserved mushrooms. Fold in the bread crumbs, lemon juice, reduced mushroom liquid, and salt and pepper to taste.

6. Pour the mixture into the prepared pan and cover the top tightly with foil. Set it in a baking pan and add hot water to come halfway up the sides. Bake in the center of the oven for 1 hour, or until it is brown on top and starting to pull away from the sides. Remove and refrigerate until completely chilled, at least 6 hours.

7. Bring to room temperature, cut into slices, and serve.

{ COOK *to* Cook }

Dried mushrooms are investments. For the best value and quality, try to smell the mushrooms before buying. Rich aroma means rich flavor. You also want large pieces of mushroom. If the mushrooms are packaged, avoid bags with crumbs and dust in them. Always turn the package upside down, and if you see any webs, look for another brand. Check dates on the bag. Dried mushrooms hold 6 months to 1 year.

Tomatillo Salsa with Fresh Cheese from El Cardenal in Mexico City

| *Serves 4 to 6* | *15 to 20 minutes prep time* | *Tomatillo salsa shines when it's freshly made.*

You know those dishes you can't get out of your head? Tomatillo salsa shows up constantly in Mexican restaurants, but the one we had in Mexico City's El Cardenal, the city's grande dame of genteel tradition, kept haunting us.

As green as a fluorescent shamrock, wonderfully tart and herbal, it came to the table in a little blue-and-white ceramic mortar with sticks of fresh cheese for dipping.

Don't let summer get away from you without trying this. Then again, it is pretty swell in winter, too. You'll love it as an opener for a Mexican menu (page 4).

1 medium **garlic clove**
4 sprigs fresh **cilantro**
½ pound fresh **tomatillos**, husks removed, quartered
1 tablespoon **onion**, coarsely chopped
¼ teaspoon **sugar**
½ to 2 fresh **serrano chiles**
Salt
8 ounces **Queso Fresco** (fresh Mexican cheese),
    feta, farmer, or firm fresh goat cheese, cut into
    ½-inch × 2-inch sticks

1. In a blender or food processor, pulse the garlic, cilantro, tomatillos, onion, sugar, and chiles to a very fine mince, until well combined but not entirely liquid. The salsa should have a slightly thickened texture to stand up to the cheese. Add salt to taste.

2. Pour the salsa into a serving bowl. Tuck some of the cheese sticks into it and have the rest on a plate. Set out in the middle of the table and have everyone dip away.

WORK NIGHT ENCORE

Tomatillo Chicken or Shrimp: Use leftover tomatillo salsa to gently poach thin slices of chicken breast or whole shrimp. Serve with a dollop of sour cream and warm corn tortillas.

Creamy Scrambled Eggs with Tomatillo Salsa: Cut leftover cheese into cubes and fold it into slow-scrambled eggs, along with a few tablespoons chopped fresh cilantro or scallions, as you finish scrambling them. Pile the eggs on a plate and spoon the leftover tomatillo salsa over them.

Dinner CONVERSATION or Not?

If you find yourself having a hard time making conversation at the dinner table, perhaps you suffer from **deipnophobia,** the abnormal fear of dining or dinner conversation. We think this is much better than having dipsophobia, the fear of drinking, or, even worse, **cenosillicaphobia,** the fear of an empty glass!

Sichuan-Inspired Pickled Vegetables

| *Makes about 3 cups* | *20 minutes prep time; 5 minutes stove time; 12 hours to 4 weeks refrigeration in marinade* | *The pickles keep for a month in the refrigerator.* |

You will love what happens to radishes and carrots in this pickle—one turns a sheer sunset pink while the other practically pulsates orange. Chinese pickles are a cook's great cheat. In an elaborate Chinese menu (page 26), they save you from having to pull off time-consuming appetizers while they tune up palates for what's to come.

MARINADE

2½ cups **white distilled vinegar**

1 teaspoon **kosher salt**

½ cup **sugar**

1 generous teaspoon medium-hot ground **chile** (such as mirasol, guajillo, New Mexico, or hot Hungarian paprika)

1 **star anise**, broken, or 1 teaspoon **anise seed**, bruised

1½-inch piece fresh **ginger**, cut into 6 pieces

3- to 4-inch **cinnamon stick**, broken into several pieces

VEGETABLES

2 to 3 medium **carrots**, cut on the diagonal into ½-inch-thick slivers (if organic, do not peel)

8 to 10 **red radishes**, cut into ⅛-inch-thick rounds

1. In a 3-quart saucepan, combine the vinegar, salt, sugar, and chile. Heat until the sugar is dissolved. Boil for 1 minute.

2. Wash and rinse two 1-pint glass jars with very hot water.

3. Divide the anise, ginger, and cinnamon between them, then place the carrots in one jar and the radishes in the other. Pour half of the vinegar mixture into each, cover, cool, and store in the refrigerator. Use after 12 hours. Keep refrigerated.

4. When ready to serve the pickles, drain them, then place in small bowls with toothpicks, or eat as finger foods.

SOUPS AND SALADS

SOUPS

Master Broth

| Makes about 7 quarts | 40 minutes prep time; 12 to 14 hours mainly unattended stove time | Keeps refrigerated 4 days and frozen 6 months

Why bother with homemade broth when there's the can? Because if you break some old broth-making rules, you will have a culinary powerhouse than no can will ever match.

New food science led to ingredients in this recipe that are never found in classic broths. But each is here for a reason. Tomatoes, wine, garlic, and fish sauce are packed with that so-called fifth taste, umami. Everything it touches tastes better.

From a Chinese cook we learned that poultry wings uniquely meld light and dark meats, their skin-to-meat balance boosts body, and the small bones break easily to release more nutrients. Add our unconventionally long, quiet simmer to tease out every last bit of taste, and you end up with a broth that's ambrosia on its own, which in cooking is the salvation of the dull and boring.

Never let the broth boil; that's the single most important thing to remember. You want the barest simmer, meaning you can count to five between bubbles. Boiling emulsifies fats into the liquid, giving you a cloudy, greasy-tasting broth. Gentle simmering can be hard to control, so don't hesitate to do this broth in the oven rather than on the stovetop.

5 to 6 pounds **turkey** or **chicken wings**

2 large **onions**, trimmed of root ends and coarsely chopped (if organic, do not peel)

2 medium **carrots**, coarsely chopped (if organic, do not peel

1 large **celery stalk** with leaves, coarsely chopped

4 large **garlic heads**, trimmed of root ends, halved horizontally, and crushed

5 whole **cloves**

3 dried **bay leaves**

1 teaspoon **Asian fish sauce**

1 cup dry **red wine**

6 canned **tomatoes**, drained

1. With a cleaver or heavy knife, cut up the wings, cracking the bones in several places. Place them in a tall 10- to 12-quart pot. Add enough cold water to cover. Over medium heat, bring the water slowly to a simmer. The meat will throw off a scum that rises to the surface. When the scum stops rising (about 10 minutes), drain the wings in a colander, rinse them with cold water, and rinse the pot.

2. Put the wings back in the pot. Add the onions, carrots, celery, garlic, cloves, bay leaves, fish sauce, wine, and tomatoes and enough cold water to cover them by 2 to 3 inches. *Most important is not to let the broth boil, ever.* Over medium-high heat, bring the water to a slow bubble. Partially cover the pot.

3. Continue to gently simmer for 12 to 14 hours on the stovetop or alternatively in the oven at 300°F., stirring and skimming off fat occasionally. Add boiling water if the broth reduces below the level of the solid ingredients. If using the oven, babysit the pot for the first hour to make sure the broth is bubbling very slowly. Adjust the heat as needed.

4. Off the heat, strain the broth through a fine sieve into a large bowl or storage container. For a clearer broth, strain it by ladling rather than pouring it, leaving behind any sediment at the bottom of the pot.

5. Before refrigerating, cool the broth as quickly as possible. Set it outside in cold weather, or chill it down in several small containers set in bowls of ice. Then refrigerate the broth for about 8 hours, or until its fat has hardened. Skim off the fat; use the broth now or freeze it in assorted-sized containers. Season the broth to taste as you use it.

Using Master Broth

New England Autumn Soup:

Heat 6 cups broth to bubbling. Stir in a tart unpeeled apple cut into ⅛-inch dice, 4 ounces smoked diced ham, and 4 ounces sharp Cheddar cheese. Season to taste with freshly grated nutmeg. Adding ½ cup hard cider would gild the lily.

Tortilla-Tomatillo Broth:

This is a good soup to make with leftover Tomatillo Salsa (page 52). Heat 6 cups broth. As it warms, thinly slice a few corn tortillas and pan-fry them in a little oil until crisp. Drain them on paper towels. Stir 6 to 8 halved grape tomatoes into the broth with tomatillo salsa to taste. Top each serving with a few tortilla strips.

(recipe continues)

Winter Sunday Soup:

Heat 10 cups broth with 2 cups diced onion and 1 cup each diced potato, butternut squash, rutabaga, mushrooms, cabbage, yams, and turnips. Add 1 cup red wine, 2 tablespoons tomato paste, 8 crushed garlic cloves, and 3 tablespoons West Indies Spice Blend (page 175). Simmer until the vegetables are tender, about 30 minutes. Stir in a little whole-milk yogurt at the table.

Tart Spanish Broth:

Heat 6 cups broth with 1 to 2 tablespoons Spanish sherry vinegar and ½ to 1 teaspoon smoked Spanish paprika (Pimenton de la Vera), either mild or hot. Add salt to taste and garnish with chopped fresh cilantro leaves and chopped toasted almonds.

Lemon-Parmigiano Broth:

Heat 6 cups broth to a slow bubble. In a small bowl, mix with a fork 1 egg, ½ cup grated Parmigiano-Reggiano cheese, and 1/16 teaspoon freshly grated nutmeg. With the broth barely simmering, use the fork to slowly stir in the egg mixture so it forms long shreds. Garnish with thinly sliced scallion (green parts only).

Chinese Chicken & Pork Master Broth

| *Makes 5 to 6 quarts* | *30 minutes prep time; 8 hours mainly unattended stove time* | *Keeps refrigerated 4 days and frozen 6 months*

Pork brings a soft, almost sweet quality to the broth. This is the broth for Chinese Hot & Sour Soup (page 68), Asian dumpling soups like wonton, or vegetable soups, and as the liquid needed in stir-fries. Sip the broth on its own, maybe with minced fresh ginger and scallion added.

3 pounds **turkey** or **chicken wings**, each cut into 4 or 5
   pieces, if possible
2½ to 3 pounds **pork country spareribs**, trimmed of
   excess fat
1-inch piece fresh **ginger**, thinly sliced
4 **scallions** (white and green parts), thinly sliced
1 tablespoon **soy sauce**

This broth cooks slightly faster than the standard master broth. Follow the directions for Master Broth (page 58), except gently simmer this broth for only 8 hours.

Cheater's Broth

| *Makes about 4 cups;* | *5 minutes prep time;* | *Keeps refrigerated 4 days and frozen*
| *doubles or triples easily* | *30 minutes stove time* | *6 months*

When time isn't on your side, this is a surprisingly fine substitute for master broth.

½ cup dry **white wine**
2 large **garlic cloves**, crushed (if organic, do not peel)
2 whole **cloves**
1 canned **tomato**
1 dried **bay leaf**, broken
½ teaspoon dried **basil**, crumbled
3 14-ounce cans low-sodium **chicken broth**
1 medium to large **onion**, trimmed of root end and
   coarsely chopped (if organic, do not peel)
½ large **celery stalk** with leaves, coarsely chopped
½ medium **carrot**, coarsely chopped (if organic, do not
   peel)

1. In a 4-quart pot, combine the wine, garlic, cloves, tomato, bay leaf, basil, broth, onion, celery, and carrot. Bring to a simmer, partially cover, and cook for 30 minutes.

2. Strain the broth through a fine sieve into a large bowl or a storage container. Refrigerate if not using immediately, or freeze.

Good manners: The noise you don't make when you're eating soup.

—BENNETT CERF

Scandinavian Broth with Scallop–Smoked Salmon Drop Dumplings

Serves 6 to 8; doubles easily | *1 hour 40 minutes prep time; 20 minutes stove time*

These scallop dumplings with their chunks of smoked salmon are pure Scandinavia, especially when you float them in a broth flavored with dill and allspice. If only all of the grand things in life came together this easily.

BROTH

3 tablespoons **unsalted butter**

1 cup minced **shallots** (8 large)

1 medium **carrot**, cut into ⅛-inch dice

1 tablespoon ground **allspice**

8 cups **Master Broth** (page 58) or **Cheater's Broth** (page 62)

½ tightly packed cup fresh **dill**, minced

Salt and freshly ground **black pepper**

DUMPLINGS

7 ounces fresh **sea scallops**

1 large **egg white**

1 tablespoon **cornstarch**

⅛ teaspoon **salt**

Freshly ground **black pepper**

$\frac{1}{16}$ teaspoon freshly grated **nutmeg**, or to taste

1½ teaspoons fresh **lemon juice**

3 ounces **hot-smoked salmon** (such as alderwood smoked, cooked through), chilled

½ cup **heavy cream**, whipped and chilled

FINAL SEASONING

2 small **lemons**, each cut into 4 wedges

Seafood dumplings are notoriously tricky to make, but not these. Make sure all the dumpling ingredients are stone-cold, use a light hand in folding in the cream, and it will be a snap.

(recipe continues)

1. Make the broth: In a 6-quart saucepan, melt the butter over medium-low heat, add the shallots and carrot, cover, and cook for 3 minutes. Stir in the allspice and cook for 1 minute. Blend in the broth and half of the dill. Raise the heat so the broth bubbles slowly, then cover and cook for 10 minutes. Add salt and pepper to taste. Set aside for 1 hour, or chill for up to 2 days.

2. Make the dumplings: Place a food processor bowl, the steel blade, and a medium mixing bowl in the freezer. Start the dumplings about 10 minutes before serving. Make sure all of the ingredients are ice-cold. In the food processor, purée the scallops, egg white, cornstarch, salt, pepper to taste, nutmeg, and lemon juice. The mixture should be absolutely smooth.

3. Break up the smoked salmon and add it to the food processor; pulse several times so the salmon is broken into small bits and mixed into the purée. Transfer the purée to the chilled mixing bowl.

4. Now for the key step to airy dumplings: Fold in the cream so the mixture stays airy. With a spatula, gently fold a third of the cold whipped cream into the scallop mixture, taking care not to overmix. Fold in the rest of the cream.

5. Bring the broth to a very gentle simmer, then scoop up a mounded teaspoon full of dumpling purée. With a second teaspoon in your other hand, bowl side down, smooth the top of the purée so you've formed an oval. Ease it into the broth. Repeat until all of the purée is used. Gently simmer the dumplings a few moments until they float—they firm up very quickly. You want them just firm, but not hard.

6. Sprinkle the soup with the remaining dill and serve immediately. Pass the lemon wedges—they give the soup a good tart finish.

A first-rate soup is more creative than a second-rate painting.

—ABRAHAM MASLOW

Chinese Hot & Sour Soup

| *Serves 8 to 12 as part of a special* | *1½ hours prep time; 10 minutes stove time*
| *Chinese menu (page 26),*
| *6 to 8 with a smaller menu, and*
| *4 to 6 as a supper on its own*

This was Lynne's favorite soup from years ago when she and her husband conjured up Chinese banquets for monthly parties. It was the era when New Yorkers were first discovering that there was Chinese food beyond chow mein, sweet-and-sour pork, and egg drop soup. Everybody loved this soup. The vinegar and pepper sharpened appetites, which was a new concept. All of the prep work can be done ahead—a gift when you're pulling off a Chinese menu (page 26), where the last-minute stir-fry is king.

MEAT AND MARINADE

- 7 ounces lean **pork** (pork steak cut from the loin or pork chops)
- 1 teaspoon **cornstarch**
- 1 tablespoon **Shao-Hsing** (Shao Xing) **Chinese rice wine** or dry **sherry**
- 1 teaspoon **soy sauce**
- ¼ teaspoon **sugar**

DRIED INGREDIENTS

- 30 dried **tiger lily buds** (lily flower buds)
- 7 dried **Chinese mushrooms** (large dried shiitake work well here)
- 2 tablespoons dried **cloud ears** or **black tree fungus** (don't be put off by the name; they taste of dark mushrooms and meat)

SOUP

- 2 tablespoons **cornstarch**
- 8 to 9 cups **Chinese Chicken & Pork Master Broth** (page 61) or **Cheater's Broth** (page 62)

Substitutions are possible here, but we think this soup is worth a trip to an Asian market. Once you buy the ingredients, they'll keep well for a year. And while you're at it, pick up some frozen Chinese flatbreads, such as scallion pancakes, to have the next day for supper with the reheated soup.

½ cup shredded fresh or canned **bamboo shoots**, cut into
⅛-inch sticks

12 whole peeled **water chestnuts**, sliced ⅛ inch thick

1 tablespoon **soy sauce**, or to taste

8 ounces firm **tofu**, rinsed and cut into ½-inch dice

3 ounces Smithfield or other **dry-cured ham** or precooked
Chinese sausages, cut into ⅛-inch sticks (optional)

1 cup shredded cooked **chicken** (optional)

3 to 5 tablespoons **white vinegar**

2 to 3 teaspoons freshly ground **black pepper**

½ teaspoon **sesame oil**, or to taste

2 large **scallions** (white and green parts), thinly sliced

1. Prepare the meat: Up to a day ahead, trim the excess fat from the pork and freeze it for 30 minutes, or until firm. Then slice it across the grain into ½-inch pieces that are almost transparent. Toss with the cornstarch, wine, soy sauce, and sugar. Cover and refrigerate for 1 hour or overnight.

2. Prepare the dried ingredients: Gather 3 coffee mugs or small bowls. Place the tiger lily buds in one, the Chinese mushrooms in another, and the cloud ears in the third. Cover with very hot tap water. Soak for 30 minutes, or until softened. Drain each cup. (You can strain their liquids and freeze them; they're delicious in soups and braises.)

3. Cut the stems away from the tiger lily buds and save the buds. With the cloud ears, feel for the hard nubs at their bases. Trim them away, then thinly slice what remains. Place the mushrooms cap side down and cut out the stems. Then slice the mushroom caps into ⅛-inch-thick slices.

4. Make the soup: In a small bowl, stir the cornstarch with 3 tablespoons water until smooth and keep handy. In a 6-quart pot, combine the tiger lily buds, Chinese mushrooms, cloud ears, broth, bamboo shoots, water chestnuts, soy sauce, and the pork with its marinade. Bring to a simmer over medium heat. Reduce the heat, cover, and cook for 4 minutes.

5. Gently stir in the tofu, ham (if using), and chicken (if using), and the smallest amounts of white vinegar and pepper. Blend in the cornstarch mixture and simmer for about 2 minutes, or until the soup thickens slightly. Taste for sour/hot balance and for salt. Add a little more white vinegar and pepper if needed, but don't overwhelm the other flavors. Sprinkle with the sesame oil and scallions and serve hot.

Moroccan Harira Red Lentil Soup

| *Serves 4 to 6 as a main-dish soup with accompaniments; doubles easily* | *40 minutes prep time; 45 to 60 minutes stove time* | *The soup can wait a day in the refrigerator. Add the final fresh cilantro garnish at the moment of serving.* |

Lustily spiced, cooled with fresh herbs, and sharpened with lemon, this type of lentil soup is what Moroccans eat to ward off the chill of the desert night. Harira looms large in Moroccan culture, often served at weddings and other celebrations, but the soup practically unites all of Morocco during the holy month of Ramadan. Then, no food or water is taken from sunrise to sunset. But once the light fades and cannons announce the end of the day's fast, that is the moment of harira, the one "break fast" dish all Moroccans eat each evening. The soup is served with dates, dried figs, fried honey cakes, and other finger foods, and each diner takes his or her harira as desired.

In this recipe, some liberties have been taken, but hopefully we have not offended tradition. The often-used lamb, chicken, chickpeas, and eggs weren't included, and our accompaniments were modified by what is to be had close to home.

Good-tasting **extra-virgin olive oil**
1 large **onion**, cut into ⅛-inch dice
1 small **carrot**, minced
⅓ tightly packed cup fresh **flat-leaf parsley stems and leaves**, chopped
½ tightly packed cup fresh **cilantro stems and leaves**, chopped
Salt
1½ teaspoons freshly ground **black pepper**
5 large **garlic cloves**, minced
2-inch piece fresh **ginger**, minced (about 2 tablespoons)
1 teaspoon ground **turmeric**
1 teaspoon ground **cinnamon**
1¼ cups dried **red lentils**

COOK *to* **Cook**

Greek walnut-and-honey baklava pastries cut into small bites can stand in for the honey-drenched fried cakes often eaten with harira in Morocco.

2 teaspoons **sweet Hungarian paprika**

1 28-ounce can whole **tomatoes** and their liquid, puréed
(do not use tomato purée)

About 8 cups **Cheater's Broth** (page 62) or canned
low-sodium **vegetable** or **chicken broth**, enough to
make a slightly thick soup

ACCOMPANIMENTS

2 **lemons**, each cut into 6 wedges

12 or more dried **figs**, halved

12 or more **dates**

3 tablespoons **cumin**, freshly ground if possible

3 tablespoons ground **hot chile**, Aleppo if possible

12 small **phyllo pastries** of honey and nuts (see
Cook to Cook)

2 tightly packed tablespoons fresh **cilantro leaves**,
chopped

1. Coat the bottom of a 6-quart pot with a thin film of oil and set it over medium-high heat. Add the onion, carrot, parsley, cilantro, and a little salt and sauté for 8 minutes, or until golden brown. Reduce the heat to medium-low; stir in the pepper, garlic, ginger, turmeric, and cinnamon and cook for 30 seconds.

2. Blend in the lentils, paprika, tomatoes, and broth. Bring to a gentle bubble, partially cover, and simmer for 45 minutes, or until the lentils have dissolved and the soup tastes rich and good. Add salt and pepper to taste. Add a little water if the soup is too thick.

3. While the soup cooks, set out small plates for each diner with the accompaniments—lemon wedges, about 2 figs and 2 dates each, a little of the ground cumin and chile, and bite-sized pieces of pastry.

4. To serve the soup, sprinkle it with the chopped cilantro and ladle into bowls.

Pintos & Red Wine Soup with 20 Cloves of Garlic

| *Serves 6 to 8 as a main dish and 8 to 12 as a first course* | *2 hours soaking time; 30 minutes prep time; 2 hours mainly unattended stove time* | *Time is on the side of this soup; it mellows with a day or two in the refrigerator and freezes well.* |

A combination of beans, their broth, wine, and more garlic than seems sane, this soup cashes in on every frugal trick dreamed up by Tuscan farmers. Lynne's Tuscan grandfather, Severino, finished this soup with a toasted piece of bread rubbed with garlic and moistened with olive oil in the bottom of the bowl, then ladling soup over it, and finishing it with a spoonful of cheese.

BEANS

2 cups dried organic **Borlotti, pinto,** or **cranberry beans**

Good-tasting **extra-virgin olive oil**

1 large **celery stalk** with lots of leaves, cut into ¼-inch dice

1 large **carrot**, cut into ¼-inch dice

1 medium **onion**, cut into ¼-inch dice

6 large **garlic cloves**, crushed

10 fresh **sage leaves**

6 whole **cloves**

½ teaspoon **salt**

SOUP

Good-tasting **extra-virgin olive oil**

1 large **onion**, cut into ½-inch dice

Salt

½ teaspoon freshly ground **black pepper**, or to taste

4 ounces **salami** (soppressata, Genoa, or cacciatore), cut into ¼-inch dice (optional)

10 or more fresh **sage leaves**, torn

4-inch sprig fresh **rosemary**

{ **COOK** *to* **Cook** }

Borlotti beans are the tradition for this sort of soup in Tuscany, but our American pintos and cranberry beans work beautifully as well. For good bean broth you need flavorful beans. Look for organic beans from a source where turnover is fast.

20 **garlic cloves**, thinly sliced

1½ cups dry **red wine**

Head of **escarole** or **curly endive**, chopped into ½-inch
  pieces

2 generous tablespoons **tomato paste**

FOR SERVING

6 to 12 ¼-inch-thick slices coarse **whole-grain bread**,
  lightly toasted (1 slice per person)

1 large **garlic clove**, halved

About ⅓ cup good-tasting **extra-virgin olive oil**

Dry **red wine**

1½ cups freshly grated young **sheep cheese** (Pecorino
  Toscano, Pecorino Crotonese, or aged Asiago;
  about 6 ounces)

1. Make the beans: In a heatproof medium bowl, cover the beans with boiling water and soak for 2 hours. Drain, rinse, drain again, and set aside.

2. Coat the bottom of a 6-quart pot with a thin film of oil and set it over medium-high heat. Stir in the celery, carrot, onion, garlic, sage, and cloves. Sauté for 5 minutes, or until golden.

3. Add the beans and enough water to cover them by 2 inches. Bring to a very slow bubble, partially cover, and cook until they're tender, but not mushy, 45 minutes to 1½ hours depending on the freshness of the beans. Stir in the salt.

4. Make the soup: While the beans cook, coat a 12-inch straight-sided sauté pan with a thin film of oil and set it over medium-high heat. Add the onion with a little salt and the pepper.

5. When the onion is golden brown, stir in the salami (if using), sage, rosemary, and garlic, and half of the wine. Boil the wine down to nothing. Cover and set aside until the beans are done.

6. Scrape the contents of the pan into the beans, adding the escarole and tomato paste. Simmer everything together for 20 to 30 minutes, uncovered. Add salt and pepper to taste.

7. To serve, heat the soup and toast 1 slice of bread per serving. Rub each slice of the toast with garlic, set 1 slice in each soup bowl, and drizzle lightly with oil. Ladle the hot soup into the bowls and finish each helping with a few tablespoons wine. Pass the cheese at the table.

High Summer Tomato-Melon Soup

| *Serves 3 to 4; doubles* | *15 minutes prep time;* | *If there's time, make the soup early in*
or triples easily | *30 minutes chill time* | *the day and refrigerate it until serving*
| | *time; serve chilled.*

Tomatoes and Vietnamese dipping sauce may not sound like a marriage for the ages, but trust us, it has possibilities. Sweet, hot, sour, and salty, the sauce does amazing things for tomatoes. This soup was a quick improvisation on a hot night, with the melon added as an afterthought. As it turned out, that ripe sweetness let the soup take off.

1 large **garlic clove**, crushed
½ **serrano chile**, thinly sliced, or to taste
¼ cup fresh **lime juice**
2 tablespoons **sugar**, or to taste
¼ teaspoon **Asian fish sauce**
1 pound fresh **tomatoes**, cored and quartered (do not seed or peel)
½ pound ripe **cantaloupe**, peeled, seeded, and cut into large chunks
½ cup **coconut milk** (optional)
2 tightly packed tablespoons fresh **Thai basil** or **regular basil leaves**
2 tightly packed tablespoons fresh **mint leaves**

1. In a small bowl, combine the garlic, chile, lime juice, sugar, and fish sauce and let stand for 10 minutes while you prep the rest of the ingredients.

2. In a food processor, purée the tomatoes and melon along with the contents of the bowl. Taste for seasoning, add coconut milk (if using), and chill for 30 minutes to several hours.

3. Serve the soup cool, but not ice-cold. Dilute it with a little water if it's too thick. Tear the basil and mint leaves into the soup 10 minutes or so before serving. Taste for seasoning and ladle into bowls.

Two Minutes to Success

It's discouraging to hear how many people feel they are failures in the kitchen, as if they're somehow cursed with a "bad cooking" gene. There is a secret and it is crazily simple: **Read the recipe.**

Do this and you'll understand the rhythm of the dish, where you have to hover and when you can go check your e-mail. A well-written recipe tells you the equipment you need (no, you can't use a saucepan when a big, shallow sauté pan is called for—the food cooks differently in each of these). A recipe should also tell you how much time it takes to complete and give you clues as to what to look, listen, and taste for.

Don't start cooking until you have all the ingredients and equipment lined up. Next, cut and measure. Then cook and enjoy.

WORK NIGHT ENCORES

Tomato-Melon Granita: Freeze leftover soup until it's slushy and serve in tumblers.

Tomato-Melon Rice Salad: Turn the soup into a dressing for rice salad. Boil rice just as you would pasta, in lots of boiling water, drain, and toss with the soup to taste. Add more lime, fresh mint and basil if you'd like, and thinly sliced scallions. Serve cool.

Supper Salad of Melon, Fresh Cheese, and Greens: On a large platter, arrange a bed of lettuces. Tuck in chunks of melon and cucumber, spoonfuls of a fresh cheese such as goat cheese or fromage fraîche, and thinly sliced onion. Scatter the salad with small tomatoes and toasted almonds or peanuts. Sprinkle with salt and pepper, and then dress the salad with the leftover soup.

SALADS

Orange Onion Salad with Warmed Coriander Oil

| *Serves 6 to 8 as a side dish* | *2 hours 20 minutes prep time; 5 minutes assembly time* | *The salad is a natural for buffets because it can stand at room temperature for a couple of hours.* |

Imagine this. Just when your dinner party guests are expecting an oh-so-common green salad, you sashay in with a platter of Mediterranean brilliance—fresh orange slices scattered with the black and red of olives and onions. The dressing? Orange zest and freshly ground coriander seed warmed in olive oil, then drizzled over the oranges with dustings of salt, sugar, and black pepper. To top it all? This is the salad that never wilts.

Ice

¾ small to medium **red onion**, halved and thinly sliced

½ cup good-tasting **extra-virgin olive oil**

2 generous tablespoons **coriander seed**, freshly ground

2 teaspoons finely grated **orange zest**

10 to 12 **navel oranges** (4 to 5 pounds), peeled and sliced into ¼-inch-thick rounds

½ cup good-tasting **black olives**

Coarse salt

Generous amount of freshly ground **black pepper**

4 to 6 teaspoons **sugar**

Warming the ground coriander (and any other spice) and orange zest in a little olive oil helps ignite their flavors.

1. Fill a medium bowl halfway with ice cubes, add the onion, and top with more ice cubes. Add cold water to cover and refrigerate for a couple of hours or overnight. Drain the onions and pat them dry with a towel.

2. In a microwave-safe bowl, combine the oil, coriander, and orange zest. Microwave on high power for 1 minute, or warm in a saucepan over medium heat for 2 minutes. Let cool.

3. To serve, arrange the orange slices and onion rings on a platter. Scatter with the olives and the oil. Finish with the salt, pepper, and sugar to taste.

Buttermilk-Garlic Slaw with Smoky Paprika

| *Serves 6 to 8; doubles easily* | *15 minutes prep time; optional overnight rest* | *Keeps refrigerated up to 4 days* |

This slaw takes the ubiquitous ranch dressing into new territory. Creamy, garlicky, and spiked with lime, you get a nice velvety kick of smokiness from Spanish paprika (also known as Pimenton de la Vera; see page 240), which hails from western Spain. If it's not to be had, you can use any chile that's sweet and gently hot, such as ancho, Aleppo, or New Mexico. A great match for grilled and roasted dishes and perfect on a sandwich; try the slaw freshly made when it's all crunch and tang, or mellowed overnight in the fridge.

DRESSING

2 generous teaspoons **smoked mild Spanish paprika** (Pimenton de la Vera), ground **ancho chile**, or **New Mexico chile**
3 tablespoons good-tasting **extra-virgin olive oil**
Juice of 2 large **limes**
4 large **garlic cloves**
1 cup **mayonnaise** (do not use low-fat)
1 cup **buttermilk**
Salt and freshly ground **black pepper**

SLAW

Head of **green cabbage** (about 2¼ pounds)
1 medium **red onion**, halved

GARNISH

⅓ tightly packed cup fresh **cilantro** or **parsley leaves**

{ COOK *to* Cook }

Since cabbage throws off a lot of liquid, drain the slaw of much of its liquid before serving, especially if choosing to refrigerate it and serve the next day.

1. Make the dressing: Open up the flavor of the paprika by gently warming it with the oil in a small skillet over medium heat. You want it to be fragrant, but not toasted. One to 2 minutes should do it.

2. Fit a food processor with the flat steel blade and turn it on. Pour in the lime juice and drop in the garlic; process for 3 seconds. Turn off the machine, scrape down the sides of the bowl, and add the mayonnaise, buttermilk, and paprika and process for another 2 seconds. Add salt and pepper to taste. (By hand, mince the garlic and blend it with the remaining dressing ingredients.)

3. Make the slaw: Replace the flat steel blade with a thin slicing disk. Slice the cabbage and onion into the dressing at the bottom of the processor bowl. Scrape the slaw into a bowl or storage container and serve, or refrigerate overnight. (By hand, thinly slice the cabbage and onion and toss with the dressing.)

4. To serve, drain off any excess liquid and taste the slaw for seasoning. Then turn it into a serving bowl and fold in the cilantro. Serve cool, but not ice-cold.

Society, my dear, is like saltwater—good to swim in, but hard to swallow.

—ARTHUR STRINGER

Cucumber & Melon Salad with Mint

Serves 2 as a main dish and 4 as a first course or side dish | *10 minutes prep time; 30 minutes rest time; 5 minutes assembly time*

Melons and cucumbers are naturals together—they're practically siblings in the botanical world—but cooks rarely pair them. Here, they get Mediterranean attitude with mint and garlic, making them into the coolest possible essence of summer-in-a-bowl.

Partner this salad with anything pulled from the grill, or have it as a light lunch on a bed of tender greens. Obviously, the better the melon, the better the salad, but don't be afraid to sweeten not-so-perfect melon with a sprinkle of sugar.

Cucumbers have a shifty habit of giving off liquid exactly when you don't want them to. You can beat them at their own game by giving them a 30-minute salted rest in the fridge before assembling this salad (see recipe).

2 medium **cucumbers**, peeled, seeded, and cut into 1-inch pieces (about 1½ cups)

Salt

1 **garlic clove**, halved

1½ cups ripe **cantaloupe** or **watermelon**, seeded and cut into 1-inch chunks

¼ tightly-packed cup fresh **spearmint leaves**, torn

1 heaping tablespoon finely snipped **chives** or **scallions** (green parts only)

1 tablespoon **white wine**, or to taste

1 tablespoon good-tasting **extra-virgin olive oil**, or to taste

Freshly ground **black pepper**

¼ to ½ teaspoon **sugar** (optional)

¼ cup crumbled young **sheep cheese** (Ricotta Salata, Cacio di Roma, Pecorino, or feta)

1. Sprinkle the cucumbers with salt, roll up the pieces in a double thickness of paper towel, and let rest in the refrigerator for 30 minutes. Unwrap and pat dry.

2. Rub a serving bowl with the garlic. Add the cucumbers, melon, spearmint, chives, 1 tablespoon wine, and 1 tablespoon oil. Gently combine. Add wine, oil, salt, pepper, and sugar (if using) to taste.

3. Serve topped with spoonfuls of crumbled cheese and eat immediately.

Watermelon: a good fruit. You eat, you drink, you wash your face.

—ENRICO CARUSO

North African Bread Salad

Serves 4 to 8 | *20 minutes prep time* | *Dressings almost always can be done hours ahead and this one's no different, but combine it with the salad ingredients just before serving.*

Summer tomatoes and green beans usually get the olive oil and vinegar treatment in the Mediterranean, but North Africa's salty-sour preserved lemons and warm spices took this into new territory. Somewhere around the end of August when you think your salad palate is totally jaded, this is the one to try.

DRESSING

2 medium **garlic cloves**, minced

¼ cup **wine vinegar** or **cider vinegar**

1 whole **Moroccan Preserved Lemon** (page 85), pulp scraped away and rind cut into ⅛-inch dice (if not available, use the grated zest of 1 lemon and the chopped pulp of ½ lemon)

½ teaspoon **sugar**

2 teaspoons **fennel seed**

1 teaspoon **sweet paprika** (Hungarian or Spanish)

1 teaspoon whole **allspice**

4 tablespoons good-tasting **extra-virgin olive oil**

SALAD

3 cups 1-inch chunks of stale chewy **bread** (multi-grain or ciabatta)

1 pound cooked **green beans**, cut into 2-inch lengths

1 large sweet **yellow pepper**, cut into ½-inch dice (optional)

3 medium delicious ripe **tomatoes**, cut into 1-inch chunks

½ cup salted whole **almonds**, coarsely chopped

Salt and freshly ground **black pepper**

{ COOK *to* Cook }

Stale bread isn't always hanging around the house, so to duplicate it in a pinch, slowly bake torn-up pieces of fresh bread in a 325°F. oven for about 30 minutes.

  Some tomatoes worth checking out for this salad, or just for good eating, are Pink Accordion, Aunt Ruby's German Green, Black Krim, Black Cherry, German Red Strawberry, and Red Zebra.

1. **Make the dressing:** Combine the garlic, wine vinegar, lemon, and sugar in a medium bowl.

2. Combine the fennel seed, paprika, and allspice in a coffee grinder or mortar and pestle and grind very fine. Transfer the mixture to a small microwave-safe bowl, add the oil, and microwave on high power for 45 seconds. Blend into the lemon mixture and set aside until needed.

3. **Assemble the salad:** In a serving bowl, gently combine the dressing with the bread chunks, green beans, yellow pepper (if using), tomatoes, and almonds. Add salt and pepper to taste and serve at room temperature.

Variation

Sweet Roasted Peppers and Tomato Salad:

Make the dressing as directed. Eliminate the green beans and increase the peppers to 4 sweet yellow peppers. Halve them, sprinkle lightly with sugar and black pepper, and roast them in a 500°F. oven or on a hot grill for 4 minutes, or until lightly browned and softened. Cool, then cut into thin strips. Tuck clusters of yellow pepper strips between overlapping slices of 3 or 4 medium tomatoes. Dust with salt and pepper and spoon the dressing over the salad.

Doctoring
Tasteless Tomatoes

We've all had to contend with the beautiful but barren tomato—
pretty as a picture but tasting like wet Styrofoam.

There are some sneaky ways to boost flavor in those lifeless orbs, which makes sense if you think about the flavor profile of a tomato. A world-class tomato is both sweet and acid, with a good dose of umami, that almost indescribable savoriness that you find in foods like soy sauce or Parmigiano-Reggiano cheese. Before you pitch that tasteless wonder, try these tricks:

1. Sprinkle slices of tomato with both salt and sugar, or a drop or two of fish sauce.

2. For a bastardized version of the Mediterranean's sun-dried tomatoes, halve or quarter the tomatoes, place them in a single layer on a parchment-lined sheet pan, and sprinkle them with salt, a bit of sugar, and a generous dose of olive oil. Roast at very low heat (250°F. to 275°F.) until the tomatoes are shriveled and smaller in size.

3. Halve or slice the tomatoes, sprinkle with salt and olive oil, and broil until they are charred around the edges.

Moroccan Preserved Lemons

| *Makes about 1 quart;* | *10 minutes prep time; minimum* | *Keep refrigerated up to a year.*
| *doubles easily* | *2 weeks preserving time* |

These spiced lemons are Sally's own, and she uses them in salads; tucked into baked sweet potatoes; cooked with greens; braised with lamb, garlic, and carrots; or with chicken and dried fruits. Her Playboy Steak's gremolata (page 261) gets all its personality from these lemons. These lemons preserved in salt, spices, and lemon juice taste like nothing else. They turn sour and salty, but something else happens in the process that gives them a unique come-hither quality that carries over into anything they touch.

1 pound organic **lemons** (4 or 5 lemons), thoroughly washed
⅓ to ½ cup **sea salt** or **kosher salt**
4-inch **cinnamon stick**
1 teaspoon **coriander seed**
1 teaspoon **cumin seed**
3 dried **bay leaves**
3 dried **red chiles**
Juice of additional 4 to 5 **lemons**, or to cover

Since you are eating the peel, please use organic lemons.

1. Wash and sterilize a 1-quart or larger glass jar. Make a large cross in the top of each lemon and continue to cut down about two thirds of the way through the lemon, leaving the stem end intact. Open each lemon slightly and stuff generous amounts of salt into and between the cut edges. Be generous. They should be heavily packed with salt.

2. Pack the lemons into the jar with the remaining salt and the cinnamon, coriander, cumin, bay leaves, and chiles. Be sure to tightly wedge the lemons together so that they don't float around the jar. Cover them with the lemon juice and seal with a lid.

3. Let them rest for 2 to 6 weeks at room temperature out of direct light. Give them a good shake every once in a while to remind them you are waiting.

4. To use, remove the remains of the pulp and rinse the rind. Slice the rind into long graceful strips or chop it into small dice.

Grilled Lettuces with Pine Nut–Parmigiano Cream & the 65° Egg

Serves 4 to 6 as a light main dish and 6 to 8 as a first course; doubles easily

Mellow the dressing at room temperature for a couple of hours or overnight in the refrigerator.

Grilling greens unleashes something primal, an earthy spunkiness you never knew a head of romaine could possess. Most lettuces take to this treatment, but putting together a mix of sweet, herbal, and peppery really shows off what they can become.

If, like Lynne, you live where grilling is a happy memory most of the year, just grill your lettuces on the stovetop.

There are two possible takes on this recipe. Serve it as a starter. For a full meal, tuck the 65° eggs between the lettuces and scatter two generous handfuls of croutons over the platter or plates.

DRESSING

3 ounces **Parmigiano-Reggiano cheese**, in chunks
½ cup **pine nuts**, toasted
¼ cup good-tasting **extra-virgin olive oil**
½ cup **half-and-half**
2 tightly packed tablespoons fresh **basil leaves**
Salt and freshly ground **black pepper**

GRILLED LETTUCES

2 **romaine hearts**, halved lengthwise, root end trimmed of dark edges, thoroughly washed and drained of excess water
2 heads of **oak leaf** or **Bibb lettuce**, halved lengthwise
2 small heads of **frisée** or **curly endive**, halved lengthwise
Good-tasting **extra-virgin olive oil**
Salt and freshly ground **black pepper**

Fennel-Herbed Croutons (recipe follows)
3 tablespoons **wine vinegar**
3 to 4 tablespoons toasted **pine nuts**
12 fresh **basil leaves**, torn

4 to 8 **65° Eggs** (recipe follows)

1. Make the dressing: In a food processor, grate the cheese and then add the pine nuts and oil and ¼ cup water. Purée until smooth. Add the half-and-half and basil and process for 1 second, or until there are even flecks of basil in the dressing. Add salt and pepper to taste. Let stand at room temperature for up to 2 hours, or refrigerate overnight.

2. Grill the lettuce: Sprinkle the lettuce halves with oil and grill over hot coals or in a hot griddle or skillet for 1 to 2 minutes, or until they're speckled with brown on both sides. Remove from the pan immediately.

3. Assemble the salad: Spoon broad streaks of the dressing across a large platter or individual plates. Arrange the lettuces atop the dressing; sprinkle with salt and pepper and more streaks of the dressing, thinning with water if necessary. Garnish with the croutons, wine vinegar, pine nuts, and basil. Serve immediately.

(recipe continues)

Buying Lettuce

When buying lettuce, forget what you learned about the old grocer's strategy of stacking the oldest produce in the very front.

According to research from the Department of Agriculture, leafy greens such as lettuce and spinach that are stored in the front of the cooler and, therefore, in the light, actually have more nutrients than those in the shadows.

Apparently photosynthesis, which is how plants keep themselves alive, occurs even in non-natural light. It turns out fluorescent bulbs can stand in for sunlight, at least where produce is concerned.

Fennel-Herbed Croutons

Makes 4 cups	*Since these go down as easily as popcorn, this is an especially generous recipe. They hold for 2 days at room temperature.*

Good-tasting **extra-virgin olive oil**
4 cups ½-inch cubes of stale, coarse **whole-grain bread**
1 teaspoon **fennel seed**, bruised
1 teaspoon dried **basil**
½ teaspoon dried **oregano**
½ teaspoon **kosher salt**
⅛ teaspoon freshly ground **black pepper**
2 large **garlic cloves**, minced

1. Generously coat a 12-inch slant-sided skillet with a film of oil and heat over medium-high heat. Add the bread, then reduce the heat to medium. Slowly pan-fry the bread, turning the pieces until they are golden.

2. Stir in the fennel seed, basil, oregano, salt, pepper, and garlic and cook, tossing the bread to coat it, for 1 to 2 minutes, or until the garlic bits are beige, but not browned. Spread the mixture on paper towels to cool. Store in an open container for up to 2 days at room temperature, or sealed in the refrigerator for up to 1 week. Serve warm or at room temperature.

The 65° Egg

| 5 minutes prep time; 2½ to 3 hours oven time | Prepare a day ahead and refrigerate, if desired.

The 65° egg is not quite like any other egg—silken, custardlike, yet holding its shape out of the shell; a very old idea that tastes very new. You bake the egg in its shell for a couple of hours at 65°C. (149°F.). French molecular gastronome and chemist Hervé This introduced us to this idea. Eggs treated this way are gently eased out of their shell and set whole on the plate. And you can do them well ahead of time.

4 to 8 large **eggs** in the shell, at room temperature

1. Preheat the oven to 149°F. (65°C.) and have an oven thermometer handy. Don't worry if the temperature is a few degrees higher, but you don't want it lower. Place the eggs on the middle oven rack and bake for 2½ to 3 hours. Remove the eggs and let them cool to room temperature. Refrigerate until needed.

2. To serve, gently crack and remove the shells and arrange the eggs on a serving platter.

Smoked Trout & Watercress Salad with Warmed Sherry Dressing

| *Serves 6 to 8* | *20 to 30 minutes prep time*

Sally's husband, Michael, introduced us to this utterly sensuous salad that demonstrates how a few carefully chosen ingredients are all you need to make something exceptional. It seems spare, but it's a perfect mix of spicy watercress slicked with mustardy vinaigrette, sweetened with nuggets of smoked trout, and finally laced with a clipping of fresh dill.

Michael is adamant that smoked trout be used, not smoked salmon, because of the sweetness the trout brings to the plate. Who are we to argue?

We know that cleaning watercress can feel maddening at times, so this is the time to rope in help if you can. Luckily, it's work even a six-year-old can do.

DRESSING

¼ cup **Spanish sherry vinegar**
1 tablespoon **Dijon mustard**
¾ cup good-tasting **extra-virgin olive oil**
Salt and freshly ground **black pepper**

SALAD

10 to 12 cups **watercress**, cleaned and sorted, thick stems and yellowed leaves removed
2 **smoked trout**, filleted and flaked into bite-sized pieces
½ cup fresh **dill**, washed and dried

After all that work, don't even think about tossing those watercress stems. Instead, boil them lightly with shallots and lemon rind to make a flavorful poaching liquid for fish, or use them as the foundation of a delicate soup for spring peas.

WINE Pair with a dry Riesling, especially one from Alsace, or in a pinch look to Austria or Australia.

1. Make the dressing: In a small bowl, combine the sherry vinegar and mustard using a fork. Slowly whisk in the oil and add salt and pepper to taste. Gently warm the dressing in a small saucepan over low heat. It should be just warmed, not hot enough to wilt the watercress.

2. Make the salad: In a large bowl, toss the watercress with the dressing. Start with half of the dressing and add more as needed. Mound the dressed greens on individual plates.

3. Top each salad with the flaked trout and a generous portion of snipped fresh dill. Serve and enjoy.

Variation

Bacon–Brussels Sprouts Sauté with Dijon–Sherry Vinegar Dressing:

In a big skillet, sauté several slices of bacon and remove them from the pan. Thinly slice about 2 pounds Brussels sprouts and a red onion and sauté until golden, then add one recipe of the warmed sherry dressing from the smoked trout salad, but use 2 tablespoons olive oil. Toss to warm through and serve over mashed potatoes.

Spring is nature's way of saying, "Let's party."

—ROBIN WILLIAMS

The Billionaire's
Vinegar

Good mysteries don't figure into a food show, but in 2008 writer Benjamin Wallace came on the show with a doozy. He's the author of *The Billionaire's Vinegar: The Mystery of the World's Most Expensive Bottle of Wine* (Crown, 2008). The tale goes like this:

In 1985, Christie's auction house in London auctioned off a single bottle of wine for the highest price in history, $156,000. If this wasn't enough, the auctioneer was one of the most revered authorities in the wine business. With Michael Broadbent bringing down the gavel, it seemed he was endorsing that wine's veracity.

Hardy Rodenstock, a former pop-band manager, had "found" the bottle in a bricked-up cellar in Paris. Etched into the glass were "1787 Lafite" and Thomas Jefferson's initials. Odd though, that he never would show anyone where he found it or how. Once that first bottle sold, he produced several more Jefferson wines. As the years went on, he continued to unearth even more great old vintages from mysterious sources. Some wine experts were skeptical, others enamored.

Then, just as the questions about the bottle's provenance became more insistent, Rodenstock started throwing wine tastings, inviting only stars of the wine world and the über wealthy. He poured only the most rare and mysterious. Fortunes were spent for the experience and for the wines. In fact, Robert Parker called one of these tastings the most incredible experience of his life.

But one buyer, the billionaire Bill Koch, wasn't convinced. He'd bought a Jefferson bottle and when he demanded written proof of its heritage, Rodenstock had none. Koch proved that the etchings on the bottle were done by a modern dentist's tool. Add that to the fact that Rodenstock never left a bottle or a cork behind after a tasting (which could be tested for age, etc.) and the later discovery of a small laboratory with etching tools and old bottles in Rodenstock's former residence. Was this the greatest wine scam ever? The jury is still out because as of this writing, Rodenstock still sells wine.

Growing Fortune Salad

| Serves 6 to 8 on a regular menu and 8 to 12 on a special Chinese menu (page 26) | 15 minutes prep time; several hours standing time | The dressing can be made 2 days ahead and refrigerated. |

You could have tipped me over with a chopstick when, in the midst of a New Year's banquet, our formidable Chinese hostess served a head of iceberg lettuce. She'd teased it open like a giant rose and poured a ginger-sesame dressing into its center. Those leaves, with their odd mix of crunch and water, countered all the richer, darker tastes on the table. But the question that niggled at me for years was what iceberg lettuce was doing on a Chinese menu, anyway?

Clarity came from Chinese food expert Grace Young in her book *The Wisdom of the Chinese Kitchen* (Simon & Schuster, 1999). Grace explains that lettuce is part of New Year celebrations because its name in Cantonese, *saang choy*, sounds like the Cantonese expression for "growing or producing fortune."

Don't be limited by its Chinese origins; treat the salad like any other bowl of greens—pair it with almost anything.

DRESSING

- ¼ cup **Japanese seasoned rice vinegar**
- 2 tablespoons **soy sauce**
- 1 teaspoon **sesame oil**
- 2 teaspoons grated fresh **ginger**
- 2 **scallions** (white and green parts), cut on the diagonal into very thin slices
- 1 teaspoon **toasted sesame seed** (optional)

SALAD

Head of **iceberg lettuce**, trimmed of all wilted and bruised leaves

Japanese seasoned rice vinegar is flavored with sugar and salt. Just check the ingredients list before buying to be sure you are getting the right one.

1. Make the dressing: In a large bowl, combine the rice vinegar, soy sauce, oil, and ginger. Let stand at room temperature for a couple of hours, or refrigerate for up to 2 days. Just before dressing the lettuce, stir in the scallions and sesame seed.

(recipe continues)

2. Make the salad: A few hours before serving, cut the top quarter off the head of lettuce and trim the root end of its dark base, but leave it intact so the head holds together. Open up the head slightly by cradling it in both hands and rapping the root end on the counter. This loosens the leaves a bit.

3. Hold the head under cold running water to wash the interior leaves. Turn upside down on a rack to drain thoroughly. Then put it in a salad spinner or a bowl with a rack at the bottom so all the moisture can drain away. Cover and refrigerate until needed.

4. Serve the salad by putting the head root side down on a platter, teasing open the leaves a bit, and drizzling the dressing over them. Cut the wedges down to the core, but not all the way through. Serve immediately.

Have a mouth as sharp as a dagger, but a heart as soft as tofu.

—CHINESE PROVERB

Hotel Survival with
Comedian George Egg

It began innocently enough, ironing pita bread in a desperate moment of hunger after a late arrival at a hotel and no open restaurant in sight.

British comedian George Egg has taken the idea of room service to new levels with his videos on hotel cooking. Don't miss his how-tos such as bread dough rising under a halogen lamp held aloft with a Gideon Bible, or tortellini tossed with crème fraîche and wilted arugula cooked in an electric teakettle. There is no stopping him. Check him out at www.georgeegg.com.

Pineapple, Greens, & Tofu with Roasted Chile–Coconut Dressing

Serves 4, possibly with	*10 minutes prep time;*	*The dressing can be made in advance*
leftover sauce	*10 minutes stove time;*	*and warmed when needed. Rice*
	5 minutes assembly time	*noodles are a good addition to this.*

Fresh, hot, sour, salty, and sweet—Thai cuisine, and this salad, hits every pleasure point. The dressing alone is like money in the bank—it improves nearly anything it touches.

Fiddling with the recipe verified something we'd suspected: when using spices in uncooked dishes, warming them gently gets rid of their raw edge and opens up all their individuality.

Inspiration for this dressing recipe came from Thai food writer and restaurateur Su-Mei Yu's cookbook *The Elements of Life* (Wiley, 2009).

ROASTED CHILE–COCONUT DRESSING

½ cup expeller-pressed **canola oil**
4 generous teaspoons coarsely ground **Aleppo chile**
 or other flavorful medium-hot to hot ground chile
4 large **garlic cloves**, finely chopped
1⅓ cups **coconut milk**, or to taste
2 to 2½ tablespoons **Asian fish sauce**
4 tablespoons **sugar**
¼ teaspoon **salt**
Juice of ½ large **lime**

SALAD

3 large handfuls **mixed tart greens**, such as the
 tender yellow hearts of escarole, arugula, frisée,
 curly endive, mizuna, watercress, purslane, lamb's
 ear, and baby spinach
8 to 10 leaves of **napa cabbage**, cut crosswise into
 thin slivers

In Thailand, this would be made with small, fiery-hot dried Thai chiles. We prefer the Aleppo chile's sweet, fruity warmth, but you could use other chiles. Use ancho for a milder chile; for more heat, try mulato, cascabel, guajillo, cayenne, or Thai.

(recipe continues)

4 **scallions** (white and green parts), thinly sliced

1½ cups bite-sized pieces fresh **pineapple**, or canned in pineapple juice and drained

½ cup roasted, salted, and broken **cashews** or **peanuts**

1½ to 2 cups diced firm **tofu** or cooked and diced **tempeh**, **chicken**, or **seafood**

½ lightly packed cup fresh **mint**, **cilantro**, or **basil leaves**, torn

Salt and freshly ground **black pepper**

Juice of 1 to 1½ large **limes**

WINE Pour yourself a glass of the super consistent and readily available dry Riesling from Washington State's Chateau Ste. Michelle.

1. Make the dressing: In a 12-inch straight-sided sauté pan, combine the oil, chile, and garlic. Heat slowly over medium heat so the flavors will open up but nothing will burn, about 2 minutes. Stir with a wooden spatula until the garlic begins to sizzle, but do not let it brown.

2. Quickly add the coconut milk, raise the heat to medium-high, and boil the coconut milk for 30 seconds, or until it's a deep red-gold. Stir in 2 tablespoons of the fish sauce, or more to taste. Then mix in the sugar and salt and boil for 30 seconds, or until the dressing is thickened with glossy bubbles and is the color of light caramel.

3. Immediately scrape the dressing into a bowl to stop the cooking. Add the juice of half a lime. Rinse and dry the pan and keep it handy for reheating the dressing.

4. Make the salad: Toss the greens and cabbage and divide them among 4 dinner plates. Divide the scallions, pineapple, cashews, tofu, and mint among the plates, scattering them over the greens. Season the salads with salt and pepper to taste.

5. Warm the dressing in the pan to a bubble, then stir in the juice of ½ lime. Drizzle the warm dressing over each serving. Squeeze generous amounts of fresh lime juice over the salads and serve.

WORK NIGHT ENCORES

Supper Spring Rolls with Roasted Chile Dressing: Moisten rice paper rounds under warm running water. When they soften, roll up some cold cooked chicken or seafood with the dressing, or with the leftover salad.

Unplugging
YOUR KITCHEN

Nearly everything in today's kitchen replaces a tool that existed long before the electric outlet was dreamed of. **Before the food processor there was the food mill,** before the vegetable peeler there was the paring knife, before the blender it was the manual ice crusher, and whisks have whipped up froths for centuries before the mixer arrived.

Using our hands and manual tools hones our instincts and our common sense. The pleasures of touch are immeasurable. Two of the most inspiring looks at slow kitchen ways can be found in *The Unplugged Kitchen* by Viana La Place (Morrow, 1996) and *Cooking by Hand* by Paul Bertolli (Clarkson Potter, 2003).

An Unusual Italian Salad

| *Serves 4 to 6* | *20 minutes prep time*

Bitter greens with candied lemon peel, pine nuts, balsamic, and Parmigiano-Reggiano cheese become a salad destined for the holidays. The idea of this salad began in a favorite source—an Italian Renaissance cookbook from 1570, *The Opera Bartolomeo Scappi* (now in translation from the University of Toronto Press, 2008). What is charming about the dish is how new it feels.

2 heads of **frisée** or **curly endive** (6 to 7 cups), washed, dried, and torn into bite-sized pieces

¼ to ½ teaspoon **salt**

⅛ teaspoon freshly ground **black pepper**

3 tablespoons good-tasting **extra-virgin olive oil**

2 tablespoons **red wine vinegar**, or to taste

About 3 ounces **Parmigiano-Reggiano cheese**, shaved into long curls

⅓ cup **Candied Lemon Peel** (recipe follows), homemade or store-bought, cut into ½-inch sticks

⅓ cup toasted **pine nuts**

¼ cup **Balsamic Syrup** (recipe follows)

WINE Salads can be tricky with wines, and this one is particularly so because of its sweetness and the intense zestiness of the vinegar. However, you can make a terrific match with a German Riesling made from ripe grapes (look for *Kabinett* or *Spätlese* on the label), but finished dry (*Trocken*) or off-dry (*Halbtrocken*).

1. Place the frisée into a large bowl and have 4 to 6 individual salad plates at hand. Sprinkle the greens with the salt, pepper, and oil. Toss and then add the wine vinegar. Toss again and taste for oil/vinegar balance.

2. Heap greens on each plate, and tuck the cheese curls and lemon peel here and there into the greens. Scatter with the pine nuts and drizzle each pile with a few streaks of balsamic syrup. Serve immediately.

(recipe continues)

Candied Lemon Peel

Makes ⅔ cup; doubles easily | 10 minutes prep time; 15 minutes stove time; 5 minutes finishing time | Keeps several weeks in an airtight container

Who knew making candied peel was so easy, and frankly satisfying! It is quite beautiful when finished and a great gift to bring to a favorite hostess, so make extra.

3 to 4 organic **lemons**, washed
2½ cups **sugar**

1. Using a vegetable peeler, remove the peel from the lemon in vertical strips, trying to leave as much of the bitter white pith behind as possible.

2. In a small saucepan, combine the peels with 2 cups cold water and bring to a boil. Immediately drain, refill the pan with water, bring to a boil, and drain again. Repeat this process three times to remove the bitterness from the peel. After the third dunking, remove the peels from the pan and set aside.

3. Measure 2 cups of the sugar into a saucepan and add 1 cup water. Set over medium-high heat, bring to a boil, and whisk until the sugar dissolves. Drop in the peels, reduce the heat to medium-low, and simmer uncovered for 10 to 15 minutes, or until the peels are tender and translucent. Drain and cool the peels. Keep the syrup for other uses.

4. Place the remaining ½ cup sugar in a large bowl and add the peels. Toss with your fingers until the peels are thoroughly coated. Remove one peel at a time, shaking off the excess sugar. Store in an airtight container.

Since you are actually eating the peel, please use organic lemons if at all possible. Be sure to save the lemon syrup, as it is delicious in iced tea.

Balsamic Syrup

| *Makes about ¼ cup;* | *5 minutes prep time;* | *Keeps refrigerated in a sealed jar*
| *doubles easily* | *4 minutes stove time* | *1 month or more*

⅔ cup **balsamic vinegar**
1 tablespoon (packed) **dark brown sugar**

Combine the balsamic vinegar and sugar in a small skillet and boil over
medium-high heat, stirring occasionally with a wood spatula, for 3 to 4 minutes,
or until glossy bubbles cover the surface. The syrup is ready when the spatula
leaves a path as you run it along the bottom of the skillet. It should be quite
thickened and syrupy. Take off the heat and cool before using.

What We Learned from the Pros—
Daniel Patterson

When asked about his favorite kitchen tool, award-winning San
Francisco chef and writer Daniel Patterson told us that two
things found in every single kitchen can give you more
information, more accurately and more consistently, than anything
else: **your hands.**

In the simplest of all illustrations, he told us to think about the difference between
tossing a salad with tongs versus using your hands, and innocently asked, "How can the
tongs tell you when the leaves are evenly coated? Only your fingers can do that."

Pomegranate-Cinnamon Tabbouleh

Serves 4 to 6 | *30 minutes prep time; 5 minutes assembly time* | *The tabbouleh can be made ahead, but do not dress it until you're ready to serve.*

This is Sally's take on a new tabbouleh she had years ago in London at the restaurant Moro. It was eye-opening as the usual characters, cucumber and tomato, were nowhere to be found. Instead, this salad was a jumble of cracked wheat bulgur; raw, bitter winter greens; nuts; and fresh parsley studded with ruby-red pomegranate seeds.

The beauty of bulgur, aside from its wheaten, nutlike taste, is that it's already cooked. It merely needs to be reconstituted with hot water.

1½ cups medium or coarsely ground **bulgur wheat**

DRESSING

1 large **garlic clove**, minced
Generous ¼ teaspoon ground **cinnamon**
3 to 4 tablespoons **pomegranate molasses**
2 to 3 tablespoons **water** or dry **white wine**
¼ teaspoon **salt**
Freshly ground **black pepper**
⅓ to ½ cup expeller-pressed **canola** or **safflower oil**

SALAD

2 **Belgian endives** or ½ medium head of **radicchio**, trimmed, cored, and coarsely chopped
1 medium **fennel bulb**, cored, quartered, and coarsely chopped, fronds reserved
½ cup chopped fresh **flat-leaf parsley**

{ COOK *to* Cook }

Find pomegranate molasses (often called pomegranate syrup) in Middle Eastern markets. It keeps for months in the refrigerator and is utterly delicious. Drizzle it over grilled lamb, garlicky chicken, or roasted eggplant, or stir the syrup into club soda as a cocktail.

If pomegranate molasses is not available, pour 3 cups pure pomegranate juice into a skillet and boil it down to a thick syrup. There should be about 6 tablespoons.

2 tightly packed tablespoons fresh **mint**, coarsely
    chopped
2 to 3 **scallions** (white parts only), thinly sliced
Generous ¼ cup shelled, salted **pistachios**, coarsely
    chopped
Seeds from 1 large **pomegranate**, white membrane
    removed
Salt and freshly ground **black pepper**

1. Soak the bulgur: Place the bulgur in a bowl and add boiling water to cover by 2 inches. Soak for 10 to 20 minutes, depending on the grind of the grain. Taste for tenderness, but be sure it's not mushy. Drain well, squeezing out as much extra moisture as possible by wrapping the grain in a clean towel and wringing it out. If time allows, spread out the bulgur on a fresh towel to help it dry a bit. Transfer the bulgur to a large bowl.

2. Make the dressing: In a medium bowl, combine the garlic, cinnamon, pomegranate molasses, water, salt, and pepper to taste. Stir well. Add ⅓ cup of the oil in a slow stream while whisking until emulsified. Taste for seasoning and to see if more oil is needed.

3. Make the salad: Toss into the bulgur the endive, fennel, parsley, mint, scallions, and pistachios. Gently fold in the pomegranate seeds and the dressing. Taste again for seasoning, garnish with the fennel fronds, and serve.

PASTA AND GRAINS

Barley Risotto with Saffron, Corn & Chives

| *Serves 4; doubles easily* | *25 minutes prep time;* | *Serve immediately.*
30 to 40 minutes stove time

Make this dish like mad when corn is in high season, but don't desert it when the weather turns; even without corn, it is still delicious.

This is a rustic take on risotto. The Arborio rice is replaced with everyday pearl barley, which manages to keep its toothiness while still becoming velvety smooth and creamy.

The pinch of saffron is a nod to Italy's classic *risotto alla Milanese*, while the handful of fresh-cut sweet corn makes this a decidedly American version. Fresh-cut corn is key in this recipe; frozen or canned simply will not make the cut.

¼ teaspoon crumbled **saffron threads**

3½ to 4 cups **Master Broth** (page 58) or **Cheater's Broth** (page 62)

3 tablespoons **unsalted butter** or good-tasting **extra-virgin olive oil**

1 medium **onion**, finely chopped

Salt and freshly ground **black pepper**

1 large **garlic clove**, minced

1 heaping cup (8 ounces) **pearl barley**

½ cup dry **white wine**

1 cup freshly shucked **sweet corn**, cut from the cob (about 2 ears)

¾ to 1 cup (4 ounces) freshly grated **Parmigiano-Reggiano cheese** or shredded American **Fontinella** or **Asiago**

2 tablespoons freshly snipped **chives**

{ **COOK** *to* **Cook** }

Branch out and try other grains in this recipe, such as farro, an heirloom wheat from Italy, or Job's Tears, an ancient tropical grain with a corn-barley flavor. Taste your way through the cooking process and add more or less liquid as needed.

WINE Look for a minimally oaky, medium to full-bodied white such as an unoaked Chardonnay from California or Australia, Chardonnay-based Mâcon from Burgundy, Pinot Blanc from Alsace, or Pinot Gris from Oregon.

1. Soak the saffron: In a coffee cup, crumble the saffron into ¼ cup hot water; steep for 15 minutes.

2. Heat the broth in a 2- to 3-quart saucepan and keep it warm.

3. Make the risotto: In a heavy 4-quart saucepan, heat the butter over medium heat, adding the onion with a light sprinkling of salt and pepper. Sauté for about 3 minutes, or until the onion is soft and clear. Blend in the garlic and barley and cook for 2 minutes, stirring often.

4. Raise the heat to medium-high. Stir in the wine and cook for about 1 minute, or until it's absorbed.

5. Add the saffron water and, using a ladle, begin adding the broth, 1 cup at a time, simmering and stirring each addition until all of the liquid is absorbed by the barley before adding the next cup. After cooking in about 2 cups, begin adding the broth in ½-cup portions. Once you start adding the broth, the cooking time will be 35 to 40 minutes. Begin tasting the barley.

6. When it's ready, the barley should be nearly tender, with a little more firmness to the bite than you'd like, and it should be soupy. Add the corn and cook until just cooked through, 2 to 3 minutes. Remove from the heat, stir in the cheese, and let stand for 2 to 3 minutes.

7. Ladle the risotto into individual heated bowls and garnish with the freshly snipped chives.

Ever wonder about those people who spend $2 apiece on those little bottles of Evian water? Try spelling Evian backward.

—GEORGE CARLIN

Midnight Pasta with Prosciutto

| Serves 4 as a main dish and 6 as a first course | 10 minutes prep time; 20 minutes stove time | The sauté can be prepared several hours ahead and tossed with the remaining ingredients just before serving. Once the pasta is in play, eat the dish while it's hot. |

Late-night forays are an ignored yet vital dining category. The assumption is that we'll stand at the open fridge forking up sustenance directly from the storage container. Well, let's put a little class into the act, as in a dish from the Italian city of Parma, where the curing of ham is taken very seriously.

Ten minutes gives you a pasta of savory ham with bright-tasting tomato, garlic, onion, and a touch of barely melted sweet butter. This is the way to smooth out the end of a long day.

4 tablespoons **extra-virgin olive oil** or **unsalted butter**

2 large **garlic cloves**, halved

1 large **onion**, minced

3 tablespoons minced fresh **flat-leaf parsley**

4 to 5 ounces **prosciutto di Parma** or **Iowa's La Quercia** or good-quality **salami**, thin sliced and cut into thin strips

1 pound freshly cooked **tagliatelle** or **fettuccine pasta**, well drained

1 tablespoon **unsalted butter**

3 to 4 good-tasting ripe **tomatoes** (about 2 pounds), diced, or 1 28-ounce can whole tomatoes and a little of their liquid

Salt and freshly ground **black pepper**

1½ cups freshly grated **Parmigiano-Reggiano cheese**

COOK *to* **Cook**

Prosciutto di Parma sets the bar high in the world of hams—never salty, it tastes of concentrated essence of good pork. Up until a while ago, no American ham matched it. Now there's Iowa's La Quercia, and no doubt more artisans will follow. Taste as you find them and see what you think. Also, prosciutto freezes well, so it's easy to keep on hand.

WINE Look for a light but ripe Italian red, like a Valpolicella Ripasso from the Veneto.

1. In a 12-inch sauté pan, heat the oil over medium heat. Add the garlic and cook, pressing it down in the oil, for 1 minute, or until slightly softened and pale golden. Do not burn. Pull the garlic from the pan and keep it handy.

2. Add the onion and parsley to the pan, cover, and cook over low heat for about 15 minutes, or until the onion is soft and clear. At this point the pan could be set aside off the heat until shortly before serving.

3. When ready to eat, return the pan to the stove and raise the heat to medium. Stir in one fourth of the prosciutto and cook for about 2 minutes. The onion should just start to color. Add the reserved garlic and toss in the cooked pasta, butter, and tomatoes and the rest of the prosciutto. Toss over medium heat to thoroughly combine. Add salt and pepper to taste.

4. Turn the pasta into a serving bowl. Pass the cheese separately, but be certain to use it, as it is the final seasoning of the dish.

PASTA IN BRIEF

1. Never add oil to the water; it won't keep the pasta from sticking, only boiling in a generous amount of water will.

2. Pasta water should taste like the sea. Be generous with the salt.

3. If the pasta box directs "rinse after boiling," put the box back on the shelf and walk away. It's a low-grade pasta.

Summer is the time of year when one sheds one's tensions with one's clothes.

—ADA LOUISE HUXTABLE

Farmer's Market Pasta

Serves 4 as a main dish | *30 minutes prep time; 10 minutes stove time*

We've all had those post–farmer's market moments when, while unloading your goodies, you remember that you actually bought *three* pounds of zucchini in an optimistic moment, and now you wonder what the heck you are going to do with it. Well, this is what.

Think of this as a lemon-garlic salad dressing tossed with pasta, vegetables, and cheese. The only stove time needed is to heat the water and cook the pasta.

SAUCE

- 6 large **garlic cloves**, finely chopped
- ½ medium **red onion**, cut into ¼-inch dice
- ⅔ cup fresh **lemon juice** (about 3 large lemons)
- 1 fresh **chile**, seeded or not, and minced, or ground chile to taste (Aleppo is one we like, and for fresh sting, a small Thai chile)
- **Salt** and freshly ground **black pepper**
- 2 to 3 **anchovy fillets**, rinsed (optional)

PASTA

- 1 pound **pasta** (fettuccine, tagliatelle, or linguine)
- 1½ pounds **zucchini** (5 medium zucchini), cut into ¼-inch × 2-inch sticks

FINISHING SEASONINGS

- ⅓ tightly packed cup fresh **basil leaves**, torn
- ¼ to ⅓ tightly packed cup fresh **mint leaves**, torn
- 1 tightly packed tablespoon fresh **oregano leaves**, torn
- ½ cup **black olives**, pitted and coarsely chopped
- 3 to 4 tablespoons good-tasting **extra-virgin olive oil**
- ½ cup whole **toasted almonds**, coarsely chopped
- 1½ cups (6 ounces) shredded medium-aged **sheep cheese** or Italian or American **Asiago**

The concept behind this recipe translates into any season. Think peas and asparagus cooked in the pasta water in spring, and broccoli or butternut squash in the winter.

WINE Simple dishes like this don't demand fancy wines, so something like an inexpensive Tuscan red (Toscano Rosso) will do well. That said, simple foods can offer a subtle backdrop that can show off complex wines without clashing, making a fine Chianti or Brunello a great choice for a more special evening.

(recipe continues)

1. **Make the sauce:** In a large serving bowl, combine the garlic, onion, lemon juice, chile, salt and pepper to taste, and anchovy (if using). Set aside.

2. **Make the pasta:** Bring 6 quarts salted water to a boil in an 8-quart pot. Drop the pasta into the boiling water. Add the zucchini to the pasta in the water 4 minutes before the pasta is done (check the box for timing). Once the pasta is tender but still has a little bite (al dente), scoop up ½ cup pasta water and set aside. Immediately drain the pasta and zucchini in a colander.

3. **Finish the pasta:** Stir the reserved hot pasta water into the lemon juice mixture along with the basil, mint, oregano, olives, and oil. Add the drained pasta and zucchini and toss to combine. Add salt and pepper to taste (be generous with the black pepper), and then toss with the almonds and cheese. Serve hot.

WORK NIGHT ENCORE

Farmer's Market Pasta Omelet: This is one way our frugal Italian ancestors turned leftover pasta into family supper. Preheat the oven to 350°F. Beat together 1 to 2 eggs per person you are serving. Add a little salt and pepper, and fresh herbs if you'd like. Heat the leftover Farmer's Market Pasta with a little hot olive oil in a 10-inch nonstick skillet with an ovenproof handle. Pour the eggs over the noodles, stir a little to combine, and slip the pan into the oven. Bake for 15 minutes, or until the eggs are firm and cooked at the center of the noodles. Sprinkle with shredded cheese, cut into wedges, and serve.

Never Is a Colander

Too Big

Don't bother buying multiple sizes. **Buy one big enough to rinse a baby** in and you will never need another.

Homemade Ricotta Gnocchi with Saffron Tomato Sauce

| *Serves 4 as a main dish; doubles easily* | *10 minutes prep time* | *Both the sauce and the gnocchi dough can be made up to 2 days in advance and refrigerated. Once cooked, serve and eat immediately.* |

This is the homemade pasta to make with little kids; anyone who can work with Play-Doh can make these gnocchi with expertise.

Tender, milky, and virtually foolproof, these little lumps no doubt had clouds as ancestors—they are that light. The saffron in the sauce opens up once the sauce and dumplings come together.

With so few ingredients, this dish hinges on their quality, which brings us to the ricotta. It's tough to find good store-bought ricotta, so make your own. It's crazily easy and the flavor will blow you away. Another advantage to using your own ricotta is that the dough becomes easier to handle than when made with store-bought.

1 recipe **Homemade Ricotta Gnocchi** (recipe follows)
1 recipe **Saffron Tomato Sauce** (recipe follows), warmed in a 12-inch skillet
1 cup (4 ounces) freshly grated **Parmigiano-Reggiano cheese**

WINE Pair this delicate pasta with a light and delicate red from Italy, such as Barbera, Pinot Nero, Valpolicella, or a fresh, young Chianti.

1. Bring 5 quarts salted water to a boil in a 6-quart pot. Drop the gnocchi into the boiling water and cook for 3 to 4 minutes, or until they rise to the surface and float.

2. Drain the gnocchi in a large colander, or scoop them out of the water with a big slotted spoon. Toss them gently in the skillet with the warmed tomato sauce until uniformly covered. Sprinkle lightly with cheese and serve.

(recipe continues)

Homemade Ricotta Gnocchi

Serves 4 as a main dish; doubles easily | *20 minutes prep time* | *Can be made up to 2 days in advance and refrigerated. Because of the delicate cheese, these do not freeze well.*

1 pound fresh **Homemade Ricotta** (about 2½ cups),
   chilled (recipe follows)
½ cup unbleached **all-purpose flour**, plus more for rolling
   the gnocchi
1 large **egg**
¼ cup freshly grated **Parmigiano-Reggiano cheese**
1 tablespoon **unsalted butter**, melted
½ teaspoon **salt**
¼ teaspoon **sugar**
⅛ teaspoon freshly grated **nutmeg**, or to taste
Freshly ground **black pepper**

1. In a large bowl and using your hands, mix the ricotta, flour, egg, cheese, butter, salt, sugar, nutmeg, and pepper to taste, adding more flour as needed until the dough is slightly sticky. Cover and refrigerate until cold, 1 hour or up to 2 days.

2. When ready to make the gnocchi, lightly sprinkle flour on a large cutting board and a rimmed large shallow pan. Transfer the dough to the floured board and cut it into 4 equal pieces. Using your hands, roll one of the pieces on the board into a long log ½ to ¾ inch wide. Don't worry if the dough isn't uniformly shaped—the gnocchi will be charmingly irregular. Take care not to pick up too much additional flour or the gnocchi will be tough. You want just enough to keep them shapeable, but still a little sticky.

3. Cut the log into ¾-inch pieces and toss them on the floured sheet pan, leaving space between them. Repeat until all the dough has been rolled and cut. Cover with plastic wrap and chill for at least 1 hour or up to 2 days.

Homemade Ricotta

| *Makes 1¼ to 1½ pounds* | *10 minutes prep time;* | *Keeps refrigerated, covered, up to*
| | *15 to 20 minutes stove time* | *3 days*

1 gallon high-quality **whole milk**
2 teaspoons **salt**
⅓ cup fresh **lemon juice** (about 1 large lemon)

1. Line a large colander with a layer of cheesecloth and place it in the sink or over a bowl if you want to save the whey. Wet the cheesecloth to hold it firmly in place.

2. Make the ricotta: In a large heavy pot, bring the milk and salt to a gentle simmer over medium-high heat. Stir in the lemon juice and continue to simmer gently for 1 to 2 minutes, or until curds begin to form and float to the top. They will first look like spatters of white, then gather into soft, cloudlike clumps. When you see the liquid begin to clear of cloudiness and the curds are firming up but not hard, scoop them out with a slotted spoon or sieve.

3. Let the curds drain thoroughly in the colander. If very soft, press gently to extract a little moisture, but take care not to dry out the cheese. Transfer the ricotta to a large bowl, cover, and chill for 1 to 2 hours.

Rinsing the pot with cold water before pouring in the milk will save you some serious cleanup! The reserved liquid whey can go into soups, stews, and curries and be used to cook pasta and rice. It will keep refrigerated for up to 3 days.

WHAT TO DO WITH HOMEMADE RICOTTA

1. Eat it warm from the colander drizzled with good olive oil.
2. Grill slices of crusty bread, rub with a clove of garlic, and top with sun-dried tomatoes, ricotta, fresh basil leaves, and liberal amounts of salt and pepper.
3. Toss with thick tubes of pasta and quickly cooked tomatoes.
4. Fill ravioli (page 122).
5. Eat for breakfast doused with milk and honey and a sprinkle of nuts.
6. Make a tart (page 310).
7. Blend with cocoa powder, ground cinnamon, and sugar and slather on slices of stone fruit that you eat with your fingers.

(recipe continues)

Saffron Tomato Sauce

| *Makes about 3 cups* | *10 minutes prep time;* | *Keeps refrigerated, covered, up to* |
| | *30 minutes stove time* | *3 days and frozen 3 months* |

Good-tasting **extra-virgin olive oil**
1 medium **onion**, minced
Generous ½ teaspoon crumbled **saffron threads**
1 28-ounce can whole **tomatoes** with their liquid
Salt and freshly ground **black pepper**

1. **Make the sauce:** Coat a straight-sided, 12-inch sauté pan with a thin film of oil. Over medium heat, gently cook the onion for 3 to 4 minutes, or until tender and translucent. Add the saffron and sauté for 30 seconds to 1 minute, or until fragrant.

2. Add the tomatoes and their liquid, crushing them with your hands as they go into the pan. Raise the heat to medium-high and simmer for 20 to 30 minutes, or until the tomatoes have lost their raw taste and have thickened in the bottom of the pan. Add salt and pepper to taste and thin with water as needed.

Never argue at the dinner table, for the one who is not hungry always gets the best of the argument.

—RICHARD WHATELY

High School
Food Police

New York City high schoolers Brenda Tam and Matt Gross
had an idea for a science project they called DNA House. They were
studying DNA bar coding, which is a method used to identify
species based on their DNA sequences. They collected 217 samples
from their homes and neighborhood grocery stores—things such
as beef jerky and dried soup mix. They then tried to isolate
animal DNA.

It turned out that 11 out of 66 of the foods tested were mislabeled. Perhaps
even worse, the pricier items turned out to be the biggest offenders. The artisan
"sheep's milk" cheese? Actually lowly cow's milk, and the "sturgeon" caviar?
The humble Mississippi paddlefish. Just for the record, these two bright
teenagers were following in the footsteps of a science project done the year
before called Sushigate. Who needs the FDA?

Paradise's Ravioli of Ricotta & Mascarpone

| Makes about 45 large ravioli; serves 8 to 12 as a first course and 7 to 8 as a main dish | The filling can be made several hours ahead and refrigerated. You can make the ravioli a couple of hours before cooking, but once they're cooked, serve them immediately. | The tomato sauce holds in the fridge for 3 days. |

Lynne's neighbor Tim Paradise plays a mean clarinet; in fact, he plays it for the Saint Paul Chamber Orchestra. But in private life, Tim's star power rests on his ravioli. He has "the hand," that instinctive feel for light pasta.

Tim makes a "platter sauce" right on the serving platter. You'll see how it's done in this recipe and will probably be improvising the sauce tonight for a bowl of spaghetti. Do try your own hand at making Tim's ravioli. Aside from what they deliver on a plate, doing your own ravioli can be your moment of Zen.

One last note: this is the recipe of a perfectionist; Tim's pasta technique is as exacting as his music.

You will need a pasta machine or rolling pin, cake racks and/or flat baskets to hold the ravioli, a food mill for making the sauce (a food processor can stand in), and a hand cheese grater for the table.

FILLING

1 cup (4 ounces) freshly grated **Parmigiano-Reggiano cheese**

2 cups (8 ounces) high-quality **ricotta**, preferably homemade (page 119)

2 cups (8 ounces) **mascarpone cheese**

1 tightly packed tablespoon fresh **mint leaves**, coarsely chopped, plus more to taste

⅛ to ¼ teaspoon freshly grated **nutmeg**

Salt and freshly ground **black pepper**

4 large **egg yolks**

WINE A relatively softly textured wine is the key to a good match for this dish. For a white, consider an Arneis from Piedmont. If looking for a red, try a Valpolicella Ripasso from Italy's Veneto region.

TOMATO SAUCE

2 28-ounce cans whole **tomatoes** and their liquid
(Tim uses Muir Glen)
Salt and freshly ground **black pepper**

PASTA

1 recipe **Tim's Fresh Pasta** (recipe follows)
1 large **egg white**

FINISHING

1 stick **unsalted butter**, at room temperature
10 sprigs fresh **basil**
Salt and freshly ground **black pepper**
8-ounce chunk of **Parmigiano-Reggiano** for grating
at the table

1. **Make the filling:** In a medium bowl, blend the
Parmigiano, ricotta, mascarpone, mint, nutmeg, salt,
and pepper and taste for seasoning. Thoroughly blend in
the egg yolks. Cover and refrigerate.

2. **Make the tomato sauce:** Put the tomatoes in a deep
6-quart pot. Simmer over medium-low heat for about
15 minutes, or until reduced by a third. Stir often. Add
salt and pepper to taste, let the tomatoes cool, and then
put them through a food mill. (In a pinch you can purée
them in a food processor.) Refrigerate or keep warm if
serving soon.

3. **Fill the ravioli:** Have cake racks and/or flat baskets
handy.

Spread out the first rolled-out strip of pasta dough
(page 125), and trim away any ragged edges. If the strip
is more than 4 inches wide, you'll make two rows of
ravioli; with a narrower strip, make one.

Place generous teaspoons of filling 1 inch in from the
edge of the dough down the length of the strip. Space
them about 1½ inches apart. With your finger, spread
egg white around each mound. Fold over the dough

**For the pasta, Tim
mixes lower-protein
and higher-protein
flours to approximate
the pasta flour used in
Rome at his favorite
trattoria. When looking
for the pastry/cake
flour, check nutrition
labels for 8% protein.
The unbleached
all-purpose flour
should be 11% to 12%.**

**High-quality ricotta
pays off here. If you
can't find any, make
your own (page 119).
If using homemade
ricotta, or if the store-
bought is very moist,
you need to protect the
ravioli from turning
soggy by removing
some of the cheese's
moisture by draining it.
Line a sieve with a thin
towel and set it over a
bowl. Add the ricotta to
the sieve and let it drain
overnight in the fridge.**

(recipe continues)

carefully to eliminate air pockets and press the edges together. Cut them apart with a zigzag cutter or a knife and lift each onto the cake racks or baskets so they don't touch. Keep the ravioli at room temperature for up to 2 hours; after that, refrigerate them. Repeat the whole process as the remaining dough is rolled out.

4. Cook and serve the ravioli: Have ready a large serving platter (warmed if possible) and a slotted spoon. Bring 5 quarts salted water to a boil in a 6-quart pot. Have the tomato sauce warm on the stove and the butter, basil, salt, and pepper nearby. Rub a little butter over the platter.

Once the water is boiling, turn it down to a lively simmer and drop in 5 or 6 of the ravioli. Cook until they float to the surface (cut off an edge of dough to taste for doneness if you like). Gently lift them out with the spoon, drain, and spread them on the platter. Rub them with a little butter.

Repeat the cooking until you have a single layer of ravioli lightly coated with butter. Sprinkle them with a little salt and pepper and scant daubs of tomato sauce. Tear a few basil leaves over the layer. Cook the rest of the ravioli, and continue layering until all of the ravioli are used.

5. Serve the ravioli: Garnish them with whole basil leaves. Serve hot. Pass the chunk of Parmigiano with a hand grater.

Tim's Fresh Pasta

Makes enough dough for about 45 large ravioli, or about 1½ pounds pasta; serves 6 to 8 as a main dish	*20 minutes prep time; 1 to 3 hours rest time; 45 minutes rolling-out time*

3 cups **pastry** or **cake flour** (8% protein and organic
   if possible), dipped and leveled (see page 304)
6 large **eggs**
2 to 3 cups unbleached **all-purpose flour** (11% to 12%
   protein and organic if possible), dipped and leveled
   (see page 304)

1. Mix the pasta dough: Put the pastry flour in a large bowl. With the back of your hand, make a well in the center. Pour the eggs into the well. Stir them together with a fork. Now gradually stir flour from the sides of the well into the eggs until everything is mixed and ragged looking.

2. Knead the dough: Flour a counter and turn the dough onto it. Gradually work in a cup or so of the unbleached flour. Do this by sprinkling flour on the dough, folding it over on itself (a pastry scraper helps here), and kneading it. The dough will become velvety on the outside and sticky in the center.

Keep kneading by lightly dusting on more flour and constantly rolling the dough over on itself, like winding a spring. Then stretch it out, roll it back up, turning a quarter turn, and repeat.

Do this for 5 to 8 minutes, or until the dough is smooth and a little soft. Its interior should be a little sticky. Rest the dough under a bowl for at least 1 hour. Before rolling, knead in another ⅓ cup unbleached flour.

3. Roll out the pasta: A rolling pin can be used—merely roll the dough to the thickness described. If working with a pasta machine, have its rollers at the widest opening. Divide the dough into thirds; keep two pieces under a towel as you work with the other.

Lightly flour the dough, shaping it into a 5-inch round. Pass it through the pasta machine's widest setting five times, folding it back on itself each time. This folding laminates the dough to make it lighter. Next, narrow the rollers and pass and fold the dough three more times. Flour the dough only if it's sticky. Keep narrowing the rollers and passing the dough until you can see shadows through it. Spread it on a lightly floured surface and fill as directed in the main recipe. Repeat the rolling out and filling with the other two pieces of dough.

Pasta Prank

In 1957, a BBC news show called Panorama (think Jim Lehrer's *NewsHour*) produced a spoof segment on the bumper spaghetti harvest in Switzerland, complete with footage of Swiss farmers picking spaghetti off trees. Hundreds of people called the BBC asking for information on how they could plant their own spaghetti trees.

The BBC's response? Place a sprig of spaghetti in a tin of tomato sauce and hope for the best.

Long-Life Noodles of Chinese Broccoli & Garlic Pork

| *Serves 6 to 8 on a Chinese menu* | *30 minutes prep time;* |
| *(page 26) or 2 to 3 as a one-dish supper* | *20 minutes stove time* |

Here a little pork makes a big point. Crisp it in a wok along with garlic, hoisin sauce, and water chestnuts for crunch, and you'll taste how a small amount of meat used solely as a seasoning can be just as satisfying as a lot of it as the main event. Toss that pork with broccoli and noodles and dinner is done. Or you have the beginning of a Chinese menu (page 26).

Nearly everything on the Chinese table is there for its meaning. Noodles symbolize long life. In many regions of China you'd never celebrate the New Year or a birthday without them. Be they hot or cold, sweet or spicy, they must never be cut—for obvious reasons.

NOODLES

8 ounces **Chinese wheat noodles** (about ⅛ inch wide) or boxed **Italian linguine**

1½ teaspoons **sesame oil**

PORK

3 large **garlic cloves**

6-ounce piece of well-marbled **pork** (butt or shoulder), cut into 1-inch chunks

2 tablespoons **rice vinegar** or **white vinegar**

1 tablespoon **soy sauce**

2 tablespoons **hoisin sauce**

Salt

3 whole **water chestnuts**, cut into ⅛-inch dice

3 **scallions** (white parts only), thinly sliced

1 tablespoon expeller-pressed **canola** or other **neutral-tasting oil**

COOK *to* Cook

Prepping ahead as much as possible is the secret to pulling off a Chinese meal. The ground pork and seasoning mixture can be done a day ahead and refrigerated. Once cooked, the pork can wait for an hour or so. Cut all the vegetables, measure seasonings, and cook the noodles. Just before serving, stir-fry the broccoli and finish the dish.

CHINESE BROCCOLI STIR-FRY

12 to 14 ounces **Chinese broccoli** (*gai lan*), washed
    and thoroughly dried
1 tablespoon **soy sauce**
1 tablespoon **Shao-Hsing** (Shao Xing) **Chinese rice
    wine**, or dry **sherry**
1 tablespoon **rice vinegar** or **white vinegar**
3 large **garlic cloves**, minced
2 tablespoons expeller-pressed **canola** or **safflower oil**
1-inch piece fresh **ginger**, thinly sliced into rounds
Salt and freshly ground **black pepper**

WINE The soft, spicy, faintly sweet character of New World Pinot Noir works very nicely with these noodles. However, if you have a hankering for a white, keep it in the family and look for Pinot Blanc or a dry-style Pinot Gris from Oregon.

1. Make the noodles: Bring 4 quarts salted water to a boil in a 6-quart pot. Drop the noodles into the boiling water, stir, and cook, stirring often, for 5 to 8 minutes, or until just tender. Drain in a colander, rinse with cold water, shake off excess water, and drain again thoroughly. Toss with the sesame oil and set aside.

2. Make the pork: In a food processor, mince the garlic. Add the pork, vinegar, soy sauce, and hoisin sauce and a generous pinch of salt. Pulse the machine until the pork is ground medium fine.

Transfer everything to a medium bowl. With a spoon, work in the water chestnuts and scallions.

3. Cook the pork: Heat a wok or large sauté pan over high heat. Swirl in the canola oil. When it's practically smoking, add the pork. Stir-fry for 3 minutes, breaking up any chunks. When the meat's browned, it's ready. Transfer the meat to a small bowl and hold until needed. Wipe out the wok or pan.

4. Make the stir-fry: To cook the Chinese broccoli, separate the leaves from the stems. Slice the stems into ½-inch lengths and set aside. Coarsely chop the leaves and put them in another pile. In a small bowl, blend the soy sauce, wine, vinegar, and garlic.

5. Just before serving, set the wok over high heat; when very hot, swirl in the canola oil and heat to barely smoking. Stir in the ginger with a generous sprinkling of salt and pepper. Stir-fry for a few seconds, until fragrant, then drop in the broccoli stems. Stir-fry for 1 minute and add the leaves. Stir-fry for another minute to 90 seconds, or until the stems pick up a little brown color. Add the soy sauce mixture and stir-fry until boiled off.

6. Immediately add the pork and stir-fry for 10 seconds. Add the noodles and keep tossing them for another 20 seconds, or until hot. Transfer to a platter and serve immediately.

Vietnamese Green Mango Noodle Salad with Grilled Pork

| Serves 4 to 8 as part of a larger menu | 1 hour prep time; 20 minutes marinating time; 5 to 10 minutes stove or grill time | The assembled salad can wait in the refrigerator for 1 to 2 hours; the noodle prep and dipping sauce can be done hours ahead. |

Gather up everything there is to love about Vietnamese food and put it in one dish and you'd probably create this salad. Tangles of sheer cellophane noodles topped with slices of grilled pork, fresh herbs, crunchy vegetables, and one unusual addition— sour-sweet green mango, which is the bridge between the sweet and the hot spicing.

Please don't be intimidated by the long list of ingredients—it is very simple to prepare and should be a staple in every hot August kitchen.

NOODLE SALAD

- 1 medium **cucumber**, peeled, seeded, and cut into ⅛- to ¼-inch × 3-inch sticks
- **Salt**
- 12 ounces **cellophane noodles** (bean threads) or mung bean noodles
- 1 large unripe **mango**, peeled and cut into ⅛- to ¼-inch × 3-inch sticks
- 4 leaves of **napa cabbage**, cut on the diagonal into long, thin strips
- 1 large **carrot**, cut into ⅛- to ¼-inch × 3-inch sticks
- 6 **scallions** (white and green parts), cut on the diagonal into long, thin strips
- 1 to 2 fresh **jalapeño chiles**, or hotter, smaller **Thai chiles**, thinly sliced lengthwise into long, thin strips
- ⅓ tightly packed cup fresh **mint leaves**
- ⅓ tightly packed cup **Vietnamese coriander leaves** (*rau ram*) (optional)
- ⅓ cup **Asian basil leaves** or **regular basil**, torn

WINE A lighter-style wine with just a hint of sweetness, served nicely chilled, is the ticket for this dish. Try a Chenin Blanc such as Vouvray, an unwooded Chardonnay, or an off-dry Riesling.

PORK

2 to 3 tablespoons minced **lemongrass** (2 to 3 lemongrass stalks)

1 tablespoon **Asian fish sauce**

1 tablespoon (packed) **light brown sugar**

3 large **garlic cloves**, minced

3 large **shallots**, minced

5 tablespoons **canola oil**, divided

⅔ pound **pork tenderloin**, untrimmed, cut across the grain into thin slices (about 2 inches wide × 4 inches long and ⅛ inch thick)

LEMON-GINGER DIPPING SAUCE

4 **garlic cloves**, minced

4-inch piece fresh **ginger**, minced (4 to 5 tablespoons)

2 to 3 fresh **jalapeño chiles**, seeded and minced

½ cup **Asian fish sauce**

½ cup fresh **lemon juice**

½ cup **granulated sugar**, or to taste

GARNISH

1 cup **toasted unsalted peanuts**, coarsely chopped

An easy way to get long thin sticks of mango is to peel the fruit, then make long cuts from the top to the bottom of the fruit, right to its wide flat pit in the center. Then just slice the fruit the other way, parallel to the pit, and you're done.

Cook with lemongrass by first stripping away the long outer leaves of the stalks (save them for tea or to flavor dishes) down to the firm 2 to 3 inches or so of the base. The heart of this base is what is minced.

1. Make the noodle salad: Spread the cucumber on a double layer of paper towels, sprinkle with a little salt, roll up, and refrigerate for at least 1 hour so the cucumber gives off all of its liquid.

2. Put the noodles in a deep bowl and cover them with very hot water. Let stand for about 5 minutes, or until they are tender, but not mushy. Drain in a strainer and rinse with cold water. Let drain again. Have all of the noodle salad ingredients ready.

3. Marinate the pork: Soak 12 to 18 8-inch bamboo skewers in water for 30 minutes. In a medium bowl, combine the lemongrass, fish sauce, brown sugar, garlic, shallots, and 2 tablespoons of the oil. Stir well to blend. Add the pork and let it marinate for 20 minutes. Thread the meat onto the skewers and set aside. Keep cold until ready to grill.

(recipe continues)

4. Make the Lemon-Ginger Dipping Sauce: In a medium serving bowl, blend the garlic, ginger, chiles, fish sauce, lemon juice, and granulated sugar and ⅓ cup water and set aside at room temperature.

5. Assemble the salad: In a large bowl, gently toss all of the noodle salad ingredients. Mound the salad on a large platter.

6. Make the pork: Preheat a grill or broiler to high heat. Oil the grill, then grill the pork slices for 3 to 4 minutes, or until the meat is cooked through and the edges are nicely charred.

7. To serve, cluster the pork skewers on the salad. Scatter with the peanuts and serve with small bowls of the Lemon-Ginger Dipping Sauce for each diner. Everyone can dress the salad to his or her own taste.

WORK NIGHT ENCORE

Heat up some broth laced with ginger, garlic, and star anise, then drop in leftover salad for an impromptu Asian soup.

At every party there are two kinds of people—those who want to go home, and those who don't. The trouble is, they are usually married to each other.

—ANN LANDERS

CASSEROLES

Cornbread Pudding with Rough Country Greens

| Serves 6 to 8 as a main dish and 8 to 12 as a side dish; doubles easily | 1 hour prep time; 1 to 2 days rest time; 2 hours oven time | The entire dish can be assembled ahead and the components made days in advance. |

Every year we do our radio broadcast *Turkey Confidential* on Thanksgiving morning. Afterward the entire crew packs up their families and comes together to celebrate with our own potluck Thanksgiving dinner.

This recipe started life as cornbread stuffing for that feast. Evolution (and leftovers) took hold and it became a favorite winter meal all on its own. It's really an offbeat bread pudding of herb-garlic cornbread chunks and peppery greens stuffed with pockets of Cheddar and finished with toasted pine nuts.

Extra-virgin olive oil

1 recipe **Herb & Garlic Cornbread** (recipe follows), cut into 1-inch pieces and dried for 1 to 2 days

2 cups (8 ounces) shredded **sharp Cheddar cheese**

1 recipe **Rough Country Greens** (recipe follows), thoroughly drained

7 large **eggs**

3½ cups **half-and-half**

½ teaspoon **salt**

¼ teaspoon freshly ground **black pepper**

¼ teaspoon freshly grated **nutmeg**, or to taste

¼ cup **pine nuts**

This recipe must be made in a 2½-quart glass baking dish. Another type will change the results.

WINE A lighter but savory wine with just a hint of fruity sweetness is what you want with this casserole. Try a young Tempranillo-based wine from Ribera del Duero in Spain.

1. Preheat the oven to 350°F. Generously oil a 2½-quart glass baking dish.

2. **Start the pudding:** Spread the cornbread pieces in the prepared pan and tuck ½ cup of the cheese around the cornbread. Spread the greens out as evenly as possible on top.

3. **Make the custard and assemble the pudding:** In a large bowl, whisk the eggs, half-and-half, salt, pepper, and nutmeg until well combined. Carefully pour the custard over the cornbread, allowing the bread to fully absorb the mixture. Let it sit for 10 minutes so the bread can take in the custard. It will be a very full pan. Top with the remaining 1½ cups cheese and the pine nuts.

4. Let the assembled pudding stand at room temperature for 30 minutes. It can be refrigerated and covered at this point and baked later, if desired.

5. **Bake the pudding:** Bring the pudding to room temperature. Cover with foil and bake for 1 hour, or until the center reaches 170°F. on an instant-read thermometer. Let it rest for 15 to 30 minutes at room temperature before serving. Enjoy the pudding hot or at room temperature.

Herb & Garlic Cornbread

| *Makes one 9-inch-square pan* | *15 minutes prep time; 30 minutes oven time* | *You should bake this a couple of days in advance and let it stale at room temperature.* |

¾ cup unbleached **all-purpose flour**, dipped and leveled (see page 304)

¾ cup coarsely ground **cornmeal**

1½ tablespoons **sugar**

1¼ teaspoons **baking powder**

1 teaspoon **kosher salt**

¼ medium **onion**, cut into ½-inch dice

Generous ½ teaspoon fresh **thyme leaves**

1 large **garlic clove**, minced

⅓ cup shredded **sharp Cheddar cheese**

3 tablespoons **unsalted butter**, melted and cooled

1 large **egg** plus 1 large **egg yolk**, beaten

¾ cup **milk**

1½ tablespoons **extra-virgin olive oil**

(recipe continues)

1. Preheat the oven to 425°F. Slip a 9-inch square, shiny metal baking pan (not a dark baking pan) into the oven.

2. In a large bowl, stir together the flour, cornmeal, sugar, baking powder, and salt with a whisk to thoroughly combine. Stir in the onion, thyme, garlic, and cheese until well blended. Set aside.

3. In another large bowl, beat the butter with the egg and egg yolk and gradually add the milk. Stir the wet ingredients into the dry ones only long enough to combine. The mixture should be a little lumpy. Don't overmix.

4. Using thick potholders to take the hot pan from the oven, add the oil and swirl it around to coat the pan. Take extra care not to burn yourself. Pour in the batter and bake for 20 to 30 minutes, or until a knife inserted in the center of the cornbread comes out clean.

5. Cool for 10 minutes in the baking pan, then turn the cornbread out onto a rack. Break it up into 1-inch chunks and spread out to dry.

Variation
Butter-Roasted Cornbread:

This is a cornbread with all the classic ingredients for a poultry stuffing already baked into it. Slice the cornbread into croutons and toast them with butter for the Ancho Cider-Glazed Hens (page 198), or on a work night, try a warm square of the cornbread with scrambled eggs.

This is a generous recipe because the croutons are good on their own and the bread freezes well for 3 months. Bake it 1 to 2 days before using in the hens recipe and keep it in the fridge.

Follow the cornbread recipe as written, but double the ingredient quantities, except for ⅔ cup toasted pine nuts and ½ cup shredded sharp Cheddar cheese. For flavorings, use 4 whole scallions, cut into ¼-inch rounds; 1 generous teaspoon fresh thyme leaves; 2 large minced garlic cloves; and 3 ounces mild or hot Italian sausage, cooked and thinly sliced. Follow the rest of the recipe as written, except use a 9 × 13-inch shiny metal baking pan.

To make butter-roasted croutons, preheat the oven to 400°F. Cut the cornbread into ½-inch cubes and melt 4 tablespoons of butter. Spread the cubes on a cookie sheet, toss them with the butter, and roast for 10 minutes, or until golden with crisp edges. Serve with drinks or with the Ancho Cider-Glazed Hens (page 198).

(recipe continues)

THE RETURN OF
Oven Betrayal

Most of us blame ourselves when a dish doesn't turn out. It's a constant lament we hear from callers to the show: **"It must be me. I did something wrong."** It is not you; most likely it is your oven. We talked about oven betrayal in our first book *How to Eat Supper,* and it bears repeating here.

Nearly every oven we've known was inaccurate, as in off by 25°F. and sometimes even 50°F. That is a failed roast and burnt cookies waiting to happen.

Buy yourself an accurate oven thermometer. Hang it in the center of the oven, let the oven preheat for 20 minutes, and check the temperature. Then adjust the oven's setting as needed, and never be betrayed again.

Rough Country Greens

| *Makes 2 cups cooked greens* | *15 minutes prep time;* | *Can be made ahead and* |
| | *20 minutes stove time* | *refrigerated* |

Good-tasting **extra-virgin olive oil**
½ medium to large **onion**, cut into 1-inch dice
Salt and freshly ground **black pepper**
1 very large or 2 smaller heads of **escarole** or **frisée**
   or **curly endive**, thoroughly washed and chopped
   into 1-inch pieces
1 10-ounce package of chopped frozen **collard**
   greens or **spinach** (no need to defrost), or fresh
   (see Cook to Cook)
4 large **garlic cloves**, minced
1 teaspoon dried **oregano**
2 teaspoons dried **basil**
⅓ cup **raisins** or dried **cranberries**

If you prefer fresh greens to frozen, use 1½ pounds fresh collard greens or 2 pounds fresh spinach. Steam either one until tender, cool, and squeeze out excess liquid.

1. Coat the bottom of a 12-inch, straight-sided sauté pan with a thin film of oil and heat over medium-high heat. Add the onion and salt and pepper to taste and cook for 3 minutes, or until the onion begins to brown. Stand back and drop in the escarole and collards.

2. Stir the greens until wilted. Cook away all of their liquid, then add the garlic, oregano, basil, and raisins and ½ cup water. Reduce the heat to medium-low and simmer, stirring occasionally. When all of the water is cooked away, add another ½ cup water and simmer it away. Repeat adding water and cooking it away for another 5 to 10 minutes, or until the greens are tender. Remove from the heat and cool. Refrigerate, covered, if not using immediately.

The Chinese Sand Pot
An All-Purpose Casserole

Call it a romantic notion, but taking on the traditional tools of a cuisine along with its recipes can become a deeply pleasurable immersion, the sort of experience that quietly reshapes instincts and sometimes even worldviews.

In the performance-for-dollars-spent department, there's an unsung gem from China called the sand pot or sandy pot. With all the coziness of a Crock-Pot, the sand pot is a lidded, bowl-shaped clay pot that gently cooks an uncountable number of dishes—rice, soups, stews, and casseroles, be they Chinese or not.

Mediterranean Clay Pot Cooking by **Paula Wolfert** (Wiley, 2009)

Sand pots work on the stovetop, in the oven, and at the table. Anything you cook in them stays especially moist and good tasting, as the clay absorbs and holds both heat and moisture. In a way the pot seasons itself, holding tastes, then subtly lending them to the next new dish that goes into it. Clay pots can do this sort of thing; they have a life rarely found in metal ones.

THE BUYING, CARE, AND FEEDING OF SAND POTS

A proper sand pot has an exterior of rough, gray, unglazed clay enclosed in a heat-conducting and protective wire cage. Interiors are smooth and glazed a dark color, but the lid's interior should also be rough, unglazed clay like the exterior. Sizes range from individual to 3 quarts, which are good for dishes serving 2 to 4, up to 12 quarts. Check carefully for cracks before buying.

To use, follow the directions that come with the pot. If there are no directions, soak the pot in warm water before each time you cook. Always have it one third or more full before putting it over heat, and always start a sand pot over very low heat, or in a cold oven. Just as with nonstick surfaces, use only wood or soft plastic utensils. Clean by washing the pot with warm water and very little soap; never use any abrasives.

Interestingly, minor cracks sometimes fill themselves in as you cook. Paula Wolfert, in her book on clay pot cooking, says she's had great luck filling any hairline cracks that develop by simmering milk in the pot. According to Paula, milk contains casein, a protein that's insoluble in water, and therefore it works like glue.

Caramelized Catfish Sand Pot

| *Serves 4 with two or three other dishes* | *20 minutes prep time; 1 hour stove time* | *Best prepared a day or two before and gently reheated when ready to serve* |

Forget everything you have ever learned about flash-cooking fish. In this southern Vietnamese *kho*, or traditional, homey braising recipe, from Vietnamese scholar and author Andrea Nguyen, catfish steaks are bubbled for an hour in a caramel sauce, resulting in deliciously dense pieces of fish cloaked in a sticky mahogany sauce.

To eat, combine a little piece of the fish, some rice, and a bit of sauce in each bite. Andrea is a masterful recipe writer; her recipe appears here untouched. It is from her book *Into the Vietnamese Kitchen: Treasured Foodways, Modern Flavors* (Ten Speed Press, 2006).

If possible, buy a whole fresh catfish (about 3 pounds cleaned weight) at a Chinese, Southeast Asian, or Latin market and ask the fishmonger to cut it into 1-inch-thick steaks. If that is not possible, frozen catfish can be used.

1½ pounds **catfish steaks**, each about 1 inch thick
2 teaspoons **light brown sugar**, tightly packed, and more as needed
½ teaspoon freshly ground **black pepper**
¼ teaspoon **salt**
2 tablespoons **Caramel Sauce** (recipe follows)
1½ tablespoons **fish sauce**, and more as needed
2 ounces **pork fatback**, cut into ½-inch dice, or 1 tablespoon **canola** or other **neutral oil**
2 large **cloves garlic**, sliced
5 **scallions**, white part only, cut into 1½-inch lengths
Brown sugar

1. Thoroughly clean the catfish steaks, removing membranes and blood that the fishmonger may have overlooked. On a dinner plate or in a bowl large enough to hold the fish, stir together the brown sugar, pepper, salt, caramel sauce, and fish sauce. Add the catfish and coat with the mixture, turning the steaks to make sure that all surfaces are evenly exposed to the seasonings. Set aside for 15 minutes to marinate.

(recipe continues)

2. Select a shallow saucepan in which the fish steaks will fit snugly in a single layer. If you are using the fatback, put it into the saucepan and cook over medium heat for about 12 minutes, or until it renders liquid fat and turns into golden cracklings; lower the heat slightly if the pan smokes too much. Pour out all but 1 tablespoon of the fat, keeping the cracklings in the pan; return the pan to medium heat. (If you are using oil, heat it in the saucepan over medium heat.) Add the garlic and scallions and sauté for about 30 seconds, or until fragrant.

3. Add the catfish and all the seasonings from the plate to the pan. There may be some intense bubbling. Adjust the heat to a simmer, cover, and cook for 10 minutes to develop the flavors, checking midway to make sure there is enough liquid in the pan. If the pan seems dry, splash in a little water. During this initial period, the fish will more or less cook in the steam trapped in the pan. Expect the liquid to bubble vigorously. Soft plumes of steam may shoot from under the lid.

4. Uncover, add water to almost cover the fish, and bring to a gentle simmer. Cover and cook for 30 minutes. The fish will be at a hard simmer. Uncover and adjust the heat, if necessary, to continue at a gentle simmer. Cook for another 15 to 18 minutes, or until the liquid has reduced by half and has thickened slightly, forming a sauce.

5. Taste the sauce and adjust the flavor with a pinch of brown sugar to remove any harsh edges, or a sprinkling of fish sauce for more savory depth. Carefully transfer the fish to a shallow bowl. Don't worry if the steaks break up a bit. Pour the sauce over the fish and serve with simple white rice.

Caramel Sauce

| *Makes about 1 cup* | *30 minutes stove time* | *Keeps indefinitely, covered*

This is a cornerstone of Vietnamese cooking. Its ability to impart incredibly savory-sweet flavors is the key to simmering meats, seafood, eggs, and/or tofu for everyday kho dishes. The inky sauce also lends rich brown color to grilled meats, much as molasses does in American barbecue.

¾ cup **water**
1 cup **sugar**

1. Select a small, heavy saucepan with a long handle. Use one with a light interior (such as stainless steel) to make monitoring the changing color of the caramel easier. Fill the sink with enough water to come halfway up the sides of the saucepan.

2. Put one quarter cup of the water and all the sugar in the saucepan and place over medium-low heat. To ensure that the sugar melts evenly, stir with a metal spoon. After about 2 minutes, when the sugar is relatively smooth and opaque, stop stirring and let the mixture cook undisturbed. Small bubbles will form at the edge of the pan and gradually grow larger and move toward the center. A good 7 minutes into cooking, bubbles will cover the entire surface and the mixture will be at a vigorous simmer. As the sugar melts, the mixture will go from opaque to clear.

If a little sugar crystallizes on the sides of the pan, don't worry. After about 15 minutes, the sugar will begin to caramelize and deepen in color. You will see a progression from champagne yellow to light tea to dark tea. When smoke starts rising, around the 20-minute mark, remove the pan from the heat and slowly swirl it. Watch the sugar closely as it will turn darker by the second; a reddish cast will set in (think the color of a big, bold red wine) as the bubbles become a lovely burnt orange. Pay attention to the color of the caramel underneath the bubbles. When the caramel is the color of black coffee or molasses, place the pan in the sink to stop the cooking. The hot pan bottom will sizzle on contact. Add the remaining one half cup water; don't worry, the sugar will seize up but later dissolve. After the dramatic bubble reaction ceases, return the pan to the stove over medium heat.

3. Heat the caramel, stirring until it dissolves into the water. Remove from the heat and let cool for 10 minutes before pouring into a small heatproof glass jar. Set aside to cool completely. The result will seem slightly viscous, while the flavor will be bittersweet. Cover and store the sauce indefinitely in your kitchen cupboard.

RECIPE FROM *Into the Vietnamese Kitchen: Treasured Foodways, Modern Flavors* by **Andrea Nguyen** (Ten Speed Press, 2006). Visit her website at www.vietworldkitchen.com. Recipe reprinted with permission.

Renaissance Lasagne

| Serves 6 to 8 as a first course and 4 to 6 as a main dish | 45 minutes prep time; 30 minutes stove time; 50 minutes oven time | The meat ragù can be made 3 days ahead and refrigerated or frozen for 2 months. The fresh pasta can be made 24 hours ahead and air-dried. The lasagne can be assembled a few hours ahead, but please don't refrigerate it as it tends to dry out. |

We hope this will be a revelation for you. It's a far cry from that brawny work night stalwart picked up in the frozen food aisle. Consider this the long-lost wayward sister of the lasagnes we've known and loved—glamorous, delicate, ethereal, and a little daring around the edges—straight out of Italy's culinary golden age, the Renaissance.

Here tomato is not a player. Instead, sheer sheets of pasta are layered with a light chicken ragù and sprinklings of nuts, raisins, spices, and cheese, with a touch of cream—echoing the bewitching mix of savory and sweet you'd taste at Renaissance banquets.

Serve this when you want to get away from the expected, yet have a dish that's easily done in advance.

An Unusual Italian Salad (page 101) is the opener you want for the lasagne.

½ cup **golden raisins**

1 recipe **Hand-Rolled Egg Pasta** (recipe follows), cut for lasagne (page 149), or 1 pound imported dried Italian lasagne noodles, the thinner the better

2 tablespoons **unsalted butter**

1 recipe **Baroque Ragù** (recipe follows)

¾ cup **heavy cream**

6 thin slices **prosciutto di Parma**, cut into finger-sized strips

1½ cups (6 ounces) freshly grated **Parmigiano-Reggiano cheese**

½ cup **pine nuts**, toasted

Ground **cinnamon**

When buying dried, boxed lasagne, look for the sheerest sheets. If using boxed pasta, use one less layer of noodles than the recipe dictates.

WINE This delicate take on lasagne can be overwhelmed by a big, ripe wine, so look within Italy's borders for a relatively light red like a Barbera, Chianti, Valpolicella, or Brunello.

(recipe continues)

1. Soak the raisins: In a small bowl, soak the raisins in hot water to cover for about 30 minutes while you prepare the other ingredients.

2. Cook the pasta: Spread a double thickness of paper towels over a large counter space. Have a large perforated skimmer handy and a large bowl of cold water sitting near the pasta cooking pot. Bring 10 quarts generously salted water to a fierce boil. Drop in about 4 pieces of pasta. Cook the fresh pasta for about 2 minutes; cook the dry pasta a bit longer. Taste the pasta, making sure it is only barely tender, as it will cook again in the baking.

3. Lift the sheets from the water with the skimmer and drop them into the cold water to stop cooking. Lift out the cooled pasta sheets and dry them on paper towels. Keep repeating the process until all of the pasta is cooked.

4. Assemble the lasagne: Have the ragù warmed. Preheat the oven to 350°F. Coat a shallow 3-quart baking dish with the butter. Drain the raisins, discarding their liquid. Spread 3 or 4 tablespoons ragù over the bottom of the baking dish. It should be sparsely covered. Cover the ragù with sheets of cooked pasta, butting them side by side, not overlapping. Spread about a third of the ragù over the pasta.

5. Top with another layer of pasta. Spread the sheets with 3 tablespoons of the cream. Sprinkle with 3 strips of the prosciutto, 6 tablespoons of the cheese, 2 tablespoons of the raisins, and 3 tablespoons of the pine nuts. Sprinkle very lightly with a pinch of cinnamon.

6. Cover with another layer of pasta. Spread another third of the ragù over the pasta sheets and cover the ragù with pasta. Again spread on 3 tablespoons of the cream, 3 strips of the prosciutto, 6 tablespoons of the cheese, 2 tablespoons of the raisins, and the remaining pine nuts. Dust with a pinch of cinnamon. Cover with a final layer of pasta, and cover it with the remaining ragù.

7. In a medium bowl, blend the remaining cream, cheese, and raisins. Stir in a pinch of cinnamon. Spoon this sauce over the ragù, making parallel diagonal stripes atop the lasagne.

8. Cover the dish with foil, taking care not to let it touch the top of the lasagne. Slip the pan into the oven and bake for 45 to 50 minutes, or until a knife inserted in the center comes out very warm or hot.

9. Uncover and bake for another 5 minutes. The top should be bubbly and creamy, not dried out or browned. Let the lasagne rest in the turned-off oven with the door ajar for about 10 minutes. Cut the lasagne into squares and serve by lifting the pieces out with a spatula. This is not a solid lasagne; it slips a bit as it is cut and placed on a dinner plate.

(recipe continues)

Lasagne is spelled with an *e*, not an *a*.

Italian Grammar Lesson
101

Hand-Rolled Egg Pasta

| *Makes the equivalent of 1 pound dried pasta* | *20 minutes prep time; 30 minutes rest*
| *(enough for a single recipe of string pasta,* | *time; about 1 hour rolling-out time;*
| *ravioli, lasagne, or any other filled pasta)* | *20 minutes minimum drying time*

Okay, this is being picky, but there's nothing quite like hand-rolled pasta. The rolling pin (as opposed to the metal rollers of a pasta machine) embeds a pebbly texture into the dough. Sauces collect in those tiny pits and crevices, achieving what Italians see as a saintly marriage of sauce to pasta.

Pasta machines give a smooth finish, which is fine, but if you're going as far as to make your own pasta, why not go all the way? Although Italian women use a long narrow pin called a *mattarello*, use any heavy rolling pin that feels right to you. Softer than most, this dough becomes appealingly light when cooked.

For richer pasta, eliminate the water and substitute 2 more eggs. For a Renaissance experience, substitute 3 tablespoons rosewater or orange flower water for part of the water measurement, and add 3 tablespoons sugar to the flour.

2¾ cups (about 14 ounces) unbleached **all-purpose flour**, plus more for rolling the pasta

3 large **eggs**

1. Making the pasta by hand: Make a mountain of the flour in the center of a work surface. Hollow out a well in the middle. Have a pastry scraper handy. Pour the eggs and ½ cup warm water into the well. With a fork, mix them together. Now start incorporating shallow scrapings of the flour from the walls of the well into the liquid.

As you work in more and more flour, the well's sides may collapse. No fear. Stop any liquids from running off with the pastry scraper, using it to incorporate the last bits of flour into the dough. It will look hopelessly rough and messy. Don't worry. Just start kneading.

2. After about 3 minutes, the dough should be slightly sticky and elastic. If very sticky, lightly dust the surface with a couple of teaspoons of flour. Continue kneading for 10 minutes, or until the dough has become satiny, elastic, and alive in your hands. If it is too sticky while kneading, work in extra flour a little at a time. Lightly wrap the dough in plastic and let it relax at room temperature for 30 minutes to 4 hours.

3. Making the pasta in a food processor: To protect the dough from overheating, have the eggs cold. Place them and ½ cup cold water in the bowl of a food processor fitted with the steel blade and pulse for a few seconds to combine. Add about 1½ cups of the flour. Pulse for no more than 5 seconds. Add all but ¼ cup of the flour, pulsing for 5 seconds more. If the dough is very sticky, pull it apart into several pieces, sprinkle with 1 tablespoon flour, and pulse again. The dough should be smooth and slightly sticky. Pulse 8 times and then scrape the dough out of the bowl. Let rest as directed in step 2.

4. Roll out the pasta: Cut the dough into quarters. Roll out one quarter at a time, keeping the rest of the dough wrapped. Very lightly flour the work surface (no more than 1½ teaspoons). Shape the dough into a ball. Roll out into a circle by stretching as well as pressing down. Stretch the dough by rolling a quarter way back onto the pin and gently pushing the pin away from you. Turn the disk a quarter turn and repeat. Do this twice more.

Keep rolling and stretching until the pasta is thin enough to see the color of your hand or this print through it. Spread the sheet out on a flat surface and dry for 20 minutes, or until it is leathery in texture, turning it several times for even drying. Repeat with the remaining dough.

5. For lasagne noodles, cut into 4 × 8-inch pieces.

(recipe continues)

Ham and eggs— a day's work for a chicken, a lifetime commitment for a pig.

—ANONYMOUS

Baroque Ragù

Makes enough sauce for 1 pound pasta | *30 minutes prep time; 1½ hours, mainly unattended stove time* | *The ragù can be made up to 3 days ahead and refrigerated until ready to use, or freeze it for up to 2 months.*

3 tablespoons **extra-virgin olive oil**
1 tablespoon **unsalted butter**
½ large **carrot**, minced
½ large **celery stalk**, minced
½ large **onion**, minced
3 ounces **pancetta**, minced
5 ounces **mild Italian sausage**, ideally without fennel
14 ounces **chicken thighs**, boned and skinned, cut into ¼- to ½-inch dice
5 ounces **turkey** or **chicken giblets** (hearts and gizzards), trimmed and finely chopped, or 5 ounces lean **ground pork**
5 ounces lean **beef chuck**, finely chopped
1 dried **bay leaf**
¾ cup dry **red wine**
⅛ teaspoon ground **cloves**
2 cups **Master Broth** (page 58) or **Cheater's Broth** (page 62)
1 **garlic clove**, crushed
2 tablespoons imported **Italian tomato paste**
⅓ cup **heavy cream**
Salt and freshly ground **black pepper**

When buying pancetta, look for a piece with equal amounts of fat to lean, and try to buy the pancetta in one big piece, which makes it easier to mince; freezing before chopping helps as well. Mincing the meats by hand makes for better browning and gives a silkier texture to the sauce.

1. In a 12-inch straight-sided sauté pan, heat the oil and butter over medium heat. Leisurely sauté the carrot, celery, onion, and pancetta for about 8 minutes, or until the onion and pancetta begin to color. Stir often.

2. Add the sausage, chicken, giblets, pork, beef, and bay leaf. Cook over high heat for about 8 minutes, or until the meat begins to color. Reduce the heat to medium and continue sautéing while stirring frequently with a wooden spatula for 10 minutes, or until the meat is a rich dark brown. It should sizzle leisurely in the pan, not pop and sputter. Slow browning protects the rich brown glaze forming on the bottom of the pan.

3. Drain off as much fat as possible by tipping the browned meat into a large sieve and shaking it to free the fat. Put the meat back into the pan. Place the pan over medium-high heat and add the wine and cloves. Cook it at a lively bubble for 3 minutes, or until the wine is evaporated. As the wine bubbles, use a wooden spatula to scrape up the brown glaze from the bottom of the pan.

4. Raise the heat to medium, add ¼ cup of the broth, and cook it down to nothing, about 3 minutes. Stir in the garlic, tomato paste, and ¼ cup of the broth, and cook it down to nothing again. Transfer the sauce to a 2½- to 3-quart saucepan.

5. Add the remaining 1½ cups broth and let it bubble very slowly, uncovered, for 30 to 45 minutes, or until the broth has reduced by about one third and the sauce is moist but not loose. Add the cream and slowly simmer for 3 to 5 minutes. Add salt and pepper to taste. Allow the ragù to cool; cover and refrigerate, or freeze. Warm it before assembling the lasagne.

A good marriage is like a caserole—only those responsible for it know what's in it.

—ANONYMOUS

The Islam Connection

This lasagne came from what you might call on-the-spot reporting, a sixteenth-century diary of banquet dishes served in the court of the Este dukes in Ferrara, the dynasty that dominated northern Italy from Ferrara to Venice. Pasta was status food then, eaten only by the rich, as were its unexpected seasonings (at least to our twenty-first-century tastes) of sugar and spice.

Medieval Cuisine of the Islamic World: A Concise History with 174 Recipes by **Lilia Zaouali** (University of California Press, 2007) Food: The History of Taste, edited by **Paul Freedman** (University of California Press, 2008)

Worked into pasta doughs were exotica such as sugar, rosewater, saffron, and crumbled spiced breads. Flavors were further built by boiling the noodles in milk and butter or in broth. It was common to layer the sheets of pasta with ingredients not very different from the kind of fillings still found in Morocco's masterpiece, the savory/sweet bisteeya pie. With bisteeya, a sheer flaky pastry called *warka* (think phyllo dough) is layered with a lemony egg omelet, pigeon or other poultry or even fish, sugar, cinnamon, and almonds. And the similarities are no accident.

Culinary threads like this one stretch all over the Mediterranean and the world. In this case the Este court in Ferrara had strong links to Venice, which in turn struck up a profitable (to put it mildly) trade with the Middle East. That trade brought to the Mediterranean (and the Este court) those spices and tastes found in both our Renaissance Lasagne and Morocco's bisteeya.

Arab culture was one of the most advanced and sophisticated in the world. Sweeping into the western Mediterranean in the late 700s, the Arabs dominated the area until 1492. Their intellectual and culinary influences spread as far north as modern Austria. You can still taste it today in our Renaissance Lasagne and at tables from Fez to Vienna.

Does food evolve in the vacuum of a single place and culture? We think not.

Moussaka of Lamb & Red Wine Ragù

| *Serves 10 to 12* | *1 hour prep time; 1 to 2 days mellowing time; 45 to 60 minutes oven time; 10 minutes rest time* | *Individual parts of the recipe can be made a day or more ahead. Moussaka's gift to the cook is that you never bake it the day you assemble it. The dish needs a day or two in the refrigerator to blossom.* |

When the Casserole Hall of Fame finally opens, the moussaka of Greece should get a wall of its very own. Moussaka stands as one of the world's mother casseroles. Practically enshrined in Greece as a national identity marker, cooks there have argued about the right way to do it since the days of mommy Medea.

Moussaka brings home the single golden rule for all casseroles: each part of the dish has to be delicious on its own.

EGGPLANT

3 to 4 large **eggplants** (3½ to 4 pounds)
Good-tasting **extra-virgin olive oil**
Salt

TOMATO SAUCE

Good-tasting **extra-virgin olive oil**
1 medium **onion**, cut into ¼-inch dice
Salt and freshly ground **black pepper**
2 tablespoons **tomato paste**
3 large **garlic cloves**, minced
1½ tablespoons dried **oregano**
4 teaspoons ground **cinnamon**
1½ tablespoons ground **allspice**
¼ tightly packed cup **flat-leaf parsley**, chopped
1 28-ounce can whole **tomatoes** with their liquid

There is none of the usual oil-soaked eggplant in this moussaka, thanks to Sally's discovery of roasting whole eggplants, slicing them, and then browning them in barely any oil. The lagniappe for us is that the eggplant tastes strikingly fresh—a new quality for a moussaka.

(recipe continues)

LAMB RAGÙ

Good-tasting **extra-virgin olive oil**
1 medium **onion**, cut into ¼-inch dice
Salt and freshly ground **black pepper**
3 large **garlic cloves**, minced
¼ tightly packed cup **flat-leaf parsley**, chopped
2 pounds **ground lamb**
1⅔ cups plus 2 tablespoons dry **red wine**
¼ cup **wine vinegar** or **cider vinegar**
¾ teaspoon freshly grated **nutmeg**
Salt and freshly ground **black pepper**
⅔ cup **Master Broth** (page 58) or low-sodium
   chicken broth

ASSEMBLY

Good-tasting **extra-virgin olive oil**
1 generous cup fresh **bread crumbs**
1½ cups grated **Greek Kefalotyri cheese** or **Italian
   Pecorino Romano** (6 to 7 ounces)
1 recipe **Béchamel Sauce** (recipe follows)
⅛ teaspoon freshly grated **nutmeg**, or to taste

WINE If you can track one down, a wine made from Greece's Agiorgitiko (St. George) will be terrific with this moussaka, but a lighter-styled Merlot from the New World will also work very nicely.

1. Make the eggplant: Preheat the oven to 400°F. Prick each eggplant several times with a fork and rub lightly with a little oil. Roast them on a baking sheet for 35 to 45 minutes, or until they are softened and a little shriveled, but not charred or collapsed. Let them stand at room temperature until cool to the touch. Remove to a cutting board and slice crosswise into ½-inch-thick rounds. (If they fall apart a bit, just nudge them back into rounds.)

2. Spread a double thickness of paper towels over the baking sheet you used for the eggplant. Coat a 12-inch, straight-sided sauté pan (a nonstick pan is helpful here) with a thin film of oil and heat over medium-high heat. Brown the eggplant slices lightly on each side in batches, replenishing the oil as you go. Sprinkle them with a little salt and drain them on the paper towels; set aside. Wipe out the sauté pan.

3. Make the tomato sauce: Coat the same sauté pan with a thin film of oil and set over medium-high heat. Add the onion with a light sprinkling of salt and a generous amount of black pepper. Stir often as you brown them, about 5 minutes.

4. Stir in the tomato paste, garlic, oregano, cinnamon, allspice, and parsley. Cook, stirring with a flat-bottomed wooden spatula, for 1 minute. Add the tomatoes with their liquid, breaking them into pieces with your hands as they go into the pan. Simmer gently, uncovered, for 5 to 10 minutes, or until thick. Taste for seasoning, transfer to a 4-quart saucepan, and set aside, covered. Wash out the pan.

5. Make the lamb ragù: Coat the pan again with a thin film of oil. Set over medium-high heat. Add the onion with a generous sprinkling of salt and pepper and sauté for about 3 minutes, or until tender. Add the garlic and parsley and half of the lamb and brown well. Add the meat mixture to the tomato sauce. Add 2 tablespoons of the wine to the pan and boil, scraping up the browned bits on the bottom of the pan. Add to the tomato mixture in the saucepan.

6. Wash out the pan, coat it with a little oil, and heat again over medium-high heat. Brown the rest of the lamb. Tip the pan and spoon off all but 2 tablespoons of fat.

7. Reduce the heat to medium, add 1 cup of the wine and all of the vinegar, and continue to cook until nearly evaporated. Season with the nutmeg and salt and pepper to taste and add to the saucepan. Stir into the saucepan the remaining ⅔ cup wine and the broth. Simmer over very low heat, partially covered, for 25 minutes. Uncover and simmer until thick. Set aside, covered.

8. Assemble the moussaka 1 to 2 days before serving. Lightly oil a 12½ × 8½ × 3-inch enameled metal or ceramic baking pan. Sprinkle half of the bread crumbs on the bottom. Cover the crumbs with half of the eggplant slices, then spread the meat mixture on top and sprinkle with half of the cheese. Add the final layer of eggplant, the béchamel, the remaining cheese and bread crumbs, and the nutmeg. Cover the casserole with plastic wrap and refrigerate for 24 to 48 hours.

9. Two hours before serving, take the moussaka out of the refrigerator. Preheat the oven to 350°F. Replace the plastic on the casserole with foil. Once the casserole is at room temperature, bake for 30 minutes, uncover, and bake for another 15 minutes, or until an instant-read thermometer inserted in the center of the moussaka reads 170°F. The top should be nicely browned; if not, briefly run it under the broiler. Let the moussaka rest out of the oven for about 10 minutes before cutting into 3- or 4-inch squares. Serve hot.

(recipe continues)

Béchamel Sauce

Makes about 3 cups	*15 minutes prep time;*	*Make up to 3 days ahead and*
	20 minutes stove time	*refrigerate. Have the sauce at room*
		temperature before using.

2½ cups **whole milk**
4 tablespoons **unsalted butter**
4 tablespoons **all-purpose flour**
Salt and freshly ground **black pepper**
¼ teaspoon ground **cinnamon**, or to taste
¼ teaspoon freshly grated **nutmeg**,
   or to taste
4 large **eggs**

1. Make the béchamel: Heat the milk in a small saucepan over medium heat until hot, but not bubbling. In a 3-quart pot over medium heat, melt the butter. When the butter is foaming, stir in the flour with a flat-bottomed wooden spatula and cook for 2 minutes, taking care not to let the roux brown. Add the hot milk and whisk quickly to combine, making sure there are no lumps.

2. Add salt and pepper to taste and the cinnamon. Bring the sauce to a simmer and cook, stirring constantly, for about 10 minutes, or until it is thick with no raw taste of flour. Add the nutmeg. You want to slightly overseason the sauce, as the eggs and baking mute the flavors. Set aside to cool.

3. In a large mixing bowl, beat the eggs together until frothy. Add the béchamel in batches, mixing in each addition until entirely smooth.

For Bargain Wine,
KNOW YOUR REAL ESTATE

When tracking down a good bottle for little money, wine writer
Matt Kramer says think real estate. Low-priced land means
low-priced grapes and that leads to low-priced wine.

   According to Matt, bargains are to be found in either "the very
new areas of grape growing regions, or the very old areas that are
being revived." He says to look to places like Bulgaria, Romania,
Hungary, Argentina, Australia, Chile, and even parts of the
United States that haven't been planted before. He believes
wine has gone global in a way the world has never seen
before, and we consumers are going to be the winners.

MAIN DISHES

VEGETARIAN AND VEGAN

Summer Tomato Pudding

Serves 4 to 6 as a main dish or 8 to 9 as a first course or side dish; doubles easily

45 minutes prep time; about 1½ hours oven time; 15 minutes rest time

Makes an 8-inch-square baking dish of pudding. The tomato sauce and custard can be done a day ahead and refrigerated.

This was Lynne's first taste of the south of France—the place she'd fantasized about since sighting her first Van Gogh in high school. When she arrived, summer was at full tilt "with tomatoes so come-hither I imagined them hanging out on street corners swinging their beads."

That first pudding was about good tomatoes, cream, bread, and cheese—a quartet that should be stenciled on kitchen walls as the ultimate can't-miss, fallback dish.

Opening the meal with Smoked Trout & Watercress Salad with Warmed Sherry Dressing (page 90) gives the pudding a proper French setting.

TOMATO SAUCE

Good-tasting **extra-virgin olive oil**
½ medium to large **onion**, cut into ¼-inch dice
Salt and freshly ground **black pepper**
Very generous pinch of **hot red pepper flakes**
2 large **garlic cloves**, minced
3 tightly packed tablespoons fresh **basil**, torn
1¾ to 2 pounds good-tasting **tomatoes**, cored and coarsely chopped (do not seed or peel), or 1 28-ounce can whole tomatoes with their liquid
Olive oil for the baking dish
7- to 8-inch piece of **baguette**, a couple of days old if possible, cut into 1-inch-thick rounds

We check meat temperatures all the time, but rarely do the same with egg dishes. Egg custards made without starch like flour, cornstarch, or bread should reach 170°F. to kill off the enzyme that makes a cooked custard liquefy after cooking. With this pudding, in which the custard is partnered with bread and sauce, it's best to take it to between 200°F. and 210°F. and then give it at least a 15-minute rest before serving.

(recipe continues)

CUSTARD

5 large **eggs**, beaten

¼ teaspoon **kosher salt**

⅛ teaspoon freshly ground **black pepper**

⅛ to ¼ teaspoon freshly grated **nutmeg**, or to taste

1 cup **half-and-half** or **heavy cream**

1 cup **whole** or **skim milk**

⅓ cup freshly grated **Parmigiano-Reggiano cheese**

FLAVORINGS

⅓ cup crumbled **feta cheese**

4 ounces firm, fresh, **whole-milk sheep** or **cow cheese**, or **cream cheese**, thinly sliced

10 fresh **basil leaves**, torn

¼ cup pitted **niçoise** or **oil-cured Moroccan olives**

1 good-tasting medium **tomato**, sliced into ½-inch rounds, or 1 cup halved, flavorful **grape tomatoes**

WINE Look for a medium-bodied, fresh red like a young Bandol or Provençal red.

1. Make the tomato sauce: Coat a 4-quart saucepan with a thin film of oil. Heat over medium-high heat. Add the onion with some salt, black pepper, and red pepper flakes and cook for 4 minutes, or until golden. Stir in the garlic and basil and cook for 30 seconds. Stir in the tomatoes, breaking them up as they go into the pan. Bring the sauce to a lively bubble and cook, uncovered, for 10 to 15 minutes, or until thick. Stir often with a flat wooden spatula to keep from sticking. Taste for seasoning. Cover and set aside for 15 to 20 minutes to mellow, or refrigerate up to 24 hours.

2. Assemble the custard: While the sauce cooks, oil an 8-inch-square ceramic baking dish. Preheat the oven to 325°F. Cover the bottom of the dish completely with the bread slices.

3. Make the custard: In a large bowl, whisk the eggs, salt, pepper, nutmeg, half-and-half, milk, and cheese. Pour half of the custard over the bread and let it soak in for 10 minutes. Sprinkle with 3 tablespoons of the feta cheese and half of the slices of the fresh cheese. Tuck in half of the basil leaves.

4. Cover everything with the tomato sauce. Pour in the rest of the custard, scatter the olives over the custard, push the sliced tomatoes and rest of the basil leaves into the custard, cover with the rest of the fresh cheese, and sprinkle with the remaining feta.

5. Cover with foil and bake for 45 minutes, then raise the heat to 375°F. and bake for 25 to 30 minutes. Finally, uncover and bake for another 20 minutes, or until an instant-read thermometer inserted near the center of the pudding reads 200°F. to 210°F. Let the pudding rest at room temperature for 15 minutes. Serve it hot or just warm.

Variations

Charred Ginger-Chile Corn Pudding:
Instead of the tomato sauce, use a batch of Charred Ginger-Chile Corn (page 286). Follow the recipe as written, using the corn instead of the tomato sauce. Puree ½ cup fresh corn and add it to the custard.

Bread and Butter Jam Pudding:
To turn the pudding into a dessert, omit everything savory. Slather each slice of baguette with butter and a generous amount of jam. Make the custard without the pepper and Parmigiano. Instead, add ½ to ⅔ cup sugar, 2 teaspoons vanilla extract, grated zest of ½ lemon, and ½ teaspoon ground allspice. Follow the recipe, using cream cheese as flavoring. Top the pudding with several teaspoons of jam. Bake as instructed.

HOW TO COOK AN
Onion

So many recipes begin with **"sauté the onion"** that one would think this is simple, right? But how you cook that onion can change how your recipe is going to taste. There are two basic approaches:

For sweet, clear, and gentle onion flavor, cook the onion, covered, in a light film of butter or oil very, very slowly over low heat. The onion will actually sweat out its essence. You can add aromatics to this process—a bay leaf, a sprig of celery leaves, parsley. Remove them when the onion is cooked and their flavors linger.

For meaty, rich flavors, brown an onion in a generous amount of oil or butter over medium to medium-high heat. Cook the onion to a deep golden brown and you have the perfect start for a robust sauté, stew, or soup.

Sweet Yam-Tamarind Curry with Basil & Lime

| *Serves 3 to 4, depending on the menu; doubles easily* | *20 minutes prep time; 30 to 35 minutes stove time* | *Even better made a day ahead. If cooking ahead, add the lime juice and basil just before taking the curry to the table.* |

You have to love the yam—it can take on any cuisine's character and seem like it was born for the role. Marshmallows and apple pie spices are fine for Thanksgiving, but when we look at a yam, our first thought is Thai curry.

Thai curries can be marathons that begin by pounding together curry pastes made with laundry lists of exotica, or they can be as immediate as this fast purée of four essentials—chile, ginger, shallots, and garlic. The next step is pretty constant from one recipe to the next. The curry paste gets cooked in delicious fat until the fat separates from the paste. Then the main ingredient goes in, along with a liquid for braising.

A medium-grain rice usually accompanies Thai curries, but rice noodles are good, too. Adding Cucumber & Melon Salad with Mint (page 80) will make a menu.

CURRY PASTE

4 fresh medium-hot to hot **chiles**, seeded if desired
   (from mild to hot: güero, Hungarian wax, jalapeño,
   Fresno Red, serrano, cayenne, bird [piquin], and
   Thai)
2-inch piece fresh **ginger**, coarsely chopped
3 large **shallots**, coarsely chopped
6 large **garlic cloves**
½ teaspoon **salt**

CURRY

2 **lemongrass stalks**
¼ cup **canola oil** (expeller-pressed if possible)
1¾ cups **coconut milk**
2 to 3 **yams** (1¾ to 2¼ pounds), peeled and cut into
   1-inch pieces

COOK *to* **Cook**

Thai basil tastes of anise, pepper, and cinnamon. You can find it in farmer's markets and Asian groceries. We buy it up when it's available and freeze it. In this recipe you want unfrozen basil. And yes, regular basil can stand in.

(recipe continues)

2 tablespoons **Asian fish sauce** (Three Crabs brand is
   one we like)
2 tablespoons **tamarind concentrate** (Tamcon is a brand
   we use)
6 branches **curly endive** or **escarole**, cut into thin shreds
Salt and freshly ground **black pepper**
½ large **lime**

GARNISH

½ cup fresh **Thai basil leaves**, or **regular basil leaves**
2 fresh **red chiles** (medium-hot to hot), seeded and
   thinly sliced

WINE Go for a Vouvray
from the Loire Valley,
which should have enough
acidity to meet the lime and
enough substance to pair
with the coconut milk. Or
try a good lager beer.

1. **Make the curry paste:** In a blender, purée the chiles, ginger, shallots, garlic,
and salt until smooth, adding a little water if needed.

2. **Prepare the lemongrass:** Trim away the tops of the lemongrass stalks to the
bottom 4 inches from the root. Pull off the fibrous parts of the stalk until you
reach the smooth heart. Trim away the root and slice, then mince the hearts very
fine. Set aside.

3. **Make the curry:** In a 6-quart pot, heat the oil over medium heat and stir in
the curry paste. Sauté, stirring with a wooden spatula, for 3 minutes. Blend ¼ cup
of the coconut milk, reduce the heat to medium-low, and continue cooking and
stirring often for 5 minutes, or until the coconut is cooked down and the curry
paste is sautéing in the coconut milk's oil. Take care not to burn. Blend in the
yams, fish sauce, lemongrass, and tamarind with the remaining 1½ cups coconut
milk and enough water to barely cover the yams.

4. Adjust the heat so the liquid bubbles slowly. Simmer uncovered for 15 minutes,
or until the yams can be pierced with a knife, but still have a little resistance.
Stir in the endive, simmer for 10 more minutes, taste for seasoning, and adjust
as needed.

5. To serve, transfer the curry to a bowl, squeeze the lime over it, and scatter
with the basil leaves and chiles.

WORK NIGHT ENCORE

Sweet Yam–Tamarind Soup with Noodles and Tofu: Prepare the curry recipe, but don't add the garnishes. Set them aside to top the soup. Dilute the curry with vegetable broth to get the number of servings you need. Then prepare the rice noodles and tofu and some additional vegetables to go into the soup (ideally fast-cooking ones such as pea pods, spinach leaves, and shavings of carrot).

For the noodles, soak thin rice noodles (1 ounce per person) in a large bowl in very hot tap water to cover. Cover with a towel and give them 8 to 15 minutes to become tender (their thickness dictates the timing). Drain them, rinse, and let drain in a colander.

Cut up 2 ounces firm tofu per person. Heat the soup, drop in the vegetables and tofu, and heat through. Rinse the noodles with hot water to warm them and divide them between large soup bowls.

Ladle in the soup. Garnish with basil leaves and sliced chiles. Serve hot.

I yam what I yam.

—POPEYE

Golden Pie of Winter Vegetables in Cinnamon Pastry

| *Makes one 14- to 16-inch pie; serves 8 as a main dish and 12 to 14 as a starter or side dish* | *1 hour prep time; 1 hour oven time for the vegetables; 45 minutes oven time for the final pie* | *The roasted vegetables and pastry can be done a day ahead and refrigerated. The finished pie reheats well.* |

When in doubt, make pie. The humblest of humble vegetables turn into stars in this party dish. Rutabaga, celeriac, parsnips, Brussels sprouts, and turnips can each or all go into the pan, as you'll see here. Just remember to balance earthy tastes with sweet and rich ones such as onion, potato, yam, or carrot. Cut the harder vegetables into smaller pieces for even cooking.

APPLES AND VEGETABLES

2 medium **apples** (such as Honeycrisp, Granny Smith, or Liberty), cored and cut into ¼-inch-thick wedges

3 medium **onions**, each cut into 6 chunks

2 medium **red-skin potatoes** (unpeeled), cut into ½-inch chunks

1 medium **rutabaga** or **celeriac**, peeled and cut into ¼-inch-thick pieces

1 pound **Brussels sprouts**, quartered

4 or 5 leaves **frisée**, **curly endive**, or **other tart green**, torn into small pieces

2 medium **parsnips** or **carrots**, cut into ¼-inch pieces

2 teaspoons ground **allspice**

⅛ teaspoon ground **hot chile** or **hot red pepper flakes**

4 sprigs fresh **thyme**

20 fresh **sage leaves**

2 tablespoons **balsamic vinegar**

2 tablespoons (packed) **dark brown sugar**

5 tablespoons **extra-virgin olive oil**

1½ teaspoons **salt**

½ teaspoon freshly ground **black pepper**
10 **garlic cloves**, crushed and coarsely chopped

1 recipe **Cinnamon Pastry** (recipe follows)

ASSEMBLY

2 generous teaspoons fresh **thyme leaves**
12 large fresh **sage leaves**, torn
Grated zest of ½ **lemon**
Juice of ½ **lemon**
½ cup low-sodium **vegetable broth**
½ cup **heavy cream**
2 cups (8 ounces) shredded **sharp Cheddar cheese**
2 large **egg yolks**, beaten with 2 tablespoons water

WINE This dish needs some fruity sweetness to hang in with the roasted vegetables. Look for a young California Pinot Noir or a Chenin Blanc from South Africa or France's Loire Valley.

1. Roast the apples and vegetables: Set one oven rack high up and a second toward the bottom of the oven. Preheat the oven to 450°F. In a large bowl, toss the apples, onions, potatoes, rutabaga, Brussels sprouts, frisée, parsnips, allspice, chile, thyme, sage, balsamic vinegar, sugar, oil, salt, and pepper.

2. Spread the vegetables on two large, shallow roasting pans (half-sheet pans are ideal). Place one on the upper rack and the other on the lower one. Roast for about 1 hour, turning several times during cooking for even browning. Use a metal spatula to scrape up any brown bits in the pan. After 30 minutes, switch the pans' positions and scatter each one with half of the garlic.

3. Remove from the oven and cool. If doing this ahead, refrigerate. Have them at room temperature for baking.

4. Assemble the pie: Preheat the oven to 400°F. Have the pastry rolled out on a pizza pan or cookie sheet and chilled as described in step 4 of the pastry recipe. In a large bowl, toss the vegetables with the thyme, sage, lemon zest, lemon juice, broth, cream, and cheese.

5. With the pizza pan on a counter, remove the top round of dough on its foil and set aside. Mound the vegetables in the center of the dough-covered pan, spreading them out so there's a 2-inch border of pastry. Brush that border with some of the beaten egg.

(recipe continues)

6. Turn the chilled second sheet of pastry over onto the vegetables, gently peel back its foil, and with the side of your hand press and seal the pastry all around the pie. Then roll up the double-layered edge to make a raised rim. Crimp it into a zigzag pattern if you like. Brush the top of the pie with more beaten egg. Scraps of dough could be cut into oval leaf shapes and placed on the crust. Brush them with egg, too.

7. Make slits in the pastry. Bake for 35 to 45 minutes, or until the pie is a rich golden brown and the center is hot. Serve hot or warm.

Sprinkle FROM ON HIGH

Chef Thomas Keller of French Laundry fame says that **to most effectively salt, hold your hand 6 to 10 inches above the piece you are salting and let it gently rain down.** You will get a more even distribution, and the bonus, we think, is that you look good in the process.

Cinnamon Pastry

Makes enough pastry	*20 minutes prep time;*	*The dough can be blended 2 days*
for one 14- to 16-inch	*10 minutes mixing time;*	*ahead and chilled, or made 3 months*
double-crust pie	*3 hours resting time*	*ahead and frozen.*

1½ cups unbleached **all-purpose flour**, dipped and
   leveled (see page 304)
1½ cups **cake flour** (not self-rising), dipped and leveled
   (see page 304)
1 teaspoon **salt**
1½ teaspoons ground **cinnamon**
2 tablespoons **sugar**
2½ sticks (10 ounces) cold **unsalted butter**, cut into
   1-inch chunks
4 ounces cold **cream cheese**, cut into 1-inch chunks
2 large cold **eggs**, beaten
4 to 6 tablespoons **ice water**
1 tablespoon **unsalted butter** for the pan

1. Make the pastry: In a food processor or large bowl, blend the flours, salt, cinnamon, and sugar.

2. Cut in the butter and cream cheese with rapid pulses in the processor, or rub between your fingertips until you have a rough-looking mixture with jelly bean–size lumps. In a small bowl, mix the eggs and 4 tablespoons of the ice water and pour over the flour mixture. Pulse or toss with a fork until the dough forms into ragged bits. If the dough is very dry, sprinkle with the remaining 2 tablespoons ice water and pulse a few more times, or toss with a fork. The dough is moist enough when you can press it between your fingers and it holds together.

3. Turn the dough onto a counter. Divide it into two equal pieces and gently nudge each into a round patty. Wrap and chill for 2 to 24 hours.

4. To assemble the pie, let the dough sit at room temperature for 30 minutes to soften a little. Butter a 14- to 16-inch pizza pan (ideally with holes) or a cookie sheet. Roll out the dough into two 18-inch rounds. Spread one over the pizza pan. There should be an overhang. Then lay a double sheet of foil over the dough and spread the second round over it. Chill for 30 minutes or overnight.

To finish the pie, go to step 4 of the main recipe.

Timbale of Sweet Peppers, Greens & Hominy

| *Serves 6 as a main dish and 10 as part of a big dinner; doubles easily* | *1 hour prep time; 30 minutes stove time; 45 minutes oven time; 10 minutes rest time* | *Make each part of the dish up to 2 days in advance. Assemble the timbale a day ahead if convenient.* |

Yellow peppers, scarlet tomatoes, and West Indies spices layered with black beans and white hominy—not a bad combination on their own. But bake them under a dome of tender collards that turn glossy and crisp in the oven and you have a centerpiece dish if there ever was one. Vegan by design, this timbale came to be because of a repeated cry we hear from our vegetable-loving listeners.

Every year on Thanksgiving morning we do *Turkey Confidential,* a live national call-in show. It's a sort of free-for-all triage for those who cook that day. So along with instructive moments, such as the roofer who stepped us through cooking a turkey in a bucket of hot tar (foil was a major player), and moments of naked panic, as with the new bride who'd never cooked before (her husband invited his entire family, then left her alone to wrestle the meal to the table—the word *divorce* was on the tip of Lynne's tongue), we have one constant year to year—non–meat eaters struggling with "Love the people; can't eat the food."

Here's our response: this pride-of-place dish for those frustrated souls, and there's an entire vegan Thanksgiving menu to go with it (page 36). Add a turkey (page 200) and the carnivores will be happy, too.

COLLARDS

1 to 2 bunches (1½ pounds) of **collard greens**, stems
　removed, leaves halved
Good-tasting **extra-virgin olive oil**

PEPPER-TOMATO SOFRITTO

Good-tasting **extra-virgin olive oil**
2 medium **onions**, cut into ¼-inch dice
2 large **sweet yellow peppers**, cut into ½-inch dice

3 to 4 long, thin-skinned **sweet red** or **pale green peppers** such as sweet Italian, Marconi, banana, sweet Hungarian, or cubanelle, or use 2 more large sweet red or yellow peppers, cut into ½-inch dice

1 to 3 fresh mild or hot **chiles**, seeded and finely chopped (optional)

Salt and freshly ground **black pepper**

Juice of 2 large **limes**

3 **garlic cloves**, minced

2 tablespoons **West Indies Spice Blend** (recipe follows)

1 28-ounce can **tomatoes** with their liquid, crushed with your hands as they go into the pot or puréed in a blender (do not use canned puréed tomatoes)

1 29-ounce can whole **hominy** (posole or maize blanco), rinsed and well drained

1½ cups **cooked rice** (½ cup raw rice)

2 14-ounce cans **black beans**, rinsed and well drained

WINE An American hard cider would pair beautifully with this dish.

1. **Make the collards:** Bring 3 quarts salted water to a boil in a 6-quart pot. Drop the collards into the boiling water and boil, uncovered, for 10 minutes, or until tender. With a long-handled strainer, scoop up the leaves and run them under cold running water to stop their cooking and set their color.

2. Gently spread the collards on towels. Generously coat the inside of a 4-quart stainless steel bowl or an enameled cast-iron casserole with oil. You will be unmolding the timbale, so remember that the bottom of your vessel will be the top of the timbale.

3. Overlap a few of the collard leaves on the bottom of the casserole, then drape the rest of the leaves over the sides so they overlap and overhang the pan by 6 or 8 inches (you want enough overhang to completely cover the filled dish).

4. **Make the Pepper-Tomato Sofritto:** Coat the bottom of a 12-inch straight-sided sauté pan with oil and set it over medium-high heat. Once it is hot, use a wooden spatula to stir in the onions, peppers, chiles (if using), and generous sprinklings of salt and pepper. Stir occasionally until the onions start to brown.

(recipe continues)

5. Blend in half of the lime juice, stirring up any glaze from the bottom of the pan, and cook off the liquid over medium-high heat. Mix in the garlic, spice blend, and tomatoes. Simmer over medium-high heat, stirring often, for 3 to 5 minutes, or until the sauté is thick and rich tasting. Taste for seasoning, remove from the heat, and cover. Hold the sofritto at room temperature for up to a few hours, or refrigerate it for up to 2 days.

6. About 1 hour before serving, preheat the oven to 400°F. and bring the sofritto to a simmer. Immediately stir in the hominy and cooked rice. Cook until just heated through.

7. Assemble the timbale: Spread half of the pepper sauté over the bottom of the collard-lined vessel. Spread the black beans over that, sprinkling them with the remaining lime juice and a little salt. Top with the rest of the pepper mixture and fold the collard greens over the casserole to cover the filling completely.

8. With your fingers, spread about 2 tablespoons oil over the collards to moisten them. Sprinkle the collards with salt and bake for 30 to 40 minutes, or until the casserole is bubbling around the edges and hot at the center.

9. Pull the casserole from the oven, let it rest for 10 minutes, then set a large heatproof serving platter upside down on top of the timbale. Using long oven mitts and great care, flip over the timbale so it slips onto the platter. Turn on the broiler and run the timbale under it for about 2 minutes so the greens are crisp, glossy, and almost blistered, but not burned. Remove the timbale from the oven and serve it hot or warm sliced in wedges.

Do vegetarians eat animal crackers?

—ANONYMOUS

West Indies Spice Blend

| *Makes about ⅓ cup* | *5 minutes prep time* | *Keeps in a cool, dark place 3 to 4 months*

Africa's Berber spice meets the jerk seasonings of Jamaica, but without the chiles (you can add them if you wish). Use this blend with yams, tomatoes, greens, and beans. It's a BBQ rub, and with salt, a dry brine. Grinding whole spices with a coffee grinder or mortar and pestle gives you bolder flavors, but ground spices can be used, too.

- 1½ generous teaspoons whole **allspice**, or 2 teaspoons ground
- 1½ teaspoons ground **ginger**
- 1 teaspoon whole **coriander seed**, ground, or 1 teaspoon ground
- 1-inch **cinnamon stick**, broken, or 1 generous teaspoon ground
- 1 tablespoon **sweet paprika**
- 1 generous tablespoon dried **basil**
- ½ teaspoon dried **thyme**

Mix all of the ingredients in a jar with a tight-fitting lid and keep in a cool, dark place.

If vegetarians eat vegetables, what do humanitarians eat?

—ANONYMOUS

Bacon Flavor
sans Pig

Bacon is the one thing most vegetarians fall off the wagon for, and deservedly so. While true duplication is impossible to get without the animal element, we've come up with a decent stunt double—garlic plus hot red pepper flakes plus Spanish smoky paprika (sweet or hot). A Spanish label for the paprika would read *Pimenton de la Vera.* Adding this trio to the beginning sauté of the dish lends a smoky and meaty air to the pot.

Spices and chiles blossom when gently warmed in oil or fat.

For a basic sauté that serves 4 to 6, use 4 minced garlic cloves, ¼ teaspoon hot red pepper flakes, and ½ to 1 teaspoon smoked paprika. Briefly sauté in oil or butter. If chile heat isn't your thing, skip the red pepper flakes and use the sweet, smoked variety of Spanish paprika, which has less heat.

Crispy Feta-Stuffed Phyllo Torte

| *Makes one large Bundt cake;* | *45 minutes prep time;* | *The torte is best eaten the day*
| *serves 8 to 10 as a main dish and* | *1¼ hours oven time;* | *it is made but reheats well up*
| *12 to 16 as a starter or dessert* | *1 to 2 hours rest time* | *to 3 days later.*

Our food-loving neighbors nominated this torte as the recipe that would make our fortunes if we launched it as the flagship of a frozen-food line. We haven't cashed in yet, but this dish delivers on so many fronts that it's the best time investment you could make for a splashy party. Really a main-dish cheesecake wrapped in incredibly buttery phyllo, the genius is in the shape—a Bundt ring that stands golden and proud. This is a dish destined for many a buffet. Serve it with salad. A little honey on the side heightens the cheeses.

Thanks to food writer Melissa Clark for sharing the recipe that launched this dish.

FILLING

2 cups (8 ounces) crumbled **feta cheese** (rinsed, dried, and crumbled first, if in liquid)

1½ cups **whole-milk cottage cheese**, drained in a sieve

1½ cups (6 ounces) shredded **Kasseri** or **Asiago cheese**

1½ cups (6 ounces) shredded **Parmigiano-Reggiano cheese**

½ medium **onion**, cut into ¼-inch dice

⅔ cup chopped fresh **dill** (not packed)

½ teaspoon freshly grated **nutmeg**, or to taste

1 teaspoon ground **cinnamon**

Grated zest of ½ **lemon**

Juice of ½ **lemon**

½ teaspoon freshly ground **black pepper**

Salt (optional)

3 large **eggs**, beaten

WINE Look for a dry-style Gewürztraminer from Italy's Alto Adige, Mendocino's Anderson Valley, or Michigan.

(recipe continues)

1 pound frozen **phyllo dough**, thawed overnight in the
   refrigerator, if necessary
3 sticks (12 ounces) **unsalted butter**, melted
5 to 7 sprigs fresh **dill** (optional)
1 cup **honey** (Greek preferred)

1. Make the filling: Preheat the oven to 375°F. Have a 12-cup Bundt pan handy. In a large bowl, lightly combine the four cheeses, onion, dill, ½ teaspoon nutmeg, the cinnamon, lemon zest, lemon juice, and pepper. Blend and taste for seasoning, adding more nutmeg and salt if necessary. Then blend in the eggs. The mixture should be a bit chunky.

2. Line the pan with phyllo: Spread out a towel on a counter, top it with a piece of plastic wrap, and unroll the phyllo dough onto it. Cover the phyllo with another piece of plastic wrap and then a dampened towel (keep the phyllo covered when you're not lifting off a sheet). Brush the Bundt pan with some of the melted butter so the inside is well coated.

3. Lay a sheet of phyllo across the pan, then crisscross another over it. Press the sheets down into the pan so they break over the center tube. Keep layering and crisscrossing the dough sheets (they should overhang the pan) so the inside of the center tube and entire pan is lined with many layers of phyllo.

4. Fill the torte: Turn the cheese filling into the pan, fold the overhanging phyllo over the cheese, and press it in very gently. Use a knife to make about 30 cuts straight down into the torte to the bottom of the Bundt pan. Pour in the melted butter and don't worry if some stays atop the torte.

5. Bake the torte: Put the Bundt pan on a cookie sheet and bake for 1¼ hours, or until the torte is puffy and golden brown. Cool it in its pan at room temperature for 1 to 2 hours.

6. To serve, place a serving platter atop the pan and flip the Bundt over onto the platter. You'll hear a reassuring *plonk*. Lift off the pan, then garnish the torte with fresh dill if using. The torte is delicious warm or at room temperature. Pass the honey at the table for drizzling over each slice.

POULTRY

Chicken in Chinese Master Sauce

Serves 6 to 8 as part of a Chinese menu and 4 as a main dish	*20 minutes prep time; 50 minutes stove time; 1 day rest time*	*The chicken can be made a couple of days ahead and refrigerated in its sauce up to 24 hours. After that, refrigerate the sauce and chicken separately. The chicken is good cool, or warmed in the sauce. Serve with rice.*

Utterly uncomplicated, this recipe may very well become your household chicken for summer picnics, sandwiches, and salads.

Master sauce plays more to fairy tale than truth—in China it is a sauce that you would use again and again to simmer different meats until it becomes your own personal ambrosia. Then, in your final hours, you pass it on to your kin. The sauce never dies; it goes on for decades and is always evolving into something more—at least that is the story.

Although the name and some ingredients change from one part of China to another, all master sauce recipes share the basics you find here. As for passing it on to your kin, just freeze the sauce between cooking stints, replenishing ingredients as needed, and put it in your will.

¾ cup **light soy sauce** (such as Kikkoman)
¾ cup **dark** or **double soy sauce** (such as Koon Chun brand)
1¼ cups **Shao-Hsing** (Shao Xing) **Chinese rice wine**, or dry **sherry**
⅔ cup (packed) **dark brown sugar**
2- to 3-inch piece fresh **ginger**, crushed
5 **scallions** (white and green parts), coarsely chopped
2½ **star anise**, bruised
3¾- to 4-pound **chicken**, organic if possible

The two essentials in this dish are using a pot that holds the bird snugly so the sauce barely covers it, and keeping the liquid at the lowest bubble possible. You should be able to count slowly to four between each eruption. You may need to put the pot on a flame tamer to mute heat transfer.

(recipe continues)

GARNISH

3 **scallions** (white and green parts), cut on an angle into 1-inch lengths
Sichuan Dipping Sauce (recipe follows), optional
Roasted Sichuan Pepper and Salt (recipe follows), optional

1. Simmer the sauce: In a 4-quart saucepan with good heat distribution (which should hold the chicken snugly with just enough room to turn it over), combine the soy sauces, wine, sugar, ginger, scallions, and star anise with 1¼ cups water. Bring to a boil.

2. Cook the chicken: Placing a long fork or cooking chopsticks in the chicken's cavity, carefully slip the chicken into the liquid, breast side up. Tuck the chicken down into the pot so the liquid almost covers the bird. Leave a third of the breast unsubmerged so it cooks more slowly and remains moist. Add a little more water if needed. Baste the liquid over the breast three or four times. Adjust the heat so a bubble surfaces every 4 or 5 seconds.

3. Cover the pot (don't worry if the lid doesn't seal) and cook for 25 minutes. Turn the chicken breast side down. Try not to break the skin. Cook at the barest bubble for another 10 to 15 minutes, or until an instant-read thermometer inserted in the thigh reads 160°F.

4. Off the heat, cool the pot, covered, for 20 minutes, or until a thigh reads 170°F. Refrigerate the chicken in its sauce for 12 to 24 hours. Baste and turn every few hours so the chicken colors evenly. The chicken keeps for about 3 days, but if it is left in the sauce that long, the sauce overwhelms the meat. Remove the chicken from the sauce after 24 hours. Skim off the sauce's fat, strain the sauce, and refrigerate the chicken and sauce separately.

{ **COOK** *to* **Cook** }

There are two soy sauces in this recipe. Dark or double soy sauce is aged, rich in color, and slightly sweet. The Koon Chun brand is worth looking for. Light or thin soy is what to use whenever simply "soy sauce" is called for. Younger and paler than the dark, it has excellent flavor. Kikkoman brand, even though Japanese, works well here. Avoid "lite" or low-sodium soy sauces. Their flavors do not measure up.

WINE The color of this sauce will tempt you to go for a red wine, but don't be fooled. The haunting sweetness of that star anise needs a wine to match. Look for an off-dry Riesling from Old World sources: Alsace, Germany, or Austria. They will be your most reliable bet.

5. Serve the chicken. Back in the 4-quart pot, warm the bird in its strained sauce over medium to medium-high heat. Serve it Chinese style by cutting into quarters. Then slice each breast crossways into four or five pieces. Separate the legs and thighs. Assemble the pieces in a single layer, skin side up, on a platter. Sprinkle with the sliced scallions. Spoon about ⅓ cup of the sauce over the meat. Accompany with Sichuan Dipping Sauce and/or Roasted Sichuan Pepper and Salt, and serve with steamed long-grain rice or with an entire Chinese menu (page 26).

Sichuan Dipping Sauce

| *Makes ¾ cup; doubles easily* | *10 minutes prep time* | *Keeps refrigerated 1 week*

Non-Chinese dishes take to this sauce, too—chicken salad, barbecue, sausages, roast chicken, and most especially the baked potato. Mash some into a baked Idaho and see what you think.

1½-inch piece fresh **ginger**, minced
2 large **garlic cloves**, minced
3 tablespoons **soy sauce** (Kikkoman is a personal choice)
1½ tablespoons **Shanxi vinegar** or **balsamic vinegar**
2 teaspoons **rice wine** or **dry sherry**
2 tablespoons **sugar**
2 tablespoons **canola oil**
½ teaspoon **hot red pepper flakes**, or to taste
2 tablespoons **Vietnamese chile sauce** (ingredients are
   chile, garlic, sugar, salt, and vinegar)

Blend all of the ingredients in a small bowl and serve at room temperature.

(recipe continues)

Roasted Sichuan Pepper and Salt

Makes ⅔ cup   *10 minutes prep time;*
5 minutes stove time

⅓ cup **Sichuan peppercorns** (sometimes labeled Dried
   Prickly Ash)
½ cup **kosher salt**

1. In a dry 10-inch skillet, toast the peppercorns over medium heat for about 2 minutes, or until fragrant and slightly darkened. Remove from the pan, cool, and use a coffee grinder or blender to grind the peppercorns to a coarse powder.

2. In the same dry skillet, roast the salt for about 3 minutes and cool.

3. Serve the salt and pepper in two separate bowls. You put a little of each on your plate and dip the chicken into the piles.

FIVE THINGS TO DO WITH MASTER SAUCE

1. Put master sauce in your will, or gift friends—very good friends—with it.
2. Baste vegetables, seafood, meats, or poultry with master sauce while grilling or roasting.
3. **Master Sauce Soba Noodles with Ginger and Chile:** Moisten hot soba noodles with warm master sauce. Then toss with minced fresh ginger, chiles, and fresh basil.
4. **Master Sauce Glazed Onions:** Simmer 1½ pounds small onions in master sauce, then marinate overnight in the refrigerator. Glaze the onions by boiling down 1½ cups sauce in a large skillet. When it's boiled down by two thirds, add the onions and keep boiling until the sauce is syrupy and the onions are coated with it. Serve hot or warm as a side dish for lamb or seafood. Turn the onions into a condiment for cheeses or sandwiches by thinly slicing the glazed onions.
5. **Slow Rolled Sweet Corn in Master Sauce:** Melt a stick of unsalted butter with 2 teaspoons minced fresh ginger. Whisk in the master sauce to taste and heat through. Pour the sauce over a platter of hot, just-cooked corn on the cob. Roll the corn in the sauce and have a wonderfully sloppy time.

Clean
AS YOU GO

We've noticed that although good cooks don't necessarily worry about the floor of the kitchen as they cook, they do clean their dishes and workspace as they cook. When you keep up with the dishes, you always know where you are and, perhaps more important, you always know where you're going.

Vinegar—
The Secret Sweetener

Vinegar is a powerhouse seasoning when you add a little heat. For instance, cook off the acid and vinegar becomes sweet. Reducing it is also a great way to bring new flavor to inexpensive vinegars and to get bonuses out of spendy ones.

Cook it with a little *fat* and it becomes syrupy, which makes it an ideal glaze for anything from savories to sweets.

When you boil it down with *sugar* to a syrup, you get a seasoning the French call *gastric*—an unfortunate name, yes, but one of the great secrets behind a proper canard a l'orange and so many of those other streaky sauces you find on your plate in fancy restaurants. Gild your own gastric by throwing spices, bits of fruit, garlic, chile, or bits of bacon into that simmering reduction and you have a fast and fabulous sauce.

Use the Cider-Glazed Chicken (opposite) and Balsamic Syrup (PAGE 103) recipes as prototypes for cooking with vinegar.

Cider-Glazed Chicken

| *Serves 4; to double,* | *30 minutes prep time; 2 hours* | *For encores, this holds well 3 days*
| *use two pans* | *rest time; 1 hour stove time* | *in the refrigerator.*

Sally credits this dish with ending years of terrible rubber-chicken karma. Who knew it was as easy as just keeping the cooking low and slow?

Just imagine yourself making risotto, adding the broth to the rice bit by bit, gently letting each addition reduce and join forces with the whole before ladling in more. Now replace the rice with chicken and the broth with cider vinegar and some cider. The result is some of the most succulent chicken you've ever eaten—bathed in a tart-sweet-garlicky glaze and finished with a handful of crisp fried sage leaves for contrast.

Pair this technique for nearly anything—poultry, pork, root vegetables.

- 3- to 3½-pound **chicken** (organic if possible), cut into 8 pieces, wing tips cut off
- 15 large fresh **sage leaves**
- 1 teaspoon **kosher salt**
- ½ teaspoon freshly ground **black pepper**
- ⅔ cup **apple cider**
- 1 cup **cider vinegar**
- 2 tablespoons good-tasting **extra-virgin olive oil**
- ⅓ cup minced **onion**
- 3 large **garlic cloves**, minced
- ½ large **Granny Smith apple**, peeled, cored, and cut into 1½-inch-long thin sticks

GARNISH

- Good-tasting **extra-virgin olive oil**
- 20 large fresh **sage leaves**
- **Salt**

A 12-inch straight-sided sauté pan is essential to this recipe's success because the chicken pieces must be spread out to glaze the way you want them. Use two smaller pans if necessary. To ensure a good glaze, don't cover the chicken at any point while cooking, and keep basting it with the pan juices.

WINE Look to Australia or New Zealand for a medium-bodied Chardonnay, preferably unoaked.

(recipe continues)

1. If possible, about 2 hours before cooking, rub the chicken with the sage leaves. Sprinkle all sides of the chicken with the salt and pepper and pile it all on a platter, tucking in the sage leaves here and there. Cover and refrigerate. When you're ready to cook, remove the sage leaves, but keep them handy. Pat the chicken dry. In a small bowl combine the cider and cider vinegar and set aside. Pat the chicken dry.

2. In a 12-inch straight-sided sauté pan (not nonstick), heat the oil over medium-high heat. Place the chicken in the pan, skin side down, so the pieces don't touch. Reduce the heat to medium or medium-low and cook the chicken for about 10 minutes, or until it is a rich golden brown on one side. To keep the chicken from sticking during browning, slip a metal spatula under each piece to loosen.

3. Turn the chicken pieces and brown the other side. Move the breast pieces to the pan's edge to slow their cooking. Remove the pan from the heat and spoon off all but 1 tablespoon fat.

4. These final steps should take about 25 minutes. Set the pan over medium heat, sprinkle the chicken with the onion, and add one third of the cider mixture to the pan. Cook slowly, uncovered, scraping up the brown glaze, and turning the chicken pieces occasionally. The idea is to keep coating the chicken with the pan juices until all of the liquid has cooked away. Keep the cider mixture simmering gently, taking care not to scorch it.

5. Repeat, slowly reducing and coating the chicken with another third of the cider mixture. Finally, add the remaining cider mixture along with the reserved sage leaves and the garlic. Spoon the pan juices over the chicken and scrape up the sticky glaze, turning the pieces to keep them moistened. Blend in ½ cup water and the apple and cook down the liquid about halfway.

6. The chicken is cooked when an instant-read thermometer inserted in the breast reads 165°F. The sauce should be syrupy and rich tasting. If not, lift out the chicken to a platter to keep warm and cook down the sauce. Scrape the sauce over the chicken and let it rest for 10 minutes.

7. Meanwhile, wipe out the pan, coat it with a thin film of oil, and set it over medium-high heat. Fry the 20 sage leaves for 3 minutes, or until crisp. Salt the leaves, lift them out with a slotted spoon, and scatter them over the chicken. Serve hot.

WORK NIGHT ENCORES

Sichuan Chicken Salad: The chicken is outstanding reheated with Sichuan Dipping Sauce (page 185) and piled on a plate of salad greens and raw vegetables. Do a fast dressing of rice vinegar, soy sauce, minced fresh ginger, and sesame oil.

Chicken in Tart and Savory Rice: Have a few cups cooked rice and the chicken cut off the bone ready to go. In a skillet, brown a chopped onion and several thick slices of chopped bacon in oil. Stir in minced fresh garlic, 2 tablespoons tomato paste, and ⅓ cup vinegar. Cook down and stir in the cooked rice and the cut-up chicken. Heat through, add fresh parsley leaves, and serve.

The way you cut your meat reflects the way you live.

—CONFUCIUS

Pine-Smoked Chicken

| Serves 4; doubles easily | 15 minutes prep time; 4 to 6 hours marinating time; 30 minutes oven time; 15 minutes grill time | Serve hot or warm. For encores, this bird is superb in salads, especially with dried cranberries.

We're always game for a good ceremonial burning. This quick-smoked grilled chicken comes together in a heartbeat, making it perfect for a post–tree trimming family meal. You need to put those branches you cut off the bottom of your tree to good use, right? Admittedly, the boughs do tend to flame (we find that exciting), but they also impart a lovely resiny scent to whatever they touch.

This recipe is started in the oven and finished over a dying charcoal fire, just hot enough to get that pine smoke going.

½ cup dry **white wine**
¼ cup **Spanish sherry wine vinegar**
6 large **garlic cloves**, minced
1 tablespoon (packed) **dark brown sugar**
1 teaspoon **liquid smoke**
Salt and freshly ground **black pepper**
3½-pound **chicken**, cut into 8 pieces
4 to 5 fresh, green **pine boughs** (1½ to 2 feet long)

GARNISH

1 to 2 **pine sprigs**

1. Combine the wine, vinegar, garlic, sugar and liquid smoke with salt and pepper to taste in a shallow dish. Pour one third of it into a storage container and reserve. Add the chicken to the remaining marinade in the dish, turning the pieces to coat them. Cover and refrigerate for 4 to 6 hours.

Since this chicken is fully cooked before it hits the grill, you can prepare it a day ahead. After roasting the chicken, store it loosely covered in the refrigerator. Bring it to room temperature before grilling.

WINE Look for a moderately rich New World Chardonnay, something with a touch of oak or less than 14 percent alcohol (which is one way to tell if something is lightly oaked).

(recipe continues)

2. Preheat the oven to 350°F. Drain the marinade into a small bowl. Pat the chicken dry and spread out the pieces in a shallow roasting pan. Roast for 30 minutes, basting often with the marinade. You want the breast to read 165°F. on an instant-read thermometer. Take the chicken from the oven and either set it aside while you ready the grill or refrigerate it for up to 24 hours.

3. Heat coals in an outdoor grill until they're covered in gray ash, or heat a gas grill to medium-high heat. Spread the coals out. Add the pine boughs and set the rack in place. If the boughs begin to flame, cover with the grill lid and let them die before adding the chicken. (You need smoke but not flames.)

4. Take advantage of the smoking boughs by quickly putting the chicken on the grill. Cover and cook, turning and basting occasionally with the marinade you set aside. The chicken should brown and crisp and come to an internal temperature of 170°F. This takes 10 to 15 minutes. Pile the chicken on a platter, garnish with pine sprigs, and serve hot or warm.

Smoke in a Bottle— PURITY REVEALED

Imagine our surprise when Nashville barbecue authority R. B. Quinn insisted that liquid smoke was an integral part of his *Cheater BBQ* book. According to R. B., liquid smoke is made by collecting the smoke from burning wood in a condenser and then cooling it until it forms a liquid. Not only is the liquid pure smoke, but all impurities and carcinogens are removed. And that is that.

Erotica is using a feather; pornography is using the whole chicken.

—ISABEL ALLENDE

The
Charcoal Brief

SETTING UP A CHARCOAL FIRE

Which Fuel to Use: Our top pick is hardwood, such as oak, cherry, hickory, apple, or mesquite. Actual wood gives wonderful flavor, even when you are not smoking (and when soaked in water, the wood will produce fragrant smoke). Wood chunks are sold in bags very much like charcoal. Find them in natural-food stores, hardware stores, supermarkets, and kitchen shops.

A close second choice is hardwood charcoal, also labeled lump charcoal or charwood. Find the brand picks of grill addicts at www.nakedwhiz.com. This is where home grillers ruthlessly test out brands and give reports that border on exposés.

Charcoal briquettes are a very distant third choice. They're often composed of compressed coal dust, borax, and petroleum binders, none of which we need in our food or the environment.

Starting the Fire: Chimney starters have it all over the old lighter fluid technique. Lighter fluid smells and tastes nasty and doesn't do much for the environment.

The chimney is a metal cylinder with a handle, and it's ridiculously easy to use. There's a grate in the middle of the cylinder where you stuff a couple of sheets of crumpled newspaper and top with the wood or charcoal. Light the paper, and the coals catch fire. Once they're red, turn them onto the bottom grate of the grill.

Creating Cooking Zones: The way you spread out the coals can open up cooking possibilities. For fast cooking of small pieces of food, spread the coals out in a single layer of red-hot coals. If you want to sear and then slowly cook things such as burgers, steaks, and vegetables, you will need two cooking zones. Make the zones by piling coals 4 inches deep on one side of the grill and leaving a single layer on the other. Now you have the same flexibility as on a stovetop except that instead of changing the temperature under the food, you move the food to the level of heat you want.

When you are long-roasting things such as ribs, whole chickens, and roasts, you want the coals pushed away from the center of the grill, leaving a bare spot so you have indirect heat. Place a drip pan in that center opening. This gives you a large cooking surface with varying heat levels.

How Hot Are the Coals? Recipes often tell you to wait for a gray ash to form over the coals. But this doesn't apply to all dishes. A good way to gauge the temperature is to hold your hand 5 to 6 inches above the cooking grate. You'll know how high your heat is by how long you can hold your hand over the heat:

      1 to 2 seconds: high heat

      3 to 4 seconds: medium heat

      5 to 6 seconds: low heat

Ancho Cider-Glazed Hens

Serves 4 to 6;
multiplies easily

30 minutes prep time;
1 to 1½ hours roasting time;
15 minutes rest time

With their sticky, spicy glaze, these hens are a diminutive riff on our holiday turkey. The birds can be served with Butter-Roasted Cornbread (page 137)—a twist on traditional stuffing, made of cornbread with sausage, nuts, and cheese baked into it, then toasted into crispy croutons. That crunch makes them irresistible. Spoon them over the hens and serve with Roasted Grapes and Winter Vegetables (page 282) and you have a dish worthy of a cover shot (see cover photo).

HENS

1 large **onion**, cut into ⅛-inch thick rounds
4 to 6 **Cornish game hens** (1 to 1¼ pounds each)
Salt and freshly ground black pepper

GLAZE

1 quart **apple cider**, boiled down to about ⅔ cup
⅓ cup **cider vinegar**
1 tablespoon **soy sauce**
1 tablespoon ground **Ancho** or other medium-hot chile, or to taste
2 tablespoons packed light **brown sugar**
4 large garlic **cloves**, minced
Salt and freshly ground black pepper to taste

ACCOMPANIMENTS

Butter-Roasted Cornbread (page 136)
Roasted Grapes and Winter Vegetables (page 282)
⅓ cup toasted pine nuts (optional)

{ **COOK** *to* **Cook** }

The cornbread can be baked 2 days ahead and refrigerated. Roast the vegetables early in the day and keep at room temperature, lightly covered. Toast the cornbread as directed in its recipe shortly before serving.

1. Make the hens: About 2 hours before serving, preheat the oven to 400°F. Cover the bottom of a large shallow baking pan (a half-sheet pan is ideal) with the onion rounds. Tie together the hens' legs with cotton string. Arrange the hens, breast side up on the onions. You want some space around each one so they can crisp up. Sprinkle the birds with salt and pepper.

2. Make the glaze: Stir together in a medium bowl the reduced apple cider, cider vinegar, soy sauce, ground chile, brown sugar, and garlic. Spoon about 2 teaspoons of the sauce over each hen.

3. Slip the pan into the oven and reduce the heat to 325°F. Roast the hens for 30 minutes, basting with their pan juices once or twice. Then raise the heat to 400°F., baste each hen with about 2 tablespoons of sauce, and continue roasting and basting with pan juices for 20 more minutes, or until the thickest part of the breast reads 160°F. on an instant-read thermometer. At this point spoon a bit more sauce over the hens and run them under the broiler briefly, so they turn a rich, deep brown. Watch them carefully so they don't burn.

4. Remove the pan from the oven, transfer the hens to a platter, and let them rest in a warm place for 10 to 15 minutes. Roast the cornbread cubes as directed in the recipe and reheat the roasted vegetables.

5. As they heat up, set the hens' roasting pan on two burners and remove the onions from the pan. Add any remaining basting sauce to the roasting pan. Raise the heat to medium-high or high. With a wood spatula, scrape any brown glaze from the pan and stir as you boil the pan sauce for 3 minutes, or until it's rich tasting and almost syrupy. Taste for seasoning, add any necessary salt and pepper, and keep hot.

6. To serve the hens, warm a large serving platter in the oven for a few minutes. Then heap the vegetables and cornbread on it and tuck in the hens. Scrape all the pan juices over the birds and vegetables, scatter with the pine nuts if you're using them, and serve the dish hot.

Crisp Roast Turkey with Garlic, Apple & Basil

Serves 10 to 14 | *40 minutes prep time; 10 to 12 hours brining time; 2¾ to 3 hours oven time (10 minutes per pound with the bird at room temperature); 20 to 30 minutes rest time*

This is our Thanksgiving turkey—brined in cider with apples and garlic, fast-roasted and crisp, and served with a gravy worthy of a swoon. Lynne is a great believer in repeating seasoning themes in different stages of cooking to build depth. This is why you find several expressions of apple (fruit, cider, and brandy) and basil in the roasting pan, in the gravy, and in the turkey.

10- to 12-pound **turkey**, organic if possible
Apple Chile Brine (recipe follows)
3 large **celery stalks**, halved crosswise
3 large **carrots**, halved lengthwise
3 medium to large **onions**, sliced into ½- to ¾-inch-thick rounds
1 large tart-sweet **apple** (such as Honeycrisp or Granny Smith), cored and coarsely chopped
2 lightly packed cups (3 ounces) fresh **basil leaves**
1 bottle dry **white wine** (Sauvignon Blanc, Pinot Grigio, or Albariño)
½ stick **unsalted butter**, softened
½ teaspoon freshly ground **black pepper**

GARNISH

7 to 9 small **crab apples**
Pine sprigs
Apple Brandy Pan Gravy (recipe follows)

Brines are no place for the flavor-shy. If you want a brine to flavor as well as moisten your bird, you have to elevate its seasonings far beyond what seems reasonable. Here, ⅓ cup chile, 2 heads of garlic, 4 apples, and 2 quarts cider season the brine, yet the final effect is subtle.

Figure 1 hour of brine time per pound of turkey.

WINE The best wines for a Thanksgiving feast are Riesling from Alsace, Pinot Noir from Burgundy, and Gran Reserva Rioja from Spain.

1. Brine the turkey: A day ahead, calculate how long you will brine the bird by figuring 1 hour brining per pound. Remove the giblets and neck and set aside for the gravy. Put the turkey into a food-safe container (a 10- to 12-quart stockpot, a tall plastic commercial food container, or a plastic roasting bag) that is large enough to hold it submerged in brine. Pour in the brine to cover. Keep the turkey cold (brine should be 33°F.) in the fridge or buried in ice in a large cooler. When the time is up, remove the turkey from the brine and keep it cold. Set out at room temperature 90 minutes before roasting.

2. Roast the turkey: For the fastest roasting time, bring the turkey to room temperature. Remove the oven's center rack and set the other one as low as possible. Preheat the oven to 450°F.

3. In the bottom of a large, shallow pan (2 inches deep is ideal; deeper will have the turkey steaming instead of roasting) create a sturdy rack for the bird by clustering together the celery, carrots, and onions. Scatter them with half of the chopped apple and two thirds of the basil. Add enough wine to fill the pan with ½ inch of liquid.

4. Set the turkey on the vegetables, breast side down, and tuck the remaining apple and basil into its cavity. Dot the turkey with butter and dust with pepper. Roast for 10 minutes per pound, or until an instant-read thermometer inserted in the thigh reads 165°F. to 170°F. As the bird cooks, add a little wine and baste the bird with the pan juices every 20 minutes.

5. After the first hour of roasting, remove the roasting pan from the oven and use two potholders to carefully turn the bird breast side up. Baste with the pan juices and continue roasting. Cover lightly with foil if the turkey threatens to burn.

6. Once the thigh reaches 165°F. to 170°F., remove the turkey to a platter and let stand in a warm place for 20 to 30 minutes. Present the turkey whole in all its glory with its garnishes of apples and pine. Carve thin slices and pass the Apple Brandy Pan Gravy.

(recipe continues)

Apple Chile Brine

Makes 4 quarts | *15 minutes prep time*

1¼ cups **kosher salt**
⅓ cup (packed) **light brown sugar**
⅓ cup medium-hot pure ground **chile**
2 **garlic heads**, trimmed of root ends
4 **large apples**, such as Granny Smith, Honeycrisp,
    Ambrosia, or Liberty (not peeled), cored and coarsely
    chopped
2 quarts cold **apple cider**

In a 10- to 12-quart bowl or stockpot, combine the salt, sugar, and chile. In a food processor, purée the garlic, apples, and 2 cups of the cider. Add them to the salt mixture along with the rest of the cider and 4 quarts cold water. Stir to dissolve the salt and sugar.

Apple Brandy Pan Gravy

Makes about 3 cups	*30 minutes prep time;*	*Keeps refrigerated up to 4 days and*
	4 to 5 hours unattended	*frozen 3 months.*
	stove time for the broth;	*The broth can be made days ahead and*
	20 minutes stove time to	*stored in the refrigerator or freezer. The*
	finish the gravy	*finished gravy reheats beautifully.*

Granted, this is a fanatic's gravy. For some of us, the turkey is only a vehicle. For deep, intense gravy flavors, "when in doubt, boil it down." Here, it means boil down the pan juices to a thick syrup, then add rich broth and boil that down again until the gravy hums with depth. You can sidestep any lumps, the gravy maker's nemesis, by making a slurry, a mixture of water and flour that is added to the boiling gravy.

BROTH

Good-tasting **extra-virgin olive oil**
Turkey neck
Turkey giblets, thinly sliced
1½ to 2 pounds **chicken legs**, or legs and thighs
1 large or 2 medium **onions**, coarsely chopped
1 medium **celery stalk** with leaves, coarsely
  chopped
1 medium **carrot**, coarsely chopped
2 large **garlic cloves**, crushed
8 whole **allspice**, crushed
2 whole **cloves**, crushed
¼ cup **apple brandy**
2 cups dry **white wine** (Sauvignon Blanc, Fume
  Blanc, or Pinot Grigio)

GRAVY

⅓ cup **apple brandy**
½ cup dry **white wine**
⅓ cup **apple cider**
1 generous tablespoon **all-purpose flour**
Salt and freshly ground **black pepper**

**For speed, you can skip
the browning step and
just combine the
poultry, vegetables,
brandy, and wine and
simmer for 5 to 6 hours.
You lose some depth,
but still get good gravy.**

(recipe continues)

1. **Make the broth:** Coat the bottom of a 12-inch straight-sided sauté pan with a thin film of oil and heat over medium-high heat. Add the turkey neck, giblets, and chicken. Brown them (adjust the heat so the glaze on the bottom of the pan doesn't burn) on both sides, then transfer to a 6-quart pot. Pour off half of the fat from the pan. Heat again over medium-high heat. Stir in the onion, celery, carrot, garlic, allspice, and cloves and sauté for 2 minutes. Add the apple brandy and wine. Bring to a boil, scraping up all the brown glaze from the bottom of the pan.

2. Transfer everything to the 6-quart pot. Cover with 1 inch water and bring to a slow bubble. Partially cover and simmer for 4 to 5 hours. Keep the solids covered with just a little liquid. Cool the broth, strain it, and refrigerate. Remove any fat before using.

3. **Make the gravy:** As the bird rests, set the roasting pan over two burners set to medium-high heat. Remove the vegetables from the roasting pan (save for another meal) and spoon off some of the fat.

4. With a flat wooden spatula, stir in the brandy, wine, and cider. Bring to a boil over high heat and scrape up all the brown bits as you reduce the pan juices down to practically a syrup, about 3 minutes. Stir in the broth and boil down by half, or until it tastes rich and deep.

5. To thicken the gravy, make a slurry. Put the flour in a tall glass and *gradually* beat in ½ to ⅔ cup cold water. Beat until there are no lumps. Whisk this into the bubbling pan liquid. Keep simmering and whisking until the gravy is smooth and thick enough to lightly coat a spoon. Now taste it. If you taste raw flour, simmer another minute. Add salt and pepper to taste and serve.

Nothing makes a holiday quite like a family row.

—NIGELLA LAWSON

The Art
of the Stash

Good cooks use everything. They stash away bits and ends of vegetables for stocks; bones, gravies, and drippings from roasts; and old bread for croutons and for making real bread crumbs. It's ultimately an exercise in creativity once you get started.

START BY KEEPING TWO BAGS IN YOUR FREEZER: one to stash vegetable bits, and the other for meat odds and ends. When the bags fill up, make your own home-brewed broth. Just put everything in a big pot, cover with water, and cook at a slow bubble for 6 to 7 hours.

Sweet-Sour Chicken Meatballs with Candied Lemon Peel

| *Serves 3 to 4 as a main dish and 6 to 8 as a first course* | *30 minutes prep time; 30 minutes stove time* | *The meatballs reheat well the next day.* |

These are meatballs like no others. Rich with spices, cheese, peppery salami, nuts, and candied fruit, this dish clearly has Arab ancestry. This particular recipe comes from Puglia, Italy, the heel of the boot, though you will find similar versions throughout southern Italy.

These meatballs are unabashedly Catholic. A celebration dish, they're traditionally served on occasions such as Christmas, Easter, and the Feast of St. Joseph, the day in the middle of Lent when people are allowed to take a break from their fasting and have a bit of fun. Believe us, the sexiness of this dish would certainly loosen things up.

MEATBALLS

- 2 large **garlic cloves**
- 2 ounces hot **capicola salami** or **pepperoni salami**
- 4 to 5 boned and skinned **chicken thighs** (about 1 pound), cut into ½-inch dice
- Half of a 10-ounce package of frozen **spinach**, defrosted and squeezed dry, or 1 pound fresh spinach, cooked, cooled, and squeezed dry
- ½ medium **onion**, coarsely chopped
- ¼ teaspoon **salt**
- ¼ teaspoon freshly ground **black pepper**
- ½ teaspoon ground **cinnamon**
- ½ cup fresh **bread crumbs**
- 1 tablespoon **red wine vinegar**
- ⅔ cup (3 ounces) grated **Fontinella** or **Asiago cheese**
- ½ cup whole **almonds**, toasted and chopped medium-fine
- Scant ⅓ cup (2¼ ounces) **Candied Lemon Peel** (page 102), minced very fine

COOK *to* **Cook**

Although candied citron is the traditional choice here, the quality of what we can find on this side of the Atlantic leaves a lot to be desired. Unless you have a source for top-tier imported citron, you're better off using homemade candied lemon peel instead.

1 large **egg**

Good-tasting **extra-virgin olive oil**

SAUCE

½ cup dry **white wine**

6 large fresh **basil leaves**, torn

1 teaspoon **sugar**

2 tablespoons **red wine vinegar**

1 cup **Master Broth** (page 58) or
  canned low-sodium **chicken broth**

SERVICE

4 cups tart **salad greens**

WINE Pair with a young, fresh red with vivid fruit, such as the Puglia wines, Salice Salentino, Primitivo, or a Salento Rosso, or serve a Tempranillo-based Ribera del Duero from Spain or a New World Pinot Noir.

1. Make the meatballs: Using a food processor or a knife, mince the garlic and capicola. Add the chicken, spinach, onion, salt, pepper, and cinnamon. Chop them very fine (but don't purée). Transfer the mixture to a bowl and blend in the bread crumbs, wine vinegar, cheese, almonds, lemon peel, and egg; blend well.

2. Check the seasonings by sautéing a little patty of the mixture over medium-high heat until it is firm. Add salt and pepper to taste. Shape the rest of the meat into 2-inch balls.

3. Cook the meatballs: Coat the bottom of a 12-inch, straight-sided sauté pan with a thin film of oil. Set the pan over medium-high heat. Add the meatballs (keep them from touching) then reduce the heat to medium. Brown them on all sides, turning gently with a spatula. Be gentle; the meatballs are very fragile.

4. Make the sauce: Tip the pan, spoon off most of the fat, and pour in the wine. Simmer until thick and syrupy. Blend in the basil, sugar, wine vinegar, and broth. Cover and simmer very gently for 15 minutes, or until the meatballs' centers have reached 170°F. on an instant-read thermometer.

5. When done, gently lift the meatballs into a shallow bowl. Boil down the pan juices, stirring with a wooden spatula, until thick and rich tasting. Nestle the meatballs on a bed of tart salad greens, pour the warmed pan juices over them, and serve hot or warm.

FISH AND SEAFOOD

Ginger Shrimp Stir-Fry with Snow Peas, Chinese Mushrooms & Baby Corn

| Serves 4 as a main dish and 8 to 10 as part of a Chinese menu | 20 minutes prep time; 30 to 40 minutes in marinade; 15 minutes stove time | Prep all the ingredients before beginning to cook. In the best of all possible worlds, serve this recipe the moment it's done to experience the incredible vitality of the stir-fry, what Canton cooks call wok hay. |

You actually rock into a stir-fry. Let yourself go and your whole body moves into the rhythm—the tossing, the adding, and the taking away.

China's southern Canton region considers this kind of dish a hallmark. For me, this is what is missing in the Chinese restaurants where most of us eat—simple, quiet dishes with well-orchestrated ingredients that speak of themselves, not of overkill sauces, sugar, and chile.

In plotting out a Chinese menu (page 26) with its essential contrasts in flavor, this sort of dish is a focal point. Around it pivots the contrasting dishes that are sweet or salty or sour or spiced.

You will need a 14- to 16-inch rolled steel or cast-iron wok.

SHRIMP AND MARINADE

1 pound large **shrimp**, shelled, tails intact (about 26 to the pound)

1-inch piece fresh **ginger**, cut into very thin 1-inch sticks (about 2 tablespoons)

1 large **garlic clove**, very thinly sliced

1 teaspoon **sesame oil**

¼ teaspoon **sugar**

¼ teaspoon freshly ground **black pepper**

⅛ teaspoon **salt**

(recipe continues)

SAUCE

2 tablespoons **rice wine** or **dry sherry**
1 teaspoon **rice vinegar** or **cider vinegar**
½ teaspoon **sugar**
1 tablespoon **soy sauce**
⅓ cup **chicken broth**
2 teaspoons **cornstarch**

STIR-FRY

8 dried **shiitake mushrooms**, soaked for 20 minutes
    in hot water
About 5 tablespoons **peanut**, **safflower**, or
    grapeseed oil
2 **scallions** (white and green parts), cut on the
    diagonal into 1-inch lengths
½-inch piece fresh **ginger**, thinly sliced into rounds
10 whole **water chestnuts**, quartered
1 small **baby bok choy**, thinly sliced crosswise
    (generous ½ cup)
12 **snow pea pods**, strings removed
½ cup frozen tiny **peas**, defrosted
7 canned whole **baby corn ears**, rinsed and drained
½ medium **carrot**, sliced into very thin 2-inch sticks

Eaters wait for stir-
fries; stir-fries wait for
no man. The time from
the wok to the table
should be seconds. So
do all the prep well
ahead, mix together
ingredients that go into
the wok together, get
your wok or pan sear-
ing hot, and then begin.

WINE This dish needs a
subtle wine; try a Pinot
Blanc from Alsace or a
Pinot Bianco from Italy's
Friuli region.

1. **Marinate the shrimp:** In a medium bowl, toss the shrimp with the marinade
ingredients and refrigerate them for 30 to 40 minutes while you prep the rest of
the dish.

2. **Make the sauce:** In a small bowl, combine the rice wine, rice vinegar, sugar,
and soy sauce. In a second small bowl, blend the broth and cornstarch.

3. **Prep the stir-fry:** Drain the soaked mushrooms, rinse them, trim away their
tough stems, and dry each with a towel. Have all of the vegetables sliced and
ready. Make sure they are all bone-dry. Keep the scallions and ginger separate.

4. **Make the stir-fry:** When you're ready to stir-fry, have a serving platter close
at hand. Heat the wok or sauté pan over high heat. You want it very hot. Swirl in
about 2 tablespoons oil. When nearly smoking, add the shrimp, spreading them in
a single layer.

Stir-fry for 1 minute, or until the shrimp are pink and barely firm. Immediately scoop them out onto the platter. Off the heat, use a wad of paper towels to wipe out the wok or pan.

5. Heat the wok or sauté pan again over high heat, and swirl in another 3 tablespoons oil. Once hot, drop in the scallions and ginger. Stir until fragrant, no more than 20 seconds, and add the vegetables, sprinkling them with salt. Stir-fry for 1 to 2 minutes.

Add the soy sauce mixture and stir-fry for another 30 seconds. Give the cornstarch mixture a quick stir and add it to the wok. Stir-fry for 20 seconds, or until the liquid is thickened and clear. Add the shrimp and warm through, 10 seconds. Immediately turn the stir-fry out onto the platter and sprint for the table.

Gourmets dig graves with their teeth.

—OLD FRENCH PROVERB

Karl's Curried Mussels

| *Serves 6 to 8* | *15 minutes prep time;* | *Serve and devour immediately.*
| | *10 minutes stove time* |

Scented with lemongrass and ginger, this coconut-milk curry is inspired by our friend Karl Benson. He is owner of the lovely cookware shop Cooks of Crocus Hill in St. Paul, Minnesota.

Karl, though a first-generation Swede, has an eerily instinctual connection to the Southeast Asian palate. He also has a houseful of kids, all first-rate eaters, and this recipe (not exactly Swedish meatballs) is based on one of the house favorites. Serve them in small bowls with a scoop of white rice on the bottom to catch the drippings.

1 13-ounce can **coconut milk**

1 large **shallot**, minced (about 4 tablespoons)

4-inch piece **lemongrass**, minced after removing the tough outer layer

2 tablespoons fresh **cilantro stems and roots** (if available), minced

3 tablespoons **Thai green curry paste**, or to taste

2 tablespoons **Asian fish sauce**, such as Three Crabs brand

1 tablespoon (packed) **dark brown sugar**

1 small fresh hot **red chile**, minced (optional)

2 **Kaffir lime leaves** (optional)

3-inch piece fresh **ginger**, minced (about 3 tablespoons)

2 pounds **mussels**, sorted (discard the open or cracked shells), rinsed, and debearded

2 tightly packed tablespoons fresh **basil leaves**, chopped

2 tightly packed tablespoons fresh **cilantro leaves**, chopped

2 tightly packed tablespoons fresh **spearmint leaves**, chopped

Juice of 1 large **lime**

1 cup **cooked rice**, any variety, though sticky rice would be traditional

WINE Look for a young Riesling from Australia or New Zealand, as these are almost all essentially dry but still ripe and fruity, which works very well with the shellfish and the Asian spicing. Alternatively, try an unwooded Chardonnay from California or Australia, whose warmer areas can produce Chardonnays with tropical fruit notes that will flatter the richness and spice of this dish.

(recipe continues)

1. In a covered pot large enough to hold the mussels, combine the coconut milk, shallot, lemongrass, cilantro stems and roots, curry paste, fish sauce, sugar, chile (if using), kaffir leaves (if using), and 2 tablespoons of the ginger. Bring to a simmer and cook for 3 to 5 minutes, or until the lemongrass and shallots begin to get slightly tender.

2. Add the mussels and steam them, tightly covered, until they open, 3 to 5 minutes depending on their size. Remove the mussels from the pot with a slotted spoon and place them in a large shallow bowl. Discard any unopened mussels.

3. Stir the remaining 1 tablespoon ginger and the basil, cilantro leaves, spearmint, and lime juice into the coconut milk and simmer to heat through, about 30 seconds. If the sauce seems too thick, thin it with a little water to a brothlike consistency. Remove the pan from the heat and pour the sauce over the mussels.

4. Serve in individual small bowls with a little rice on the bottom of each bowl.

A converted cannibal is one who, on Fridays, eats only fishermen.

—EMILY LOTNEY

Mussel
Glue

The next time you see a mass of barnacles stuck to the side of a boat or are wrestling to debeard your mussels before throwing them in a pot, stop and think about how those shelled creatures hang on so tightly. Believe it or not, they can actually stick to nonstick surfaces, and wet ones at that. And it's not by suction.

According to our guest **Dr. Jonathan Wilker,** associate professor of inorganic chemistry at Purdue University, most shellfish like oysters, mussels, and barnacles stick by secreting a small amount of adhesive and stringing a thread to it that is attached to their bodies. That "beard" we trim off is just a collection of those threads.

Scientists such as Dr. Wilker, who research this shellfish sticking power, are intrigued with what could be created once the code to shellfish adhesive is cracked—imagine a day when your appendectomy is sealed up with help from a bivalve.

Flash-Sautéed Squid with Peppers & Garlic

| *Serves 3 to 4* | *20 minutes prep time; 1 hour marinating time; 10 minutes stove time* | *Squid is best served right after cooking.* |

These garlicky squid cook in a flash. They're tossed in a hot pan with chiles, peppers, onions, and a whisper of anchovy to bring out the very essence of the sea.

People have a funny squeamishness about squid, even though it is one of the least "fishy" of all seafood; it sleeps happily frozen in your freezer and thaws out in a snap under cold running water.

1 pound cleaned small **squid with tentacles**, defrosted if frozen

1 medium-hot fresh **chile** (red or green jalapeño, small Hungarian, or serrano), seeded

5 large **garlic cloves**

3 whole **anchovies**, rinsed (optional)

¼ tightly packed cup **flat-leaf parsley leaves**

3 tablespoons **extra-virgin olive oil**

1 medium **red onion**, cut into 6 wedges

1 large **sweet yellow pepper**, seeded and cut into 1-inch strips

Salt and freshly ground **black pepper**

2 medium **lemons**, each cut into 6 wedges

Cook squid for seconds or for hours; anything in between yields you rubber bands. You will find squid a bargain in the frozen section of Asian markets, usually tucked in next to octopus tentacles.

WINE Pair the squid with a Pinot Gris from Alsace.

1. Marinate the squid: Rinse the squid and pat it dry. Trim the squid tentacles into 1-inch pieces. Split the squid in half lengthwise and open it up like a book. With a sharp knife, lightly score the inside of the body with a crosshatch pattern. Mince the chile, garlic, anchovies (if using), and parsley and transfer to a medium bowl. Blend in the oil. Put half of the chile mixture in another medium bowl. Toss that with the squid. Cover and refrigerate the squid mixture for 1 hour. Add the onion and yellow pepper to the remaining chile mixture. Cover and refrigerate for 1 hour.

2. Remove the squid mixture from the refrigerator and put a large griddle or skillet on the stove. Have a serving platter handy. Turn the heat to high.

3. Cook the squid: When the griddle or skillet is smoking, spread the tentacles and squid on the surface, cut side down, with any seasonings that are clinging to them. Cook for 10 seconds, sprinkling with salt and pepper. With a metal spatula, turn and cook for another 10 seconds. Immediately remove the squid and its seasonings to the serving platter, squeezing 2 to 3 lemon wedges over it.

4. Reduce the heat to medium and toss the onion mixture on the grill or skillet until crisp-tender, 3 to 5 minutes.

5. Taste for seasoning and arrange the onion mixture with the finished squid. Serve hot or warm garnished with the remaining lemon wedges.

A woman without a man is like a fish without a bicycle.

—GLORIA STEINEM

Smoke-Roasted Salmon

| *Serves 6 to 12, depending on* | *10 minutes prep time; 25 to 30 minutes* |
| *the size of the fillet* | *grill time; 10 minutes rest time* |

This fish, with its haunting edge of smoke, is a showcase recipe for a beautiful piece of salmon or other oil-rich fish. Smoke-roasted slowly on a grill over an indirect fire, the salmon burnishes to a golden glaze and nearly melts on your fork.

Serve the salmon whole, with tender leaves of butter lettuce tucked around its edges. The lettuce will wilt a little in the salmon juices, creating a new pairing—warm salmon and cool, sweet greens. Serve with French Radish Sauté (page 270).

Good-tasting **extra-virgin olive oil**
3- to 7-pound **salmon fillet**, if possible 2½ to
   3 inches thick, or other oil-rich fish, such as
   cobia, mackerel, or trout, chilled
Coarse salt and freshly ground **black pepper**
3 cups **wood chips** (hickory, fruitwood, or
   grapevine), soaked in water to cover for
   30 minutes, then drained
5 or 6 leaves of **butter** or **Bibb lettuce**
¼ cup fresh **tarragon sprigs**

1. Prepare your grill for a two-zone fire (see The Charcoal Brief on page 196). If using a gas grill, set one burner on high and one burner on low.

2. Double a piece of heavy-duty foil large enough to fit the fish with another 4 to 6 inches on each side, to act as handles. Perforate the foil with small holes no larger than the width of a pencil to allow the smoke to surround the fish. Generously oil the foil and both sides of the fish. Place the salmon on the foil, skin side down.

To avoid heartbreak, before buying your side of salmon, measure your grill to be certain it will fit! And before heading out for your fish, check www .seafoodwatch.org for ecologically sound choices and www.edf .org for concerns about contamination.

WINE The richness of this fish demands a rich wine to match. Look to a Chardonnay from California or Australia or, if you prefer a red, try a young West Coast Pinot Noir.

(recipe continues)

Sprinkle it with salt and pepper to taste. Loosely crimp the foil up and around the sides of the salmon so that some of the smoke can be captured around the fish.

3. When the coals are medium-hot, throw ½ cup of the soaked and drained wood chips on the hottest part of the fire. Quickly place the salmon in its foil on the grate, with the thick side closest to the hottest portion of the grill. Put the lid on the grill, making sure the vents are wide open on the lid and at the base of the grill.

4. Add more wood chips and charcoal as needed to keep the fire burning and the wood chips smoking to the point that smoke is billowing out. If the fire seems to be dying, blow a little on the coals and give it a bit more oxygen to get it going again.

5. A 2½- to 3-inch-thick piece of salmon will cook in 25 to 30 minutes. The salmon is done when it's colored to a burnished gold, the oils are beginning to pool on the surface, and the flesh is nearly opaque at the center of the thickest part of the fillet.

6. Using oven mitts, carefully lift the foil with salmon from the grill by grasping the foil's ends. Set it on a serving platter and let it rest for 10 minutes.

7. To serve, trim the foil away from the edges of the fish with scissors and tuck the lettuce around the sides. Sprinkle with the tarragon.

WORK NIGHT ENCORES

Home-Smoked Salmon Mousse: For every 1½ cups crumbled salmon, measure one eighth of a medium onion, about 3 tablespoons mayonnaise, and lemon juice to taste. Purée the ingredients in a food processor and serve in a crock for spreading on cucumber slices and crackers.

Salmon Niçoise on Red-Skin Potatoes: Boil 1 small to medium potato per person until tender, but not falling apart. Drop the potatoes in ice water, cool for 5 minutes, and peel. Thinly slice each potato and fan it on a dinner plate. Sprinkle with good-tasting olive oil, salt, pepper, and a little wine vinegar. Meanwhile, take the chill off the leftover salmon by warming it in a skillet. In a bowl, toss it with 1 or 2 tablespoons capers, a little grated lemon zest, some chopped pitted niçoise or Kalamata olives, chopped scallion, parsley, and fresh lemon juice to taste. Make mounds of the salmon in the center of each plate and serve.

Smoke
Roasting

According to lifelong griller John Willoughby, anything you roast in the oven is even better cooked outside with a little smoke. Think whole fish and chicken, pork roasts and lamb, and, of course, the Thanksgiving bird.

John has a couple of tricks. First, you need a grill with a lid that is at least 22 inches in diameter. You never want what you're grilling to cook over more than a scattering of coals. **Smoke roasting is all about indirect heat.** He also warns that people tend to use "way too many coals." You need only enough coals to fit in a shoe box, about three or four handfuls, and you need to replenish them every 30 minutes to keep up a steady heat.

Recipes like Smoke-Roasted Salmon (page 219) are places to try wood chips, scavenged vines, or fruitwood trimmings . . . or as in the case of our Pine-Smoked Chicken (page 193), the Christmas tree.

PORK

Yucatán Pork in Banana Leaves

(Cochinita Pibil)

| *Serves 8 to 10* | *30 minutes prep time; overnight refrigeration; 1 hour at room temperature; 2½ to 3 hours cook time* | *You can start the pork 2 days before serving because it needs an overnight seasoning before cooking, and once cooked it is even better the day after.* |

Banana leaves are one of the most sensual things to have in your kitchen. They are glossy and tender, redolent with the smell of the jungle, and impressively enormous with a beautiful rich green color. Can you tell we're in love?

This dish quickly became first-class party food at Sally's house. It's a classic dish from Mexico's Yucatán but a bit on the unusual side for non-Latin palates, as it mixes the earthy red annatto seed with the unctuousness of the fresh banana leaves that cradle the pork as it roasts. It's incredibly simple to pull off once you've gathered the ingredients.

Please note, this is a gringo's take. There are as many recipes for this dish as there are salsas. For a more in-depth interpretation, take a look at the work of the Mexican scholars (see page 9).

SEASONING PASTE

- 1 teaspoon **black peppercorns**
- 1 teaspoon **cumin seed**
- ½ teaspoon whole **allspice**
- 3 tablespoons whole **annatto seed** (also called achiote)
- 6 **garlic cloves**
- 1 teaspoon dried **oregano**, Mexican if possible
- 1 tablespoon **salt**

You can usually find banana leaves where Latino ingredients are sold. They're usually sold frozen, folded into flat, square packages. To use the leaves, defrost them, gently unfold them (they're as long as a big beach towel), and begin wrapping the pork. Sally spreads the leaves out as her tablecloth when she serves the pork; Lynne threatens to wear them as a matching caftan and hat.

(recipe continues)

3 tablespoons **Seville orange juice** (bitter orange juice) or a blend of equal parts **orange**, **lime**, and **grapefruit juices**

PORK

6-pound boneless **pork shoulder**, or butt, well marbled
¾ cup **Seville orange juice** or a blend of equal parts **orange**, **lime**, and **grapefruit juices**
Zest of 1 **orange**, sliced into thin strips
1 large red **onion**, halved and sliced into half moons
3 to 5 **banana leaves**, defrosted
Salt and freshly ground **black pepper**

ACCOMPANIMENTS

30 **corn tortillas**, warmed
Garlic-Oregano Pickled Onions (recipe follows)
3 **limes**, cut into wedges

WINE Look for a relatively light, fruity red, such as Pinot Noir from California, Garnacha from Spain, or Dolcetto from Italy.

1. **Make the seasoning paste:** In a small skillet over medium heat, toast the peppercorns, cumin, and allspice for about 3 minutes, or until fragrant. Cool, then transfer to a spice grinder or mortar and pestle along with the annatto and grind into a powder. Annatto seed is hard and takes a bit of scraping down and repeated grindings to break up. Add the garlic, oregano, salt, and the orange juice and process into a paste.

2. **Make the pork:** In a large bowl, rub the pork with the seasoning paste, 5 tablespoons of the juice, and the orange zest and onion, taking care to rub the mixture into the folds of the meat.

3. Use a Dutch oven large enough to hold the pork; a 5- to 6-quart one should work. Line the pot with overlapping banana leaves, leaving 8 to 10 inches overhanging the edges of the pot. You will be wrapping the leaves around the pork. Place the pork in the pot with all of its marinade. Swaddle the pork with the banana leaves to completely enclose it. Cover the pot with foil and refrigerate overnight.

4. About 1 hour before cooking, pull the pork out of the refrigerator and bring to room temperature. Place a rack in the middle of the oven and preheat the oven to 350°F.

5. Pour ½ cup water around the meat, cover tightly, and roast in the oven for 2½ to 3 hours, or until fall-apart tender. Check the liquid levels occasionally, adding water as needed.

6. When the pork is fork-tender and falling apart, remove it to a cutting board and pour the pot juices into a medium saucepan. Put the meat back into the pot and let it rest while you work with the pot liquid.

7. Spoon off the fat that rises to the top of the pot juices. Depending on how much liquid is left, boil down the pot juices until ½ to ¾ cup remains. Add salt and pepper to taste, and add the remaining ½ cup orange juice at the end of cooking.

8. With two forks, pull apart the pork into shreds and bite-sized pieces. Sprinkle with salt and drizzle the reduced sauce over the meat. Serve with the corn tortillas, pickled onions, and fresh squeezes of lime.

Garlic-Oregano Pickled Onions

| *Makes about 3 cups* | *15 minutes prep time; 2 to 3 hours marinating time* | *Keeps refrigerated several days* |

2 medium to large **red onions**, sliced into thin rings
1 cup **white vinegar**
1 generous teaspoon dried **oregano**, Mexican if possible
1 teaspoon **salt**
2 **garlic cloves**, thinly sliced

1. Combine all of the ingredients in a medium bowl and marinate, stirring occasionally, for a couple of hours.

2. Serve at room temperature with the Yucatán pork, with refried beans, or on sandwiches.

OJ
REDUCTION—
Gold from the Refrigerator Door

Whenever you need a punch of sweet, tart, and fruity, go directly to your refrigerator and reach for the orange juice. Pour some in a skillet and boil it down to a syrup, season with salt and pepper, and begin anointing a salad, a piece of fish such as Smoke-Roasted Salmon (page 219), Slow-Roasted Pork with Glazed Orange Slices (page 232), or Flash-Sautéed Squid with Peppers & Garlic (page 216), steamed broccoli, pork chops, grilled chicken, yams, ice cream, fingers . . . you get the idea. The OJ reduction holds a week in the fridge.

Spices—

THE SACRED AND THE PROFANE

If you've wondered why Europeans of long ago clawed their way around the globe to get to the great spice sources of Malaysia and Indonesia, it had to be the flavors in these recipes, not to mention the vast wealth spices could bring.

The single most powerful commodity to change the course of history was not gold or silver or even oil, it was spices. This comes out of the research of Yale historian Paul Freedman, who specializes in medieval social history and is the author of *Out of the East: Spices and the Medieval Imagination* (Yale University Press, 2008).

Freedman dashes the theory that spices were valued because they preserved foods. No. In the medieval world spices were magical, even holy. Not only were they delicious and exotic cures for the ailing, they were considered links to terrestrial paradise. Saints' bodies were said to give off the fragrance of spices when exhumed. The ointment poured over Christ's body was scented with them, and spices that were scraped from mummies demanded small fortunes.

Tasting
Islam in Mexico
—RACHEL LAUDAN

When Octavio Paz, Mexico's distinguished intellectual and Nobel Prize winner, was sent to India as an ambassador in the 1960s, he was immediately struck by the parallels between his country's beloved moles and India's beloved curries. It makes complete sense to food historian Rachel Laudan. She sees both dishes, essentially stews based on onion and intense spices, as the "two ends of a chain of cuisine that radiated out from Baghdad in the Middle Ages."

You can still taste that influence every day in Mexico. The delicious and addictive *agua frescas,* or fruit waters, that are served day and night there owe their provenance to the Spanish conquistadores of the sixteenth century (remember that Spain was once a part of the Islamic world). They brought to Mexico these Islamic drinks of nuts, fruits, and flowers, combined with the then-precious sugar for a refreshing nonalcoholic beverage that conformed to Islamic religious beliefs.

Rest assured, you will not miss the alcohol. This is some of the most refreshing and delicious sipping around.

WATERMELON WATER
(Agua de Sandia)

Makes 1 gallon

Because the quality of this drink depends on the quality of the fruit, buy a ripe, deep-colored watermelon in season. You are after a consistency not much thicker than lemonade, so adjust the water accordingly.

This will keep for a couple of days in the refrigerator and will be safe to drink for longer than that, but the texture changes and the taste fades, so it's best when used the same day. For a party, it's lovely to make another batch using a yellow watermelon or a cantaloupe, and a pale green one with honeydew melon.

4 to 6 cups **watermelon,** peeled, chopped into chunks, and seeded
    (or use a seedless melon, or blend with the seeds and let the debris
      settle to the bottom of the blender before pouring into the pitcher)
About ½ cup **sugar,** or to taste
Few drops **lemon** or **lime juice** to taste (optional)

1. Place the watermelon in a blender with 3 cups water and blend until smooth. Pour into a gallon pitcher and add more water to make a gallon of beverage.
2. Taste the drink and add sugar to taste if it is needed, stirring until it's dissolved. If the watermelon is not quite at its peak and the flavor needs brightening, add lemon or lime juice to taste. Chill. Stir before serving.

RECIPE COURTESY OF RACHEL LAUDAN

Malaysian Spiced Pork

| *Serves 6 to 8; doubles* | *45 minutes prep time;* | *This is twice the dish when allowed to*
easily | *1½ to 2 hours stove time;* | *rest overnight, though it's nearly*
| *30 minutes rest time* | *impossible to resist the scent while*
cooking. Serve with rice.

This heady stew of pork simmered with cinnamon sticks, cloves, anise, and galangal is actually grandmother cooking, but imagine a very sexy grandmother. She was a Nyonya, one of the many Malaysian women who married early Chinese immigrants to give Malaysia its hybrid Nyonya cuisine. Those long-ago marriages left a legacy of richly spiced and fragrant recipes like this one, adapted from James Oseland's book *Cradle of Flavor* (Norton, 2001).

The list of ingredients is long, but we encourage you to make an adventure out of this dish. Head to a good Asian market with your friends or your kids and take the dive. Once ingredients are on hand, it's a simple process of long, slow cooking.

15 to 20 **shallots**, coarsely chopped (about 1 cup)

2 tablespoons **peanut oil**, plus more as needed

3-inch piece **galangal** (fresh or frozen and defrosted), peeled, thinly sliced with the grain, and cut into sturdy matchsticks (about 6 tablespoons total), or fresh **ginger**

4 3- to 4-inch **cinnamon sticks**, broken in half

8 whole **cloves**

4 whole **star anise**

4 pounds boneless **pork shoulder**, cut into 2-inch cubes

6 tablespoons **palm**, **cider**, or **rice vinegar**

4 tablespoons **double black soy sauce** (*kecap*)

3 tablespoons **sugar**

Galangal is a relative of ginger and looks a lot like fresh ginger, but tastes of pepper, pine, and ginger. If you can't find it, fresh ginger can stand in. Palm vinegar from Malaysia and the Philippines is as good in salads and other dishes as wine or cider vinegars, so don't let the bottle sit in the cupboard for years.

WINE This is delicious with a chilled Pinot Gris from Oregon.

4 fresh **red, long chiles** (cayenne or milder), sliced into
matchsticks for garnish

1. In a food processor, pulse the shallots to a smooth paste, adding a small amount of water if necessary to get an even grind.

2. Cook the spices: Heat the oil in a 6- to 8-quart Dutch oven over medium heat. Add the galangal and cook, stirring often, for about 3 minutes, or until the pieces are lightly brown at the edges and fragrant.

Stir in the shallot paste and sauté, stirring often, for 4 to 5 minutes, or until the paste no longer smells raw and begins to thicken and turn golden, taking care not to burn it. Keeping the heat at medium or lower so the ingredients do not burn, add the cinnamon, cloves, and star anise. Continue to sauté for 1 to 2 minutes, or until the spices are fragrant.

3. Brown the pork: Pushing the paste to the edges of the pan and adding more oil if necessary, add the pork to the pan and sauté until each piece has picked up some browning. If the pieces are crowded, do this step in two batches. The browning should take 7 to 10 minutes, and again, take care not to burn the glaze forming on the bottom of the pot.

4. Cook the pork: Place all of the pork in the pot. Add 2 cups water and the palm vinegar, soy sauce, and sugar, stirring well to blend and scraping the bottom of the pot to loosen the glaze. Bring the liquid to a steady bubble, then immediately reduce the heat to low, so the liquid throws up only the occasional bubble (you should be able to count slowly to four between eruptions).

5. Partially cover the pot and continue to slowly and steadily cook the pork over low heat for 1½ to 2 hours, stirring occasionally and carefully until the meat is fork-tender. The meat should not be falling apart or mushy.

6. Remove the lid and lift meat chunks out of the pan and set aside. Now intensify the sauce's flavor by reducing it. Raise the heat to medium, bringing the liquid to a rapid simmer, stirring often. Continue cooking for 30 to 40 minutes, or until nearly all of the liquid has bubbled away and the sauce is thick and rich tasting.

7. Depending on the cut of pork you use, there may be a lot of rendered fat in the pan at this point. You could spoon it off if you wish (we like to leave most of it in). Place the pork back in the sauce; there should be enough to moisten but not drown it. If serving right away, heat the pork; if not, refrigerate overnight.

8. To serve, transfer the hot pork to a serving dish and allow it to rest for 30 minutes. Garnish with the chiles. Serve the meat warm or at room temperature.

Slow-Roasted Pork with Glazed Orange Slices

| Serves 8 to 12 | 30 minutes prep time; 3 days seasoning time; 2½ hours oven time; 10 to 15 minutes rest time | So forgiving, you can calibrate this roast around your needs instead of the usual other way around. It will hold happily in a low oven (180°F. or so) for 1 hour.

Evocative, warming, welcoming—this is the dish to share during those dark days of December when things slow for the holidays and the house is filled with candlelight.

Heady with Christmas-cake spices and orange slices turned chewy and tender in syrupy pan juices, this roast began with a Christmas recipe from Scandinavian cook Andreas Viedstadt, author of *Kitchen of Light* (Artisan, 2003). One doesn't think about Scandinavian food as being deeply spiced beyond dill, but don't forget what great sailors and adventurers they were and where their trade routes lay. Take a look at A Winter Holiday Dinner (page 32) for some pairing ideas.

SEASONING

6- to 7-pound boneless **pork shoulder**
   or **Boston butt**, well marbled
1 generous teaspoon whole **cloves**,
   or 1 level teaspoon ground
1 generous teaspoon whole **allspice**,
   or 1 level teaspoon ground
1 generous teaspoon **coriander seed**,
   or 1 level teaspoon ground
1 generous teaspoon **black peppercorns**,
   or 1 level teaspoon ground **black pepper**
2½-inch **cinnamon stick**, broken,
   or 2 teaspoons ground
1 tablespoon **kosher salt**
6 large **garlic cloves**, thinly sliced
⅓ cup good-tasting **extra-virgin olive oil**
1⅓ cups **orange juice**
1½ cups dry **red wine**

ROASTING AND FINISHING

2 tightly packed tablespoons fresh **rosemary leaves**
½ medium **onion**, chopped
½ teaspoon **salt**
1 tablespoon **extra-virgin olive oil**
1 thin-skinned **orange**, such as Valencia, Temple, or
    Hamlin, unpeeled, sliced into thin rounds

1. Marinate the meat: Three days before cooking,
make deep wide cuts into the meat. Then grind the
whole cloves, allspice, coriander, peppercorns, and
cinnamon stick in a coffee grinder or mortar and pestle,
or blend the ground spices. In a medium bowl, mix the
spices with the salt, garlic, oil, ⅔ cup of the orange juice,
and ½ cup of the wine. Stuff the mixture into the slits
and the meat's crevices and rub into the pork on all
sides. Tuck the roast into a shallow dish, cover, and
refrigerate for 3 days, turning three or four times.

2. Roast the meat: Take the meat out of the refrigerator and preheat the oven to 400°F. Purée the rosemary,
onion, salt, and oil, and stuff the mixture into the
roast's crevices.

3. Roll up the roast into a loose cylinder. Put it in a
large shallow pan, fat side up (we like a half-sheet pan),
scrape any remaining marinade over it, and scatter the
orange slices around the pan. Roast for 30 minutes, then
pour in the remaining 1 cup wine.

4. Turn the heat down to 325°F., pour in the remaining
⅔ cup orange juice, and roast for another 90 minutes,
basting the pan juices and the orange slices over the
meat several times. If the pan juices threaten to burn,
blend in a little water. You want them to end up being
syrupy, but not burned.

5. Test the internal temperature of the meat with an
instant-read thermometer. Once it reaches 145°F. to
150°F., reduce the heat to 200°F. for another 30 minutes,

**Why recipes still call
for pork loin as a
celebration roast we
can't imagine. Over-
priced and underper-
forming, the typical
commercial loin comes
off dry and tasteless.
Much cheaper shoulder
cuts, like the pork in
this recipe, have the
essential marbling for
succulent eating, and
no roast is as easy on a
cook. Short of blasting
(and toughening) them
in too hot an oven (keep
the temperature at
350°F. or lower), you
can't ruin a shoulder
roast.**

  **Start the roast 3 days
ahead with the season-
ings.**

WINE Try a Chenin Blanc
from South Africa with this
dish. They tend to be more
reliably dry than those from
the Loire and have a bit
more fruit, yet are not
overtly sweet.

(recipe continues)

or until the meat's internal temperature is 155°F. Remove the pork from the oven and let it rest in a warm place for 10 to 15 minutes before slicing.

6. The pan juices should be syrupy. If needed, set the pan over two burners, skim off a little excess fat, and cook down the juices, stirring with a wooden spatula.

7. To serve, thinly slice the pork across the grain, moistening the slices with the pan sauce and bits of roasted orange. Don't be put off if the meat is a pinkish beige; it is safe and so succulent. Serve the pork hot.

WORK NIGHT ENCORE

Pan-Browned Pork with Mom's Apple Sauerkraut: Slice the leftover pork roast into sticks about 3 inches long by 1 inch thick. Coat a big skillet with a thin film of olive oil, get it hot, and quickly brown the pork. Take the meat out of the pan and set aside.

Wipe out the pan, coat it with a thin film of olive oil, and heat it over medium-high heat. Brown a chopped large onion and a sprig of rosemary in it along with a cut-up large apple. Blend in 2 minced garlic cloves, several cups rinsed and drained sauerkraut, and a generous splash of white wine. Stir up the brown glaze in the pan as you cook down the wine. Blend in any pan juices left from the pork and the pork pieces. Have the dish hot and serve it with boiled potatoes or toasted, chewy dark bread.

LAMB

Charred Lamb with Smoked Romesco

| *Serves 6 to 8* | *30 to 45 minutes prep time;* | *The lamb needs a 10-minute rest*
| | *12 to 15 minutes grill time;* | *after it comes off the grill and*
| | *10 minutes rest time* | *before it's sliced.*

How do you cook a leg of lamb in 15 minutes and serve it with a sauce that could take pesto off its pedestal? This lamb is fast because it is cut into pieces. With this method you get ten times the surface to grill or roast into caramelized crusty bits.

Sally's romesco is Spain's grand uncooked sauce made by crushing together tomatoes, peppers, and smoky paprika with fried bread, almonds, and garlic. With it the lamb sails into new territory. Corn on the cob was made for this lamb (and this sauce).

2½ to 3 pounds boned **leg of lamb**, roughly cut into
    2- to 3-inch chunks
3 tablespoons good-tasting **extra-virgin olive oil**
1 teaspoon **coarse salt**
2 tablespoons (packed) **dark brown sugar**
½ teaspoon freshly ground **black pepper**
Smoked Romesco Sauce (recipe follows)
⅓ cup whole **toasted almonds**, coarsely chopped

The romesco recipe is especially generous because we think it's what you'll want the next day smeared on bread with your scrambled eggs, or topping your lover's fingers.

WINE Try a Ribera del Duero from Spain or a good-quality Dolcetto from Piedmonte.

1. Make the lamb: Prepare your grill for a two-zone fire (see The Charcoal Brief on page 196). If using a gas grill, set one burner on high and one burner on low.

2. In a large bowl, toss the lamb with the oil, salt, sugar, and pepper. Set the chunks over the high-heat zone of the grill. Cook for about 2 minutes per side to brown. With tongs, move the lamb to the low-heat zone and grill for 5 to 8 minutes, or until the thickest chunks reach 130°F. on an instant-read thermometer (this gives you medium-rare lamb; if you want it cooked more, grill to 140°F.). Transfer

(recipe continues)

the lamb to a large serving platter and let rest for 10 minutes—the internal temperature will rise, giving you pink, juicy lamb.

3. If using an oven, preheat it to 350°F. Toss the lamb with the oil, salt, sugar, and pepper. Spread the pieces out on a shallow pan and roast, turning them once or twice, for about 15 minutes, or until the meat reaches an internal temperature of 130°F. You'll have medium-rare meat at this temperature. If you want it more done, cook until it reaches 135°F. to 140°F. If the meat needs browning, broil the meat for a few moments. Remove it from the oven and let it rest for 10 minutes.

4. To serve the lamb, thinly slice the chunks across the grain and fan around a serving platter, leaving the center empty. Pour any juices over the lamb, and spoon a generous amount of romesco sauce into the center of the platter. Scatter the almonds over the meat and serve the meat hot. Pass the rest of the romesco at the table.

Smoked Romesco Sauce

| *Makes about 3 cups* | *30 minutes prep time* | *Keeps refrigerated, covered, 3 days*

This dreamy sauce is at its pinnacle the day it is made.

Good-tasting **extra-virgin olive oil** for frying the bread
  plus ½ cup
2 pieces of sturdy **bread**, such as ciabatta, about
  5 inches x 3 inches x 1 inch thick
½ cup unsalted whole **almonds**, roasted
4 medium **garlic cloves**
1 teaspoon **hot red pepper flakes**
1 teaspoon mild smoked **Spanish paprika**
3 medium **tomatoes**, cored and quartered, or 2 cups
  canned tomatoes, drained
1 tablespoon **flat-leaf parsley leaves**
1 **sweet red pepper**, roasted
½ cup **Spanish sherry vinegar**
Salt to taste

1. Coat a 10-inch skillet with a thin film of oil and put over medium-high heat. Fry the bread until crisp and browned on both sides. Remove the bread from the pan and cool. In a food processor, grind the bread, almonds, and garlic into a rough paste.

2. Add the red pepper flakes, paprika, tomatoes, parsley, and roasted pepper and process into a smooth paste. With the machine running, gradually add the sherry vinegar. When the vinegar is incorporated, slowly add the remaining ½ cup olive oil. Add salt to taste.

Set the sauce aside, covered, and let rest for about 20 minutes to mellow the garlic and blend the flavors. When the lamb is ready, spoon some sauce onto the platter and pass the rest at the table.

Spain's Special Sauce

Before McDonald's, even before Goya and Don Quixote, **Spain gave the world romesco.** Make this once and we promise that romesco is going to take up permanent residence in your fridge.

WHAT TO DO WITH EXTRA ROMESCO:

- Smear it on roasted onions.
- Dip steamed shrimp and shellfish in it.
- Toss with canned tuna and celery for a Spanish tuna salad.
- Thin with water and olive oil and dress fresh greens.
- Spread on crostini with a dollop of crème fraîche or yogurt.
- Top an omelet.
- Mound on a plate and cover with warm, melting fresh cheese.

Translating
Spanish Paprika
(Pimenton)

Paprika used to be so easy. If the recipe said *paprika,* **you picked it up at the supermarket and you were done. No matter how you used it, you got color but no taste. Then along came Spain's traditional paprikas with a lot of flavor and a little bit of confusion.**

Spain's paprikas come in three varieties—sweet *(dulce),* **bittersweet** *(agri dulce)* **and hot** *(picante),* and either smoked or unsmoked.

The most famous smoked paprika is the officially designated Pimenton de la Vera, meaning it comes from the La Vera area of western Spain. It's smoked over wood fires.

USING SPANISH PAPRIKA: Even hot varieties possess an underlying sweetness and a velvety quality that work in a lot of recipes, be they Spanish or not.

Sweet or spicier unsmoked paprikas go with Mediterranean vegetable dishes, soups, nut sauces, tomato recipes, the whole cabbage family, and onions, and rubbed into fish before cooking. Use the dulce variety when a recipe calls for sweet paprika.

Smoked paprika of any strength is good in potatoes, rice, yams, in bean dishes, and with eggs, and in meat dishes, especially with sausages and ham. But take care with smoked paprika because its aggressiveness can override other flavors.

Store all paprika in the refrigerator for up to 6 months.

Leg of Lamb with Honey & Moroccan Table Spices

| *Serves 6 to 8* | *30 to 40 minutes prep time; 8 to 12 hours marinating time; 2 hours oven time* | *Start the lamb a day before roasting by making the marinade. Because the acids in the marinade slow down browning, a finish of a fast broil is needed.* |

This lamb can be your savior on those evenings when you've got a bunch of strangers around the table and the mood feels as lighthearted as in a dentist's waiting room.

Serve up the lamb Moroccan style, with its bowls of table herbs and spices, and a plate of lettuce leaves. The idea is that everyone has permission to eat with their fingers and try the lamb with different combinations of spices, fresh herbs, pan sauce, and even honey all rolled up in the lettuce. Conversations can't help but take off.

You will need a large, very shallow pan; a half-sheet pan is ideal. Deep pans cut airflow around food, encouraging more steaming than roasting. Shallow pans give ingredients a chance to crisp, brown, and get that singular roasted taste.

MARINADE

4 large **garlic cloves**
⅓ tightly packed cup **flat-leaf parsley leaves**
⅓ tightly packed cup fresh **cilantro leaves**
⅓ tightly packed cup fresh **basil leaves**
1 teaspoon ground **cumin**
1 teaspoon **sweet paprika**
1 teaspoon **Aleppo pepper** or other hot ground chile
¾ teaspoon ground **allspice**
¾ teaspoon ground **ginger**
⅓ cup good-tasting **extra-virgin olive oil**
3 tablespoons **honey**
½ cup fresh **lemon juice**, or as needed
1 medium **onion**, coarsely chopped
½ teaspoon freshly ground **black pepper**
5- to 6-pound boned **leg of lamb**, trimmed of most surface fat

(recipe continues)

TABLE HERBS AND SPICES

2 to 3 hearts of **romaine**, leaves separated
⅓ cup **coarse salt**
⅓ cup ground **cumin**, freshly ground if possible
⅓ cup **Aleppo pepper** or other hot ground chile
½ cup **honey**
2 **lemons**, each cut into 6 wedges
1 large bunch of fresh **mint**
1 large bunch of **watercress**
1 large bunch of fresh **cilantro**

PAN SAUCE

½ cup dry **red wine**

WINE Try a Grenache-based wine from the southern Rhône such as Châteauneuf-du-Pape, Vacqueyras, or a good Côtes du Rhône.

1. Marinate the meat: Season the lamb a day ahead by combining all of the marinade ingredients in a food processor or blender and puréeing. Taste for a distinct snap of lemon and a hint of chile heat, adding what you think is needed.

2. Spread the lamb out in a shallow dish. Make about 12 deep slits in the meat and stuff in spoonfuls of the marinade. Pour the rest of it over the lamb, turning the meat to thoroughly coat it. Cover and refrigerate overnight. Take the lamb out of the refrigerator 1 hour before cooking.

3. Roast the meat: About 2¼ hours before you want to serve the lamb, preheat the oven to 400°F. The lamb takes a total of 1½ to 2 hours to cook and needs a 15-minute rest before serving.

Spread the meat out, fat side up, on a large, very shallow pan (a half-sheet pan is ideal). Pour in enough of the marinade to coat the meat. Reserve the rest. Roast the lamb for 15 minutes, then reduce the heat to 300°F. and roast for another 15 minutes.

4. Pour the rest of the marinade over the meat and continue roasting the lamb, basting often with the pan juices, for 1 more hour, or until it is 10°F. below the doneness you want. (Final temperatures: 130°F. to 135°F. for rare, 135°F to 140°F. for medium rare, or 145°F for medium.)

5. As the lamb roasts, pile the romaine leaves on a platter, cover, and chill until serving. Place the salt, cumin, Aleppo pepper, honey, and lemon wedges in small individual serving bowls to pass at the table. Pile the mint, watercress, and cilantro on a plate and refrigerate, covered, with the romaine. Set everything out on the table when the lamb comes out of the oven.

(recipe continues)

6. Once the lamb is about 10°F. below the final doneness you want, brown it by turning on the broiler. Broil for 5 minutes, or until crusty; turn the meat over and repeat. Transfer the lamb to a platter and keep warm at room temperature for 10 to 15 minutes to let the juices settle and the meat finish cooking.

7. While the lamb rests, make the pan sauce by putting the roasting pan over two burners turned to high heat. With a wooden spatula, stir in the wine, bringing the pan juices to a boil as you scrape up any crusty bits. Cook the sauce, stirring, for about 2 minutes, or until the sauce is thick and rich tasting (keep the sauce hot over low heat). Thinly slice the lamb across the grain, arranging pieces on a serving platter. Pour the pan sauce over the lamb, garnish with a few sprigs of the herbs, and serve hot.

Variations

Roast Lamb with Rutabaga and Potato:

Change the lamb marinade to ½ cup dry red wine, ¼ cup olive oil, 2 tablespoons tomato paste, 1 tablespoon fresh thyme leaves, 3 large chopped garlic cloves, 12 fresh sage leaves, and 2 teaspoons grated lemon zest. Marinate overnight as directed. Add to the roasting pan 1 large rutabaga cut into 1-inch dice and 2 large red-skin potatoes cut into 2-inch dice. Roast the lamb as directed, basting with the marinade and another ½ cup red wine.

Brown Sugar–Chile Roast Lamb:

Make the lamb as described, substituting Brown Sugar–Chile Rub (page 252) for the marinade. Baste the lamb as it roasts with a combination of equal parts vinegar and pineapple juice.

WORK NIGHT ENCORE

Lamb on Chile-Honey Bruschetta: Toast thick slices of a rugged whole-grain bread over a burner and rub them with a split garlic clove. Place each slice on a dinner plate, sprinkle with a pinch of hot red pepper flakes, then drizzle with a teaspoon of honey and about the same amount of olive oil. Pile leftover fresh herbs (coriander, mint, or watercress) on the slices. Warm the leftover lamb slices gently with their pan juices and spread them over the herbs. Serve warm.

Wedding Lamb Biriyani

Serves 6 to 8	*1¼ hours prep time;*	*The lamb is at its best made at a leisurely*
	1½ hours stove time;	*pace, with parts of the recipe done over a*
	1 hour oven time	*couple of days (maybe by friends), and*
		then on the day you want to eat, you bake
		the biriyani with the rice.

If the test of a great dish is that you taste something new and delicious with each mouthful, then this northern Indian masterpiece is in the first ranks. It's special-occasion food there and it should be for us, too.

Biriyani is a wonderful lesson in how to tease out unimaginable flavors from our spices. Slow sautéing as you add one ingredient after another keeps building flavor upon flavor, which is what makes Indian food so glorious.

LAMB

Canola oil

3 to 4 medium to large **onions**, thinly sliced

Salt and freshly ground **black pepper**

3 to 3½ pounds boneless **lamb shoulder**, trimmed of
  excess fat and cut into 1-inch cubes

Biriyani Spice Blend (recipe follows)

1½ cups **plain low-fat yogurt** (not nonfat)

2 cups whole canned **tomatoes** with their liquid, crushed

Ginger-Garlic-Nut Purée (recipe follows)

RICE

4 cups **basmati** or **other long-grain rice**

4 tablespoons **salt**

½ teaspoon **saffron threads**, or a generous
  ¼ teaspoon ground **turmeric**

⅓ cup **milk**

Unsalted butter for the baking dish

(recipe continues)

GARNISHES

¼ cup **canola oil**
3 tablespoons **unsalted butter**
1 medium to large **onion**, thinly sliced
Salt
½ cup **raisins**
¾ cup **roasted cashews** or **almonds**
1 recipe **Yogurt Raita** (recipe follows)

1. Make the lamb: One or 2 days before serving, place a 12-inch straight-sided sauté pan over medium-high heat, coat it with a thin film of oil, and add the sliced onions with a generous sprinkling of salt and pepper. Sauté the onions over medium-high to high heat until they turn golden with lots of dark, crisp edges, about 6 minutes.

Push the onions to the edges of the pan and spread out the lamb in the center. Reduce the heat to medium. Sear the lamb on all sides. It will throw off some liquid; let it cook away. Adjust the heat so the onions don't burn. Once the meat is seared, stir in the spice blend and cook until it is aromatic, about 3 minutes.

2. Add the yogurt to the lamb, ½ cup at a time, simmering each addition for 2 minutes, or until it disappears into the sauté. Stir in the tomatoes, the ginger purée, and enough water to barely cover the meat. Adjust the heat so the sauce simmers very slowly and cook, uncovered, for 1 to 1½ hours, or until the meat is tender and the sauce is reduced and rich tasting. There will be a generous amount of it.

3. Make the rice: The day the biriyani is served, rinse the rice in several changes of water, until the water is clear. Then soak the rice in enough water to cover (with 1 tablespoon of the salt added) for 30 minutes to 6 hours. Drain.

{ COOK to Cook }

Carefully frying down the ginger and garlic purée as instructed in step 1 is very important to the balance of this dish. The paste, when treated this way, becomes thoroughly caramelized and ultraconcentrated, both of which mean bigger, bolder flavors.

Feel free to put your imagination to work on this biriyani. Substitute vegetables or poultry for the lamb, and use whatever spices, nuts, and fruits you'd like. Using the techniques outlined here will ensure you'll have flavor by the truckload.

For a complete menu, you only need serve the biriyani with Yogurt Raita (page 250).

WINE Both red and white work with this dish. Try a Pinot Gris or a Pinot Noir from New Zealand.

(recipe continues)

4. Lightly toast the saffron for 30 seconds to 1 minute in a small, dry saucepan over medium heat. Immediately add the milk. Pull the pan from the heat and set aside to steep for a minimum of 20 minutes.

5. Fill a 6-quart pot two thirds full of water. Add the remaining 3 tablespoons salt and bring the water to a boil. Drop in the rice and cook it like pasta for about 5 minutes, or until it's tender but with a slight firmness. Drain in a sieve immediately and spread the rice out on a towel or cookie sheet so it cools quickly.

6. Assemble the biriyani: Take the lamb out of the refrigerator and preheat the oven to 325°F. You are going to dome the lamb, covered with the rice, in a baking dish; tent it with foil; and bake until it's heated through.

Butter the inside of a shallow 3- to 3½-quart baking dish. Mound the lamb in the center and cover it with the rice, patting it with a spatula into a smooth dome. Drizzle the rice with the saffron milk.

7. Tent foil over the dome so that it does not touch the rice. Seal it around the edges of the dish, then bake the biriyani for 45 minutes to 1 hour, or until it is hot at its center.

8. Make the garnishes: While the biriyani bakes, prepare several layers of paper towels on a baking sheet next to the stove. In a 10-inch skillet over medium-high heat, warm the oil and butter and fry the onion until crisp. Lift the onion out with a slotted spoon, spread on the paper towels, and sprinkle with salt to taste. In the same oil, fry the raisins until they puff, and scoop them out onto the towels. Finally, briefly fry the nuts until golden, then cool them on the towels. You are done!

To serve the biriyani, remove it from the oven, lift off the foil, and scatter the garnishes over the top. Serve it hot, making sure each helping has some of the garnishes. Pass the yogurt raita.

Biriyani Spice Blend

| *Makes about 3 cups* | *10 minutes prep time* | *Can be made a day ahead, covered, and kept at room temperature.*

8 whole **cloves**
8 whole **green cardamom pods**, lightly crushed
4-inch **cinnamon stick**, broken
1 generous tablespoon ground **coriander**
1 tablespoon ground **cumin**
½ teaspoon freshly ground **black pepper**
¼ teaspoon **cayenne**, or to taste
½ teaspoon freshly grated **nutmeg**

Blend all of the ingredients in a small bowl.

Ginger-Garlic-Nut Purée

| *Makes about ⅔ cup* | *15 minutes prep time; 20 minutes stove time* | *This can be made up to 2 days ahead and refrigerated.*

½ medium **onion**, cut into chunks
6 large **garlic cloves**
2½-inch piece fresh **ginger**, cut into pieces
⅓ cup **salted broken cashews**
1 fresh **serrano chile**, or to taste
Canola oil

1. Make the purée by combining the onion, garlic, ginger, cashews, and chile in a food processor and puréeing to a paste. Generously coat the bottom of a 12-inch, straight-sided sauté pan with oil.

(recipe continues)

2. Heat the pan over medium heat, stir in the ginger-garlic-nut paste, and sauté, stirring and scraping up any brown bits that are sticking to the pan for about 18 minutes. Watch carefully that the paste doesn't burn. You want it to become dark golden brown and have a rich, spicy aroma. Adjust the heat as needed, and stir often. Scrape the paste from the pan, adding a little water to collect all the glaze and browned bits from the bottom of the pan. Set the paste aside or refrigerate it for up to 2 days.

Yogurt Raita

Serves 6 to 8; doubles easily | *10 minutes prep time* | *Keeps refrigerated, covered, up to 4 days*

2 cups **plain yogurt**, whisked
1 large **cucumber**, peeled, seeded, and shredded
2 fresh **green** or **red chiles**, seeded and minced
1 **garlic clove**, minced
¾ firmly packed cup **mint leaves**, finely chopped
1 teaspoon **salt**

In a medium serving bowl, combine all of the ingredients. Serve chilled or at room temperature.

BEEF

Brown Sugar–
Chile Flank Steak

Serves 3 to 4; doubles or triples easily

15 minutes prep time; overnight refrigeration in marinade; 15 to 20 minutes grill time; 10 minutes rest time

Crispy bits and chewy ends are why we love grilled flank steak. The cut pairs perfectly with this rough rub of garlic, onion, brown sugar, and three incarnations of pepper inspired by Lynne's cowgirl days in Colorado.

BROWN SUGAR–CHILE RUB

- ⅓ cup (packed) **dark brown sugar**
- 1 generous tablespoon freshly ground **black pepper**
- 7 large **garlic cloves**, crushed
- 2 tablespoons plus 1 teaspoon **sweet paprika** (Hungarian or Spanish)
- ½ large **onion**, coarsely chopped
- 1 tablespoon **soy sauce**
- 2 tablespoons **canola oil**
- ½ to 1 teaspoon ground **hot chile** or **hot red pepper flakes**

MEAT

- 1½- to 2-pound **flank steak**
- **Coarse salt**

Good (and sometimes cheaper) substitutes for the flank steak include flatiron steak, top round steak, hanger steak, and skirt steak. Serve these whole, like other steaks, and you'll be chewing for a long time. Thinly slice them at an angle across the grain and they're instantly tender.

WINE Try a cold, rich Belgian Triple beer or an Australian Grenache or GSM-style blend (Grenache-Shiraz-Mourvedre).

1. **Make the rub:** In a food processor, combine all of the rub ingredients and grind down to a rough paste. Transfer the rub to a resealable plastic bag large enough to hold the steak.

2. Add the steak to the bag and thoroughly massage the marinade into all of the sides and nooks and crannies of the meat. Refrigerate overnight. You will cook the steak cold.

3. **Cook the meat:** Prepare your grill for a two-zone fire (see The Charcoal Brief on page 196). If using a gas grill, set one burner on high and one burner on low. When the fire is ready, sear the steak over the hottest part of the fire, about 2 minutes per side, until the steak has a nice crust. Move the steak to the slower part of the fire and flip often until the steak is cooked to your liking, about 130°F. on an instant-read thermometer for medium-rare. Add salt to taste.

4. Remove the meat from the fire and let it rest on a cutting board for 10 minutes. To serve, cut on an angle into thin slices across the grain of the meat.

How to Deal
with Nosy Guests

Amy Sedaris, author of *I Like You: Hospitality Under the Influence* (Warner Books, 2006), obviously a seminal entertaining guide, came up with a gem of a solution for guests who love to poke into your personal life—**put marbles in your medicine cabinet.**

Lynne's
Beef Stew
Caper

The beef stew, a simple dish, right? Well, yes and no. Maybe you have to be a little nuts to dive into rethinking everything you know about a dish so you can end up with the stew to end all stews. But here was the problem: stew can be unforgettably good, yet in all the years of trying recipes, none had gotten me there.

There had to be a different code, things nobody told us. So in a fit of obsession I began to experiment. The unforgettable stew, for me, is beautifully cooked meat, not tasteless and falling apart, but still succulent with flavors that are so deep you turn into a baritone after two bites. And those meat chunks are coated with a sauce you want to lick off the plate.

My usual stew began with cut-up beef chuck, marinated overnight in red wine, and herbs; slow browned, then cooked in its marinade with vegetables. The stew to end all stews was not happening. This book was the excuse to dig in. For the results, go to The Quintessential Beef Stew (page 256). For those who enjoy process, read on:

Building a Dream Stew
The following is amalgamated from the work of food scientists, mainly Harold McGee and British chef Hugh Fearnley-Whittingstall, along with techniques found in old French cookbooks.

Don't Buy What Recipes Tell You: The best choice is not what you've always been told, that is to use meat with lots of wavy fat marbled into it. Fat actually isn't what you need; you need the natural gelatin called collagen. Collagen shows up in curlicues, not waves, and it gives sauces remarkable silkiness and flavor, plus as it melts in slow cooking, those curlicues tenderize the meat.

The cut you want is from the leg of the animal, be it called the shank, shin, or soup meat. You want the leg's meat, but the bone is as important. Once browned, it will be a major player in flavoring the stew, as will its creamy marrow.

You also want some of the fat and lean of pork for flavor, as well as its skin to add body and more silkiness to the sauce. This means lean salt pork.

Marinate After Cooking, Not Before: This was one of those "aha" moments. It's a waste of time to marinate meat before cooking a stew; the flavors don't penetrate. Marinate the stew in its sauce after cooking. Do it overnight, or for a day or two. The payoff is immense because now flavors really do seep into the meat.

Big Tastes and How to Get Them: Okay, this is a fanatic's approach, but if you have read this far, you are probably one, too. Give the stew more depth by simply oven-browning the marrow bones and cooking them in the stew. Also cutting meat into big chunks enriches flavors because it needs longer cooking.

Stuffing meat chunks with a purée of orange zest, garlic, parsley, and salt pork makes for extra juiciness, and gorgeous flavors develop as the purée melts into the stew.

Slow browning of the meat builds up the deep, deep flavors of caramelization. There's no substitute for this.

Wine, vegetables, and tomatoes each act as flavor catalysts. Alcohol releases a special family of flavors; celery, carrot, and onion balance meat's intensity; and tomatoes are loaded with umami, the so-called fifth taste that lifts the character of everything it touches.

When to Trim the Fat: Get rid of the fat after its work is done—that is, at the end of cooking. And don't take it all away; leave a little for flavor.

Most Important of All: For juicy, tender meat, never boil a stew while the meat is in the pot. Keep the liquid at a tremor, with the occasional bubble breaking the surface, and check the meat's internal temperature. You want it at 160°F., no higher. Cooking the stew in a covered pot in a low oven (250°F. to start and then down to 175°F.) does the job.

If you've ever wondered how meat cooked in liquid can end up tasting dry and stringy, it is because the meat's been cooked at too high a temperature.

The Finish: After the overnight mellowing, get the meat and vegetables out of the liquid. Boil that liquid down until it's thick enough to coat a spoon and tastes rich, put back the meat and vegetables to just warm them, and serve up your masterpiece.

The Quintessential Beef Stew

Serves 6 to 10	*90 minutes prep time;*	*Make the stew 1 to 2 days ahead*
	1 to 1½ hours stove time;	*and serve it with rice or boiled*
	3½ hours oven time; 12 to	*potatoes to sop up its sauce.*
	48 hours mellowing time	

Sometimes the best recipes happen because you decide to wipe away everything you think you know and take a completely new look at it. That's how this stew began, and it ended up changing a lot of assumptions.

You see, there's a dream stew for Lynne—sumptuous meat in a sauce so voluptuous it's almost embarrassing to eat it in public. In short, the stew to end all stews. Lynne had never quite gotten there until she went back to look at old cookbooks and the work of scientists, master chefs, and butchers (see Lynne's Beef Stew Caper, page 254). So here, in all its time-consuming glory, is that stew. Use it as a model for those times when you want the most out of the ordinary.

WINE Look for a red from the southern Rhône such as Châteauneuf-du-Pape, Rusteau, or a good Côtes du Rhône or Provençal red like Bandol.

MEAT

8 ounces thick-cut **bacon**, cut into 1-inch pieces
Good-tasting **extra-virgin olive oil**
4 ounces lean **salt pork** (trim away any skin and reserve), cut into ½-inch cubes
5 pounds **Orange-Garlic-Stuffed Beef Chunks** (recipe follows)

VEGETABLES

1 large **onion**, cut into ½-inch dice
1 large **carrot**, cut into ½-inch-thick chunks
1 large **celery stalk with leaves**, cut into ½-inch slices
Salt and freshly ground **black pepper**

FLAVORINGS

- 2 4-inch sprigs fresh **rosemary**
- 4 large sprigs fresh **thyme**
- 4 large sprigs fresh **oregano**
- 4 large sprigs fresh **flat-leaf parsley**
- 4 dried **bay leaves**, broken
- Zest of ½ **orange**
- 6 large **garlic cloves**, crushed
- 5 cups (1⅔ bottles) rich **red wine**, such as Côtes du Rhône, Syrah, Zinfandel, or Cabernet Sauvignon
- 2 cups whole canned **tomatoes** with their liquid, crushed
- 8 whole **cloves**
- 12 whole **allspice**
- 1 heaping teaspoon **sweet paprika** (Hungarian or Spanish) (not smoked)
- ½ teaspoon freshly grated **nutmeg**
- ½ teaspoon freshly ground **black pepper**
- 2 ounces **salt pork**, rinsed and cut into ¼-inch cubes
- Reserved **salt pork skins**
- **Roasted Beef Shank Bones** (recipe follows)
- Grated zest of ½ **orange**

1. **Prepare the bacon:** Preheat the oven to 250°F. Have ready one 10-quart or two 5- to 6-quart heavy ovenproof Dutch ovens or casserole pots. Boil the bacon to mute its smokiness by simmering it for 1 minute in a small saucepan in water to cover. Drain the bacon and pat it dry.

2. **Brown the meat:** Coat the bottom of a 12-inch straight-sided sauté pan with a thin film of oil (browning in two sauté pans will speed things up). Set over medium-high heat. Add the salt pork and bacon, reduce the heat to medium, and cook just until they've released much of their fat and begin to pick up color. Remove them to the pots.

COOK *to* **Cook**

The silky sauce comes from using beef shank, which often shows up in the meat case as "soup meat." You can tell it's the right cut by checking to see if the round or half-round bone has marrow at its center. Attached to that bone should be chunks of meat with curlicues of white connective tissue lacing through the lean.

Following a piece of French genius found in an old Provence cookbook, you'll stuff the meat chunks before cooking with orange zest, parsley, salt pork, and garlic. Browning the stuffed chunks of meat to dark and crusty sets up the stew for brilliant success.

(recipe continues)

3. With the pan(s) over medium-high heat, spread out the stuffed beef chunks so they don't touch. Take care not to get spattered. Reduce the heat to medium and brown the meat until it's crusty and dark on all sides. Adjust the heat so the brown glaze on the pan bottom(s) doesn't burn. If working with one pan, brown the meat in two batches. As it finishes browning, put the meat in the casserole(s).

4. Sauté the vegetables: In the same pan(s), cook the vegetables, with generous sprinklings of salt and pepper, to a golden brown, being careful not to let the glaze on the bottom of the pan burn. With a wooden spatula, stir in the rosemary, thyme, oregano, parsley, bay leaves, orange zest, garlic, and 1 cup of the wine. Boil the wine down to nothing, then repeat with 1 more cup of the wine. Finally, stir in the tomatoes, cloves, allspice, paprika, nutmeg, and pepper, and simmer for 3 minutes.

5. Start the simmer: Pour the remaining 3 cups wine into the pan(s), add the salt pork and reserved skin, and bring the wine to a simmer. Transfer the contents of the pan(s) to the casserole(s), adding the roasted beef shank bones and enough water to cover everything by ½ inch. Stir and bring to a very slow bubble on top of the stove (you should be able to slowly count to five between bubbles). *It's important to never ever boil the stew.*

6. The stew is ready for its final cooking (at last). Cover the casserole(s) and place them in the oven for 30 minutes. Reduce the heat to 175°F. and cook, covered, for 2½ to 3 hours. Check to make sure the stew never boils, but cooks with its liquid trembling and occasionally throwing up a bubble (an instant-read thermometer inserted in the meat shouldn't go higher than 160°F.). You want the meat to be firm enough to slightly resist when you spear it with a paring knife.

7. Marinate the stew: Remove the pot(s) from the oven. Uncover and cool the stew for 20 minutes, then remove the bones and discard. Transfer the stew to covered containers and refrigerate overnight. This is when the meat absorbs the sauce's goodness. The next day, skim off about two thirds of the fat from the stew. Over medium heat, warm the stew in a heavy 6-quart pot to liquefy the pan sauce. Lift out the meat and vegetables with a slotted spoon. Set them aside.

8. Finish the stew: Add the grated orange zest to the pot, raise the heat to high, and boil down the pan sauce for 45 minutes, or until it's reduced by two thirds. You want very rich flavors and the sauce to be syrupy enough to coat a spoon. Reduce the heat to medium, gently stir in the meat and vegetables, and heat them. Serve the stew in a shallow bowl.

Orange-Garlic-Stuffed Beef Chunks

15 minutes prep time

2 ounces lean **salt pork**, trimmed of any skin and rinsed
    (save the skin for the stew)
3 large sprigs fresh **flat-leaf parsley**
3 large **garlic cloves**
Grated zest of ½ medium **orange** (you will need
    1½ oranges for the entire recipe)
8 to 9 pounds **bone-in beef shank**, cut into 3-inch lengths
    (supermarkets will do this for you), meat separated
    from the bones, both set aside

Stuff the beef chunks: In a food processor, purée the salt pork, parsley, garlic, and orange zest. With a paring knife, make a deep wide slit into each piece of meat and stuff the pesto in with a teaspoon, tamping down with the handle of the spoon. Cover and chill the beef until needed (up to 24 hours). Pat the chunks dry before browning.

Roasted Beef Shank Bones

10 minutes prep time; | *These can be roasted a day before*
20 minutes oven time | *starting the stew and refrigerated.*

Bones from 8 to 9 pounds **beef shanks**, with meat
    trimmed away
3 to 4 tablespoons good-tasting **extra-virgin olive oil**
1 teaspoon **salt**

Preheat the oven to 500°F. Have a large, shallow pan handy (a half-sheet pan is ideal). Rub the bones with the oil, spread them on the pan, and sprinkle lightly with the salt. Put them in the oven to brown for about 20 minutes. Turn with tongs to brown evenly and make sure they are a dark, crusty brown, but not burned. Once they are browned, remove them from the oven and set aside to cool.

Playboy Steak with Preserved-Lemon Gremolata

| *Serves 4 to 6* | *15 minutes prep time;* | *Serve the steaks as soon as they've*
| | *20 minutes cook time;* | *been sliced.*
| | *5 to 10 minutes rest time* |

This steak is done in a Mediterranean style, ardently cooked over wood charcoal, carved into thick slices, and then reassembled, as if a puzzle, on a platter around the bone.

We gild the lily in this version by bathing the cooked steak in olive oil with a sprinkle of bright gremolata made with our preserved lemon.

A porterhouse is the cut to track down. It's a workhorse of a steak, a slab of beef that is both a top strip sirloin and a tenderloin all in one.

GREMOLATA

- 1 **Moroccan Preserved Lemon** (page 85), or the grated zest of ½ large lemon
- ½ tightly packed cup **flat-leaf parsley**
- 3 large **garlic cloves**
- ¼ teaspoon freshly ground **black pepper**
- 2 tablespoons fresh **lemon juice**, or to taste
- ½ cup good-tasting **extra-virgin olive oil**

STEAKS

- 2 chilled **porterhouse steaks** (about 2 pounds each), cut 2½ to 3 inches thick, or a thick-cut flatiron steak
- Good-tasting **extra-virgin olive oil**
- Coarse **salt** and freshly ground **black pepper**

WINE This dish needs a red with plenty of acidity to work with the citrus from the preserved lemon. A Xinomavro from northern Greece or a Barolo or Barbaresco from Italy would be best, but if these prove too pricey or hard to find, a wine from any of the Chianti districts will do very nicely.

1. Make the gremolata: First trim away the pulp of the preserved lemon (if using) and rinse the rind. Then chop together by hand (food processors don't get the right texture) the preserved lemon or fresh zest, parsley, garlic, and pepper.

(recipe continues)

Squeeze some lemon juice over the top to taste. Pour the oil into the bottom of a shallow platter large enough to hold the cooked steak. Stir half of the gremolata into the oil, and reserve the remaining gremolata.

2. Cook the meat: Prepare your grill for a two-zone fire (see The Charcoal Brief on page 196). If using a gas grill, set one burner on high and one burner on low. Generously season the steaks with salt and pepper. Brush oil on the grate and grill the steaks over high heat for about 2 minutes per side, or until nicely charred. Take care not to move them too much in this initial sear. Move them to the lower level of fire and continue cooking, turning often, until they reach their desired temperature (7 to 10 minutes total per side for rare, or 130°F. internal temperature; medium rare is 140°F. and well done around 150°F.).

3. Remove the steaks from the grill and immediately dunk them into the oil-gremolata bath, turning to coat both sides with the mixture. Let the steaks rest for 5 to 10 minutes.

4. To carve and serve, remove the meat from the platter and place on a cutting board. Cut the tenderloin and top loin off the bone in two separate pieces. Slice each piece across the grain into ½-inch-thick slices and reassemble them around their respective bones. Spoon the oil over the top of the slices, and drizzle the remaining gremolata over the meat.

5. If cooking the steaks at the stove, preheat the oven to 325°F. Coat the bottom of a 12-inch straight-sided sauté pan with a heatproof handle with a thin film of oil. Heat the pan over high heat. Season the steaks and add them to the pan. Brown on both sides, then slip the pan into the oven. Rare steaks will take 15 to 20 minutes, medium close to 30 minutes. Check the steaks with an instant-read thermometer. Continue with the directions, starting at step 4.

COOK to Cook

We learned a surprising trick for keeping steak at its tender best from food scientist Harold McGee. Hal posits that we forget that it takes time for heat to move inward from the surface to the center of whatever we're cooking.

To do that, we need to cook with more than one level of heat. He suggests starting with cold meat and a high temperature to brown it and then switching to very low heat to gently finish cooking the interior, and flipping the meat often to ensure even cooking. This is sound advice that makes sense, whether you are working with a grill or on a stovetop.

For half the price of a porterhouse, but with little loss of flavor, substitute a thick-cut flatiron steak.

What Makes a
Good Knife Now

Forget what you've heard about knives. Existing theories were pretty much dashed when we talked with Chad Ward, a chef who became obsessed with what really makes for a good knife today. He is the author of *An Edge in the Kitchen* (Morrow, 2008). He says the advances in modern steel and manufacturing technologies "make conventional wisdom about knives look like medieval dentistry."

For instance, the style of knife that was snubbed years ago—that is, the stamped blade rather than the hand-honed one—is now an excellent choice because of that new technology.

Chad thinks this is a win-win situation for consumers, as there are knives today that are lighter, sturdier, and sharper than anything we had in the past. When shopping for a knife, Chad recommends the following:

First and foremost, find a knife that fits your hand.

Go and test-drive a few at a store where you can handle the knife.

Look at both of the two basic styles—the thicker German/French style like the knives by Sabatier, Henckels, and Wüsthof—and the thinner, lighter, and harder Japanese knives. Chad likens the difference between the two to the difference between an SUV and a sports car.

Chad's favorite entry-level knife is an 8-inch Victorinox/Forschner, model number 40520, which costs about $20.

What Good Cooks Know—
Pan Drippings

What a can of cream of mushroom soup is to some, pan drippings and cooking juices are to others. They're packed with intense flavor that makes just about anything they touch taste better, and they freeze beautifully.

To save them, stir a little water into the roasting pan or sauté pan and scrape up all the liquid and brown bits. Scoop them into a freezer bag. When a soup or some vegetables need a lift, break off some of the frozen juices and let them go to work. **A little goes a long way.**

Les Is More Burgers

| *Serves 4; doubles easily* | *For the burgers, 10 minutes prep time; 15 minutes stove time* | *The sauce can be prepared days ahead; cook and eat the burgers immediately.*

Lynne's burger-obsessed friend Les Meltzer has waxed on forever about his pinnacle burger experience from years ago in Minot, North Dakota. There, a certain bar would practically burn their burgers on the grill to get them extra crusty and brown, then dropped them into a vat of simmering BBQ sauce to finish.

It's divine inspiration in these times of required well-done patties that end up as dry as dirt.

1 pound **ground chuck**, 85% lean, organic and grass-fed if possible

1 fresh **jalapeño chile**, minced

½ medium **onion**, minced

½ teaspoon **salt**

¼ teaspoon freshly ground **black pepper**

BBQ Sauce (recipe follows)

Extra-virgin olive oil

4 **hamburger buns**

Condiments of choice

WINE Try a big California Zinfandel, slightly chilled to tamp down the alcohol and freshen the wine.

1. With a light hand, blend the chuck with the chile, onion, salt, and pepper. Gently pat the meat into 4 equal patties about 1¼ inches thick, and set aside.

2. Put the BBQ sauce in a deep 6-quart pot and bring to a gentle simmer.

3. Coat a large skillet with a thin film of oil, and set it over high heat. When the oil is hot, add the burgers and cook for about 2 minutes per side, or until they are a deep, crusty brown. Remove the burgers from the skillet and slip them into the simmering BBQ sauce. Simmer at a slow bubble for 6 to 7 minutes for medium (140°F. to 145°F. on an instant-read thermometer) and 8 to 9 minutes for medium to medium-well.

4. Remove the meat from the BBQ sauce and assemble the burgers on the buns. Garnish with condiments as you please.

(recipe continues)

BBQ Sauce

| Makes about 8 cups | 20 minutes prep time; 50 to 60 minutes stove time; keeps refrigerated 2 weeks | You need this much sauce to cover the burgers while they simmer, but the leftover sauce can be frozen for 6 months. |

Canola oil
2 medium **onions**, minced
¼ teaspoon **salt**
3 large **garlic cloves**, minced
1 teaspoon freshly ground **black pepper**
2 teaspoons ground **allspice**
2 3-inch **cinnamon sticks**, broken
1 teaspoon ground **cloves**
½ teaspoon ground **ginger**
2 tablespoons **sweet paprika**
1 cup **pineapple juice**
1 cup **cider vinegar**
2 28-ounce cans whole **tomatoes**, puréed
2 tablespoons **tomato paste**
1⅓ cups (packed) **dark brown sugar**
1 tablespoon **Tabasco sauce**
1 tablespoon **Worcestershire sauce**
¼ cup grainy dark **mustard**
½ cup **molasses**
1 stick **unsalted butter**

1. Coat the bottom of a 6-quart pot with a thin film of oil. Set it over medium-high heat and sauté the onions with the salt until they are golden brown. Stir in the garlic, pepper, allspice, cinnamon, cloves, ginger, paprika, pineapple juice, and cider vinegar. Cook down to just a thick glaze on the bottom of the pan.

2. Add the tomatoes, tomato paste, sugar, Tabasco, Worcestershire, mustard, molasses, and butter. Cook at a slow bubble, uncovered, for 50 minutes, or until thick. Taste for seasoning. Remove the cinnamon and refrigerate for up to 2 weeks.

A Mere Tablespoon of
Flavor

Great-tasting fat should never be ignored, and although science may go back and forth about how different types affect our bodies, our mouths never lie. If you use fat, go for the big hit of flavor, which usually means it's far better to add a little at the end rather than the beginning of a recipe.

That fat you've skimmed off the stew or soup along with bacon drippings, lard, salt pork, butter, and chicken fat are all fair game, and delicious. Remember the can of saved fats on the back of Great-Grandma's stove? She knew what she was doing. These days, for safety's sake, store Great-Grandma's can in the fridge.

Then for tastes that sing, stir in just a tablespoon a moment before the pot comes off the stove.

SIDES

French Radish Sauté

Serves 4; doubles easily | *15 minutes prep time; 10 minutes stove time; 5 to 10 minutes mellowing time*

Leave it to the French to one-up nature's masterpiece—the fresh radish. In this take, briefly tossed in a hot pan with butter, vermouth, and fresh herbs, they turn into glazed marbles, mellow and savory but still with that hallmark crunch.

These pair well with many dishes, including Brown Sugar–Chile Flank Steak (page 252) and Smoke-Roasted Salmon (page 219).

2 bunches of small **red radishes** (about 20), trimmed of greens and tips
1½ tablespoons plus 2 teaspoons **unsalted butter**
Salt and freshly ground **black pepper**
⅓ cup dry **white vermouth**
2 tablespoons chopped fresh **tarragon leaves**

1. If the radishes are large, halve them on the diagonal. Melt 1½ tablespoons of the butter in a 12-inch skillet over medium-high heat. Add the radishes and salt and pepper to taste. Sauté for 3 minutes, or until pale pink. Don't let the butter brown.

2. Add the vermouth and continue cooking until it's boiled away, about 3 minutes. Toss the radishes with the remaining 2 teaspoons butter and the tarragon; taste for salt. Turn the radishes into a serving bowl and let rest for about 5 minutes before serving.

{ COOK *to* Cook }

With the all-American obsession for serving everything piping hot, we sometimes forget that flavors can build in a dish that's left to sit. In other countries, dishes are often served warm or at room temperature. We know a 10-minute rest makes all the difference in a steak or roast; it works the same way with some vegetables.

It is uncanny how waiting 5 minutes to serve these radishes opens their sweetness and mellows the butter and tarragon. You'll taste the difference.

The Ultimate
Plantarians

Move over vegans and raw food enthusiasts—have you heard of the Astomis?

Pliny the Elder was the scholar of ancient Rome who wrote the famous and still-quoted *Encyclopedia of Natural History.* In it, he told the story of a tribe of men covered with hair, without mouths, and who nourished themselves solely on the scents of plants.

Now Pliny, who was a stickler for writing about only those things observed firsthand, must have been as charmed by the idea as we are, as he trusted an obviously imaginative Greek historian who claimed that the tribe hailed from eastern India and were so sensitive to scent that a strong odor could do them in.

Farmhouse Roasted Potatoes

Serves 6 to 8	*15 minutes prep time;*	*You can hold the finished potatoes in a*
	8 minutes stove time;	*200°F. oven up to 30 minutes. Or roast*
	2 hours oven time	*them several hours ahead, hold at room*
		temperature, and reheat for 15 minutes
		at 400°F. before serving.

These potatoes, seasoned the way central Italy flavors its famous roast pork, or *porcetta,* are sure to become a house favorite. There are a couple of tricks that make them extra crispy.

First, give the potatoes plenty of elbow room in the pan so they roast and don't steam. Second, lightly coat them with a thin film of olive oil a couple of times as they roast, instead of coating them with all of the oil right at the beginning of cooking. Doing it little by little is the trick to getting the crispiest of crisp.

4 pounds medium **red-skin potatoes**

About ½ cup good-tasting **extra-virgin olive oil**

Salt and freshly ground **black pepper** (use a coarse sea salt if possible)

2 to 3 teaspoons **fennel seed**, bruised

2 to 3 teaspoons dried **basil**

1 to 2 teaspoons dried **oregano**

2 large **garlic cloves**, minced

3 to 4 ounces **pancetta**, **guanciale**, **smoked pork jowl**, or **bacon**, cut into ¼-inch pieces (optional)

1. Preheat the oven to 425°F. Slip a large shallow pan (a half-sheet pan is ideal) into the oven to heat.

2. Scrub the potatoes, cutting away any eyes and bruised areas. Do not peel. Put them in a 6-quart pot, cover with cold water, and bring to a fast boil. Cook the potatoes for 8 minutes and drain them in a colander. Rinse with cold water to cool the potatoes, then cut them into quarters. Don't peel them.

{ **COOK** *to* **Cook** }

Pancetta is Italy's slow-cured, rolled-up pork belly, and guanciale is slow-cured pork jowl. Because American chefs are falling all over themselves to get good pancetta and guanciale, domestic versions are taking off.

3. In a large bowl, gently combine the potatoes with about 3 tablespoons oil, 1 teaspoon salt, and ¼ teaspoon pepper. Turn the potatoes onto the hot baking pan and roast, occasionally turning them with a metal spatula so they don't stick to the pan, until they brown evenly. After 45 minutes, sprinkle with about 2 tablespoons oil, turning to coat. Continue roasting and turning for another 45 minutes.

4. Sprinkle the potatoes with another 3 tablespoons oil and the fennel seed, basil, oregano, garlic, and pancetta (if using); toss to coat with the seasonings and roast for another 30 minutes. The potatoes should be a rich golden brown and crusty. Taste for salt and pepper. Serve them hot with the browned bits from the baking pan.

Why do potatoes make good detectives? Because they have their eyes peeled.

—ANONYMOUS

Gingered Purée of Winter Roots

| Serves 6 to 8 | 15 minutes prep time; 30 minutes cook time | This purée reheats nicely and holds for a couple of days in the fridge, but it is prime the day it's cooked. |

Ginger and root vegetables? Trust us on this recipe, it will inspire a new appreciation of what winter can deliver. The yellow turnips called for here are not essential, but try them if you can. Sweet and mild, they sidestep the earthiness of white varieties and tame down that other good-tasting but earthy root that's usually left at the store—the rutabaga.

1¼ pounds **rutabaga**, peeled and very thinly sliced
¾ pound **turnips** (yellow preferred), peeled and thinly sliced
1¼ pounds **red-skin potatoes**, peeled and thinly sliced
Salt
4 tablespoons **unsalted butter**
3-inch piece fresh **ginger**, finely minced (about 3 tablespoons)
Freshly ground **black pepper**

{ **COOK** *to* **Cook** }

The method for using ginger in this recipe is worth remembering. Not only does sautéing aromatics open up their flavor and tame their rough raw edges, the infused butter or oil helps transport their fragrances throughout the dish.

1. Place the rutabaga, turnips, and potatoes into a 6-quart pot. Cover with water by 1 or 2 inches and sprinkle with about 2 teaspoons salt. Simmer for 25 minutes, or until the vegetable slices are tender.

2. Meanwhile, in a small skillet, melt the butter over medium heat and add the ginger, gently warming it (don't sauté or brown), until it's fragrant. Cover the skillet and set aside.

3. When the vegetables are tender, drain them well in a colander. Purée in a food processor with the ginger butter. Add salt and pepper to taste. Serve hot.

Move Over,
Johnny Appleseed

Ethnobiologist and MacArthur genius Gary Nabhan told us the story of Nikolay Vavilov, the Russian botanist Gary claims was the world's greatest plant explorer.

Vavilov collected more seeds than any other person in human history. His fifty-year career took him to sixty-five countries on five continents, where he learned to speak fifteen languages. Those languages were the key to his doing what no scientist had done before—learning firsthand from peasant farmers how seed diversity was used in their fields. Nabhan believes that all of our notions about biological diversity sprung from Vavilov's work, whose ultimate goal was to end world hunger.

This alone makes Vavilov a fascinating character, but the story becomes even more compelling when you learn the fate of his work.

All 350,000 of Vavilov's seeds went into a government-run seed bank in St. Petersburg. Then came World War II and the Nazi siege on the city. Joseph Stalin had Vavilov imprisoned as the scapegoat for Stalin's own failed farming policies. There, after a year and a half of eating moldy cabbage and rotten flour, the man who fought to end world hunger in the world died of starvation.

Meanwhile, Vavilov's scientists at the seed bank locked themselves in the building to save the seeds from the Nazis and the hungry local population. Surrounded by food they never touched, twelve of the scientists starved to death. Today you will find pictures of Vavilov's scientists on the walls of that seed bank.

Where Our Food Comes From: Retracing Nikolay Vavilov's Quest to End Famine
by **Gary Paul Nabhan**
(Island Press, 2009)

West Indies Green Beans

| *Serves 3 to 4; doubles* | *20 minutes prep time;* | *Boil the beans a day ahead if you'd like;* |
| *or triples easily* | *5 minutes stove time* | *serve them hot or at room temperature.* |

It's an old trick to boil or steam your vegetables ahead and just before they make their appearance at the table, to heat them in a quick flavorful sauté. Seasoning is totally your call and it can have as much attitude as you'd like, as in these warm-tasting spices of the West Indies and a garlic-tomato sauté.

1 pound **green beans**, stem ends trimmed away
Good-tasting **extra-virgin olive oil**
2 large **garlic cloves**, thinly sliced
Salt and freshly ground **black pepper**
1 teaspoon **West Indies Spice Blend** (page 175)
¼ teaspoon ground **cinnamon**
½ to ⅔ cup finely chopped fresh or canned
   tomatoes with their liquid

{ **COOK** *to* **Cook** }

The West Indies Spice Blend recipe gives you more than you will need here, so store the remainder in a jar and use it with abandon to bring life to all kinds of meats, fish, and veggies. Just remember, for the most flavor, always begin by warming the spice blend in a little oil.

1. Bring 4 quarts salted water to a boil in a 6-quart pot. Boil the beans in the water, uncovered, for about 3 minutes, or until tender. Drain the beans immediately in a colander and cool quickly under cold running water. Drain well and set aside.

2. Coat the bottom of a 12-inch slant-sided skillet with a thin film of oil and set it over medium heat. With a wooden spatula, stir in the garlic with a generous sprinkling of salt and pepper. Adjust the heat so the garlic doesn't burn and stir for 1 minute, or until the garlic is soft, but not colored.

3. Blend in the spice blend and cinnamon and stir over low heat for another few seconds, until aromatic. Add the tomatoes and cook until their moisture is gone.

4. Add the beans to the skillet, tossing to heat them through and coat with the sauté. Once the beans are hot, taste them for seasoning and transfer them to a serving platter, scraping all their flavorings over them. Serve hot or at room temperature.

Shallot-Thyme Green Beans:

Cook the beans as directed. For the sauté use olive oil, but replace the garlic with 2 large sliced shallots and replace the spices with 3 sprigs fresh thyme. Replace the tomatoes with ⅓ cup dry white wine, boil it down to nothing, and then add ½ cup chicken broth and cook that down to a syrupy consistency. Finally, heat the beans in the sauce.

Walnut-Mortadella Green Beans:

Cook the beans as directed. For the sauté, use olive oil and sauté ⅔ cup mortadella sausage cut into ¼-inch dice to heat it through. Add the beans and ½ cup toasted walnuts.

Green Beans in Spiced Orange Reduction:

Cook the beans as directed, then heat them in the orange juice reduction on page 226. Just before serving, stir in minced fresh chile to taste.

WORK NIGHT ENCORE

West Indies Beans with Yellow Rice: Cook the rice as you would pasta in a large pot of boiling, salted water, tinted with 1 teaspoon ground turmeric, for 6 to 8 minutes, until the rice is tender, but still a little firm. Drain the rice in a sieve and toss it with the reheated West Indies beans.

The Spice Rack Scam

Don't fall for the scam of buying a complete spice set with every herb and spice known to humankind. The only thing you'll be guaranteed to have is a complete collection of dead flavors. Instead, buy as you go, in small quantities, and for the fullest flavors, buy whole spices and grind them yourself. The difference is amazing.

Dried herbs and ground spices are in their prime for 3 months; whole spices are good for a year.

ONE MORE THING: You know those nicely designed spice racks that hang over your stove? Forget them, too. Heat and light are the enemy of seasonings. Could anyone have designed a worse place to hang a spice rack?

How about starting a new household tradition at the New Year? Get family and friends together and pitch out all of the past year's spices, or better yet, do a ceremonial burning in the fireplace, or outside in the snow.

Rosemary-Orange Cauliflower

| *Serves 6 to 8; halves easily* | *20 minutes prep time; 15 minutes stove time* | *Best eaten the day it's cooked, but holds for several days in the refrigerator; reheats easily*

Think of this lovely green purée of cauliflower and kale as a sexed-up, dead easy stand-in for mashed potatoes. Try it with steak, salad, or Thanksgiving turkey.

1 large **cauliflower** (2½ to 3 pounds) with its greens
¼ pound **Tuscan kale** (about 6 leaves) or regular kale, ribs removed and leaves torn
1 large **onion**, thinly sliced
6 **garlic cloves**, crushed
1½ tightly packed teaspoons fresh **rosemary leaves**, or more to taste
Finely grated zest of ⅔ large **orange**, or to taste
Salt and freshly ground **black pepper**
3 to 4 tablespoons good-tasting **extra-virgin olive oil**
2 tablespoons **unsalted butter**

1. Cut the cauliflower into florets, then thinly slice its green stalks.

2. Place 3 inches water in an 8-quart pot. Insert a collapsible steamer. Bring the water to a boil and pile in the cauliflower greens, then the florets, layering them with the kale, onion, garlic, rosemary, and orange zest. Sprinkle with some salt and pepper.

3. Steam for about 10 minutes, or until the cauliflower is almost falling apart. Drain in a colander and let stand for 5 minutes. Place everything into a food processor along with the oil and butter. Purée, then taste for additional seasoning, be it salt, rosemary, orange zest, or pepper.

Oven-Roasted Carrots with Preserved Lemon & Allspice

| *Serves 4 to 6* | *10 minutes prep time; 20 to 25 minutes oven time* | *Best eaten the same day they are cooked, but can be served at room temperature* |

The sweetness and earthiness of carrots get a boost when they are roasted at high heat. Here we take toothy chunks of carrots, parboil them, fast-roast them in the oven with allspice, and finish them off with a garnish of minced preserved lemon and fresh garlic. Wait until a dish is fully cooked before adding a decisive seasoning like preserved lemon—it's hard to go back.

If preserved lemon isn't to be had, plain grated lemon zest can be used. It's not the same, but the dish will still be delicious.

3 pounds **carrots**, cut on the diagonal into 2-inch chunks
About 3 tablespoons good-tasting **extra-virgin olive oil**
½ to 1 teaspoon freshly ground **allspice**
Salt and freshly ground **black pepper**
4 large **garlic cloves**, minced
Peel of ⅔ to 1 whole **Moroccan Preserved Lemon** (page 85), inside pulp removed and discarded, the peel rinsed under cold water and finely minced, or shredded zest of 1 medium lemon

Roasted carrots shrink shockingly, so although the raw pile may seem enormous, rest assured that they will shrink into a manageable stack on a platter.

1. Preheat the oven to 450°F.

2. Bring 6 quarts of salted water to a boil in an 8-quart pot and cook the carrots for about 10 minutes, or until they are nearly fork-tender, but still have some firmness. Drain thoroughly.

3. On a large half-sheet pan, toss the carrots with enough oil to coat them generously, then toss them with the allspice and salt and pepper to taste. Roast for 20 to 25 minutes, or until nicely seared and browned here and there, shaking and turning often.

(recipe continues)

4. Remove the pan from the oven and while the carrots are still in it, add the garlic and lemon (preserved or zest), tossing to combine. Add salt and pepper to taste and serve.

Variations

Roasted Grapes and Winter Vegetables:

Try these paired with Ancho Cider-Glazed Hens (page 198) or any roasted meat or fish. Preheat the oven to 425°F. Instead of 3 pounds of carrots, reduce to 1 pound (if possible, the little multi-colored ones with about 1 inch of their tops). Cut them lengthwise in half or quarters. Add 1 pound Brussels sprouts, halved; ½ pound green seedless grapes; 4 to 5 branches thyme; and 4 crushed garlic cloves. Toss everything with 3 to 4 tablespoons olive oil and salt and freshly ground pepper to taste. Roast, turning often, for 45 minutes to 1¼ hours, or until the vegetables are browned and tender.

Hot and Sour Roasted Carrots:

Follow the recipe as written. Season the carrots halfway through cooking with ground hot chile or smoked hot Spanish paprika. Instead of sprinkling the cooked carrots with the preserved lemon, sprinkle them with sherry or cider vinegar.

Shall I not have intelligence with the earth? Am I not partly leaves and vegetable mould myself?

—HENRY DAVID THOREAU

Braised Belgian Endive

| Serves 6 to 8 | 5 minutes prep time; 90 minutes cook time | Can be made ahead and gently reheated before serving

We Americans underappreciate the pleasure of cooked lettuces. In Belgium, where endive is a high art, you'll find four different grades when they're in season. Although it is delicious raw, we think this classic take is a good place to expand your endive appreciation.

This recipe is the essence of simplicity and yields tender, slippery halves tinged with caramel edges, all held together by the bitter nature of the lettuce. Be patient; a long roast is necessary.

6 **Belgian endives** (1½ to 2 pounds), root ends trimmed, cored and cut in half
1 cup low-sodium **chicken stock**
3 tablespoons **unsalted butter**, cut into ½-inch pieces
Salt and freshly ground **black pepper**
⅛ teaspoon freshly grated **nutmeg**, or to taste

Be sure to select endives that are relatively the same size to ensure even cooking.

1. Preheat the oven to 350°F. In a shallow, ceramic, ovenproof baking dish large enough to snugly hold the endives in a single layer, place the endives, cut side up. Pour in the stock, dot with enough butter chunks to equal about 2 tablespoons, and season to taste with the salt, pepper, and nutmeg.

2. Cover the dish with a lid or tight-fitting foil and bake for 1 hour, checking the liquid level every 15 minutes and turning the endive in the broth. If the pan begins to dry out, add more water or broth to keep it moist. Cook until the endive is fork-tender, then remove the cover and continue to roast for another 15 to 20 minutes, depending on how much liquid remains. Remove the pan from the oven, sprinkle on the remaining butter, and set aside.

3. If a lot of moisture remains before final buttering, carefully spoon out the juices and reduce them in a small skillet over high heat until big glossy bubbles form and it begins to get syrupy. Remove from the heat, stir in the remaining 1 tablespoon butter, pour over the endive, and serve hot or at room temperature.

Mustard-Glazed
Red Cabbage with Apple

| *Serves 6 to 8* | *15 minutes prep time; 20 minutes stove time* | *Sautéing the cabbage ahead, even a day ahead, works well, but finish it with the butter and mustard just before serving.* |

Cabbage is not a sexy vegetable, but this treatment gives it hope. The piquant and the voluptuous—grainy mustard and a little sweet butter—glaze the cabbage just before it goes into the bowl, an inspiration from New York chef Tom Valenti.

Serve it as a side to anything autumnal, but if partnered with roasted potatoes and a fresh salad, it would make a meal all on its own.

Good-tasting **extra-virgin olive oil**

½ medium **onion**, cut into ¼-inch dice

1 head of **red cabbage** (2½ pounds), cut into 1½-inch chunks

Salt and freshly ground **black pepper**

6 6-inch sprigs fresh **thyme**, or 1½ to 2 teaspoons dried

2 dried **bay leaves**

1 medium **apple** (not peeled), cored and cut into ¼-inch dice

6 tablespoons **cider vinegar**

¼ cup dry **red wine**

4 cups low-sodium **vegetable** or **chicken broth**

1 tablespoon **unsalted butter**

3 to 4 heaping tablespoons grainy **dark mustard**

1. Coat a straight-sided 12-inch sauté pan with a thin film of oil. Heat over medium-high heat; add the onion and cabbage and a sprinkling of salt and pepper. Sauté, stirring with a wooden spatula, to brown the onions and get the cabbage to pick up golden edges. Adjust the heat so the pan glaze doesn't burn.

2. Stir in the thyme, bay leaves, apple, and half of the vinegar, scraping up any glaze on the pan's bottom. Boil the vinegar down to nothing.

3. Pour in the wine and broth, bring to a slow bubble, cover, and cook for about 10 minutes, or until the cabbage is nearly tender. Uncover and boil away the liquid, stirring in the remaining vinegar toward the end of the boil so it moistens the cabbage.

4. Just before serving, taste the cabbage for seasoning. Fold in the butter and mustard and serve hot.

Variations

Replace the cabbage with other vegetables or a combination of them. Try green beans, Brussels sprouts, parsnips, carrots, turnips, burdock, rutabaga, celery root, kohlrabi, kale, collards, mustard greens, or potatoes. Vary the cooking time as needed.

> In the night the cabbages catch the moon, the leaves drip silver, the rows of cabbages are a series of little silver waterfalls in the moon.
>
> —CARL SANDBURG

Charred Ginger-Chile Corn

Serves 2 to 4 | *20 minutes prep time; 20 minutes stove time*

You know those delicious, over-charred ears of grilled corn you eat at county fairs in the summer? If you are like us and request the ones with the most burned bits, this recipe is for you.

Here, freshly cut corn kernels are charred until sizzling and popping in a flaming-hot cast-iron skillet and finished with a mince of ginger, fresh garlic, and chiles. The hardest thing about this dish is learning to *not* stir or fiddle with it while it's incinerating.

3 tablespoons expeller-pressed **canola oil**
3 cups fresh **corn kernels** cut from the cob
  (4 to 5 ears)
2½ tablespoons minced fresh **ginger**
1 medium **jalapeño chile**, seeded and minced
  (about 2 tablespoons)
4 large **garlic cloves**, minced
Salt and freshly ground **black pepper**

The choice of pan is critical here. It needs to be cast iron, and the bigger the better. If using a smaller pan, be sure to scorch the corn in small batches or there will be too much liquid thrown off to ever get the proper sear.

Also, the rule for wok cookery holds true here: hot wok, cold oil. Add the oil to the hot pan for best results.

1. Heat the skillet over high heat until smoking.

2. Add the oil and let it heat briefly. Toss in the corn, making sure it is evenly spread out in the pan. The corn must not be crowded (see Cook to Cook). Do not stir for at least 1 minute, to allow the corn to severely char and pop.

3. Stir in the ginger and chile, again allowing them to char with very little stirring, about 1 minute. The corn is done when a fourth to a third of the kernels are flecked with brown (depending on your taste). Stir in the garlic and remove from the heat.

4. Add salt and pepper to taste and serve immediately.

Not Boston Baked Beans

| Serves 6 to 8; doubles easily | 10 minutes prep time; 2 hours soaking time; 1 to 1¼ hours stove time; 1½ hours oven time | The beans can be made ahead as they reheat beautifully. |

Boston doesn't know what it's missing. These beans are an outrageous riff on Beantown's very proper classic. Long and languid cooking in brown sugar, bacon, vinegar, garlic, and Tabasco make these beans the kind that you tiptoe into the kitchen for at midnight. Although Memorial Day barbecues and July Fourth picnics come to mind, don't ignore what these beans can do for a wintry Saturday night with a side of cornbread.

SIMMERING

1 pound dried organic **pinto beans** (2½ cups), covered with boiling water and soaked 2 hours
1 tablespoon ground **allspice**
6 whole **cloves**, crushed
6 large **garlic cloves**, coarsely chopped
4 medium to large **onions**, cut into ½-inch dice
1 teaspoon **salt**

BAKING

Good-tasting **extra-virgin olive oil**
1 pound good-quality sliced **bacon**, sliced into 1-inch pieces
1½ cups **cider vinegar**, plus more as needed
1⅓ cups (packed) **dark brown sugar**, plus more as needed
1½ teaspoons **salt**, plus more as needed
½ teaspoon freshly ground **black pepper**
¾ cup **dark brown mustard** (not flavored), plus more as needed
1½ tablespoons **Tabasco** or **Sriracha sauce**, or to taste

COOK *to* **Cook**

You could cook the beans one day, bake them the next, and reheat them up to 3 days after that. Any bean works in this recipe. Try some New England favorites like Jacob's Cattle, Yellow Eye, Marfax, Mayflower, Soldier, navy, red cranberry, and Great Northern.

1. Make the beans: Drain the soaked beans, then transfer them to a heavy 6-quart pot that can go from stovetop to oven to table. Add water to cover by 3 inches. Stir in 1 teaspoon of the allspice, all of the cloves, a third of the garlic, a fourth of the onions, and the salt. Simmer, partially covered, for 30 minutes to 1 hour, or until tender but not falling apart. Drain the beans and reserve the liquid. Clean out the pot. The beans can be cooked 2 days in advance and refrigerated until needed.

2. To bake the beans, preheat the oven to 325°F. Set the cleaned pot over medium heat and coat it with a thin film of oil. Add the bacon. Slowly cook it until the bacon has given off most of its fat, but isn't crisp. If the fat is excessive, spoon off all but about 5 tablespoons. Stir in the remaining onions and raise the heat to medium-high. Cook, stirring often, for about 7 minutes, or until the onion begins to brown, taking care not to burn the brown glaze on the bottom of the pan.

3. Pour in ½ cup of the cider vinegar and scrape up the brown glaze as you cook down the vinegar to almost nothing. Then stir in another ½ cup of the vinegar, the remaining 2 teaspoons allspice, and the remaining garlic. Blend in the sugar, salt, pepper, mustard, and Tabasco. Blend in 2 cups of the bean liquid. Now taste the liquid for a balance between tart, sweet, heat, and spice. Bring to a simmer.

4. Cover the pot and bake in the oven for 30 minutes. Uncover, stir in another ½ cup of the vinegar, then taste and add more mustard, salt, and sugar as needed (the beans should be spicy and sweet-tart).

5. Raise the heat to 400°F. and bake the beans, uncovered, for 1 hour longer, or until they are very thick and glazed. Taste for seasoning again. Serve hot.

SWEETS

Stirred Old-Fashioned Lemon Ice Cream

| *Serves 8 to 10* | *15 minutes prep time; 4 to 5 hours freezer time*

Lemon and cream make up one of the all-time, surefire duos, especially when the lemon is aggressive and tangy, which brings us to this puckery-sweet lemon ice cream. Before you turn away because you don't have an ice cream maker, read on.

Eons ago when not everyone possessed every gadget imaginable, there was icebox ice cream. Instead of freezing in an ice cream maker, you poured the ice cream mix into ice cube trays and stirred every so often with a fork as it froze. Of course it was icier and denser than the machine-made stuff, but that was part of its charm.

This is Lynne's mother's recipe. She made it to go with summer fruit, but Lynne loves it with caramelized pears (page 299) or apples or slightly melted as an extra-plush lemon Slurpee.

⅔ to 1 cup fresh **lemon juice** (3 to 4 large lemons)
1 generous tablespoon grated **lemon zest**
¼ teaspoon **salt**
2 cups **sugar**
4 cups **heavy cream**

1. In a shallow plastic container with a lid, stir together the lemon juice, lemon zest, salt, and sugar. Gradually stir in the cream until the mixture is smooth. Taste for sweet/tart contrast. It should be sharp, because freezing mutes flavors. Adjust the lemon/sugar balance as necessary.

2. Cover and freeze for about 1 hour. Once the rim of the ice cream freezes, stir it into the center of the cream. Repeat two or three times more, waiting about 1 hour between checks. The final result should be a frozen yet creamy consistency.

3. To make ahead, let the ice cream freeze solid, then break it up and refreeze, stirring every 30 minutes before serving.

Add ½ teaspoon hot ground chile, or more to taste, to the recipe. Two tablespoons crushed fresh or dried lavender or chopped fresh lemon balm or lemon verbena is good, too.

Ice cream is exquisite— what a pity it isn't illegal.

—VOLTAIRE

Iced Fudge Lollies

| *Makes 6 to 8 pops;* | *10 minutes prep time;* | *Popsicle molds are inexpensive, but don't*
| *doubles easily* | *4 hours to 2 weeks* | *hesitate to turn the whole batch into a*
| | *freezer time* | *large container and serve it as sorbet.*

Let's keep this short and sweet: these frozen pops are indecently delicious and easy. The angels had to be on Sally's shoulders when she conjured this one up.

There's such an intense hit of chocolate and they're just the comic relief needed at the end of an impressive meal.

1 cup **sugar**
1 cup high-quality **cocoa powder**
½ **vanilla bean**, split
Pinch of **salt**

1. In a 3-quart saucepan over medium heat, dissolve the sugar in 2 cups water. Once dissolved, whisk in the cocoa powder, vanilla, and salt. Bring to a simmer and cook for 3 to 5 minutes, or until the mixture thickens slightly and is smooth.

2. Remove from the heat, then remove the vanilla bean and cool. Pour the mixture into popsicle molds and freeze for at least 4 hours.

Variations

Try coating the tips of the lollies with nuts or coconut by packing it in the bottoms of the mold before pouring in the chocolate mixture.

Or serve them with little dishes of whipped cream and crushed salted pistachio nuts at each place. You dip, eat, dip, and eat.

COOK *to* Cook

High-quality cocoa powder is a must here to get that velvety can't-be-fat-free texture (Pernigotti, Valrhona, and Michel Cluizel are some worth looking for). And don't forget the pinch of salt—it really lifts the flavor.

Double Pear Pudding Cake with Warm Caramel-Cognac Sauce

Serves 10 to 12

2 to 3 hours prep time; 2 hours oven time; 3 to 8 hours cooling time; 24 hours rest time

This cake is better with a day of rest, tightly wrapped, kept at room temperature, or it keeps frozen up to 6 months. You can marinate the fruits, caramelize the pears, and make the sauce ahead.

Standing proud and tall on a plate, retro Bundt cakes are impressive. Fall is written all over this one—the warming spices, the autumn fruits, the warm caramel sauce filling in the crevices—here is a great baking project for that first cool weekend.

You'll get to practice the old fruit-on-fruit trick. You soak dried pears in Cognac and sauté fresh ones in butter and caramel. Pretty fancy.

Unsalted butter and flour

MARINATED FRUITS

1½ cups **raisins**

½ cup finely chopped mixed **dried pears and apricots**, or just dried pears

½ cup **Cognac** or **brandy**

1 recipe **Caramelized Pears** (recipe follows)

CAKE

3⅛ cups (16 ounces) unbleached **all-purpose flour**, dipped and leveled (see page 304), then sifted

¾ teaspoon **baking soda**

1 tablespoon **baking powder**

1¾ teaspoons **salt**

4 teaspoons ground **cinnamon**

2 teaspoons ground **ginger**

WINE The deep flavors and massiveness of this cake pose a challenge best answered by an oak-aged dessert wine like Sauternes or Barsac from Bordeaux. A great alternative that can hold its own with the Cognac sauce would be Muscat de Beaumes de Venise from France's Rhône Valley.

1½ teaspoons ground **allspice**

½ teaspoon ground **cloves**

¾ cup (12 tablespoons) **unsalted butter**, at room temperature

1½ cups (packed) **dark brown sugar**

3 large **eggs**, at room temperature

1½ cups **buttermilk**, at room temperature

1 cup whole **blanched almonds**, toasted and coarsely chopped

Caramel-Cognac Sauce (recipe follows)

1. Butter and flour a 10-inch Bundt pan.

2. **Marinate the dried fruits:** In a medium bowl, combine the raisins, dried pears and apricots, and Cognac and let stand for several hours or overnight.

3. Purée about one quarter of the caramelized pears, combine with the remaining caramelized pears in a bowl, and set aside.

4. **Make the cake:** Place a sifter or large strainer over a large bowl. Add the sifted flour, baking soda, baking powder, salt, cinnamon, ginger, allspice, and cloves and sift into the bowl. Believe it or not, sifting doesn't mix dry ingredients well enough. So to be sure they will evenly leaven and flavor the cake, stir them several times with a whisk. Set the dry ingredients aside.

5. Preheat the oven to 350°F. In a stand mixer fitted with the paddle attachment, or using a handheld electric beater and a large bowl, beat the butter at medium speed for about 5 minutes, or until light and fluffy. Scrape down the sides of the bowl a few times. Add the sugar and continue beating at medium speed for 3 to 5 minutes, or until very fluffy. Still at medium speed, beat in the eggs, one at a time, until each is just blended. Then beat in the pear purée.

6. In this step it's crucial not to overbeat the batter or the cake will toughen. Set the mixer at low speed and

{ **COOK** *to* **Cook** }

Picky though it may seem, the butter's temperature is crucial in a cake recipe. At the right temperature, you can beat it up to three times its original volume. This is how cakes get their height and lightness. The butter has to be soft enough to fluff into pockets of air, and cool and firm enough to securely hold it (65°F. to 68°F.). Tuck an instant-read thermometer in your butter as you're bringing it to room temperature and you'll know exactly where you are.

Also, for the most volume, never beat butter faster than at medium speed. Lastly, have all ingredients at room temperature before starting to mix.

(recipe continues)

beat in about one third of the sifted dry ingredients (flour, leaveners, and spices) from step 4 until just blended. Add half of the buttermilk and beat only to blend. Repeat with half of the remaining dry ingredients, then the last of the buttermilk and, finally, the rest of the dry ingredients. Do not overbeat.

7. By hand, using a big spatula, fold into the batter the caramelized pears and all of their liquid, along with the almonds and the dried fruits with any of their liquid. Fold only long enough to blend. Turn into the prepared pan and bake for 1 hour.

Reduce the heat to 325°F. and bake for 1 more hour, or until a tester inserted about an inch from the rim of the pan comes out clean. The center of the cake should still be moist. Let the cake cool in the pan on a rack for 15 minutes. Run a knife around the edge of the pan, turn the cake out onto the rack, and cool for 3 to 8 hours. Wrap tightly and keep at room temperature for at least 1 day.

8. To serve, set the cake on a platter and spoon some of the warmed caramel-Cognac sauce over it so it runs down the sides and puddles on the platter. Pass the remaining sauce at the table.

Variation

A Cake for All Seasons:

As the year passes, replace the pears with apples, cherries, apricots, peaches, and nectarines. Always pair the fresh fruit with its dried sibling.

One of the most private things in the world is an egg until it's broken.

—M.F.K. FISHER

Caramelized Pears

| *Makes 3 to 4 cups* | *15 minutes prep time;* | *The pears can be made ahead and*
| | *20 minutes stove time* | *refrigerated.*

These pears become a dessert when served on their own or spooned over Homemade Ricotta (page 119) or Stirred Old-Fashioned Lemon Ice Cream (page 292).

5 tablespoons **unsalted butter**
5 medium firm-ripe **Bosc pears**, peeled, cored, and cut
   into 1-inch chunks
1 cup **sugar**
Grated zest of 2 large **lemons**
Juice of 1 **lemon**

1. Heat the butter in a 12-inch heavy skillet over high heat, taking care not to let it burn. Add the pears and cook quickly, gently stirring often, until golden brown.

2. Raise the heat to medium-high, stir in the sugar, and cook for 1 minute, or until the sugar has turned thick and amber colored (do not let it burn). Stir in the lemon zest, remove the pan from the heat, and stand back as you add 2 tablespoons of water to the pan as a precaution against burning. Gently stir in.

3. Transfer the pears to a bowl, cool for 10 minutes, blend in the lemon juice, and cool.

(recipe continues)

Caramel-Cognac Sauce

| *Makes about 1½ cups* | *5 minutes prep time;* | *Warm before serving.*
| | *20 minutes stove time* |

Delicious warmed and poured over nearly everything: Fresh Ricotta Tart (page 310), ice creams, fruits, and even French toast.

1 cup **sugar**
2 tablespoons **light corn syrup**
⅔ cup **heavy cream**
2 tablespoons **unsalted butter**
2 tablespoons **Cognac** or **brandy**
1 teaspoon **vanilla extract**
¼ teaspoon **salt**

1. Make the caramel sauce by combining the sugar and corn syrup and 3 tablespoons water in a 3-quart saucepan. Set over medium-high heat and bring to a bubble. Do not stir at all, but do use a heatproof brush dipped in water to wash down the sides of the pan often.

2. Once the bubbles are clear, large, and shiny, the syrup will start to color. Cook it another 30 seconds, or until it's the color of caramel candy, but not dark brown. Immediately pull the pan off the heat and stand back while you pour in the cream. The syrup will fiercely bubble up and then settle down. Stir in the butter, Cognac, vanilla, and salt. Scrape the sauce into a medium metal or heatproof bowl, cool, and refrigerate it if holding for more than a few hours.

TO
Tantalize

The word *tantalize* comes from the Greek story of Tantalus, who was punished for feeding human flesh to the gods. He was condemned to stand in a river up to his neck with fruit trees hanging overhead. As if that weren't enough, he was also cursed with insatiable hunger and thirst.

Every time he reached for the fruit, a wind blew the branches away, and when he tried to drink the water, it receded to the sandy bottom. That tale surely gives our modern usage of the word *tantalize* new weight, does it not?

Chile-Spiked Mexican Wedding Cakes

Makes 24 to 30 cookies	*10 minutes prep time;*	*The dough can be made 2 to 3 days*
	2 hours to overnight	*ahead and refrigerated. Finished*
	refrigeration;	*cookies keep 1 week in a cool place, or*
	12 minutes oven time	*frozen for up to 6 months.*

This is an amped-up version of Mexican Wedding Cake cookies by Sally's mother, Ricki.

What the daughter of Italian mining immigrants in Ely, Minnesota, was doing with a Mexican cookie in her arsenal remains a mystery. The story she told was that these were actually classic Russian sweets, and "when things started going south with the Soviets," they started calling them Mexican Wedding Cakes. Wacky? Well, so was she.

1 cup **pecan pieces**, lightly toasted
1 cup **unsalted butter**, softened
½ cup **sugar**
2 teaspoons **vanilla extract**
2 cups **all-purpose flour**
½ teaspoon **salt**
½ teaspoon **cayenne**
¼ teaspoon ground **cinnamon**
½ cup **confectioners' sugar**

WINE Arguments have broken out at the table as to whether light and effervescent Moscato d'Asti or a soft and rich late-harvest wine offers a better pairing. These are very different, but both wonderfully flattering with the cookies, which should assure you that any sweet wine will work well. Here's to further study.

1. In a food processor, pulse the pecans until coarsely ground. Add the butter and pulse until combined. Mix in the sugar and vanilla. Add the flour, salt, cayenne, and cinnamon and pulse just to combine.

2. Gather the dough into a ball and wrap in plastic. Refrigerate until firm, at least 2 hours and preferably overnight.

3. Preheat the oven to 350°F. Line two baking sheets with parchment.

4. When ready to bake, let the dough warm to room temperature so that it is pliable but still cold. Using about 1 tablespoon dough per cookie, roll the dough into balls. Place them on the baking sheet about 1 inch apart and flatten slightly with the palm of your hand or the bottom of a glass to keep them from rolling.

5. Bake until slightly browned on the bottom, about 12 minutes. Let them cool completely. Sift the confectioners' sugar over the cooled cookies and dust with additional spices if desired.

Seize the moment. Remember all those women on the *Titanic* who waved off the dessert cart.

—ERMA BOMBECK

Essential
Baking 101
How You Measure Your Flour

How you measure flour can make a recipe fly or fail.
**A single leveled measuring cup of flour can hold
3½ to 5 ounces of flour,** which is a huge difference in
a recipe for brownies or birthday cake.

All of our recipes use the "dip and level" method,
which yields a 5-ounce cup. The technique is simple: dip the
measuring cup into the flour and lift it out with the flour heaping,
then sweep a straight edge, like the back of a knife, over the cup
to level it off. Don't tap or tamp.

Five-Nut Caramel Tart

| Serves 8 to 10 | 1 hour and 25 minutes prep time; 10 minutes stove time; 40 minutes oven time; 4 to 5 hours cooling time | The tart holds 4 days, but is best served the day it's baked.

For the pastry shy, this tart is salvation. It looks like jewels set in amber, with its candy bar mosaic of five kinds of nuts embedded in buttery, salty caramel slicked over a tender crust, which is where salvation comes in. There is no rolling pin in sight. You pat the crust into the tart tin with your fingers.

{ COOK *to* **Cook }**

Make the pastry 1 day in advance.

PASTRY

- 1¼ cups unbleached **all-purpose flour** (organic preferred), dipped and leveled (opposite page)
- 3 tablespoons **granulated sugar**
- ¼ teaspoon **salt**
- 1 stick (4 ounces) cold **unsalted butter**, cut into pieces, plus more for buttering the pan
- 1½ large **egg yolks** blended with 1½ tablespoons **ice water**

FILLING

- 1 stick (4 ounces) **unsalted butter**
- ½ cup (packed) **dark brown sugar**
- ¼ cup **honey**
- 2 tablespoons **granulated sugar**
- 1 cup **toasted salted cashews** (about 4 ounces)
- ⅔ cup **toasted salted macadamia nuts** (about 3½ ounces)
- ½ cup whole **blanched almonds** (about 2¼ ounces)
- ⅓ cup **salted shelled pistachios** (about 1½ ounces)
- ¼ cup **pine nuts** (about 1 ounce)
- 2 tablespoons **heavy cream**
- 1½ teaspoons **coarse salt**

(recipe continues)

1. **Make the pastry:** Place the flour, granulated sugar, and salt in a food processor and pulse a few times to combine. Add the butter and pulse until the mixture resembles coarse meal. Add the egg yolk mixture and pulse until a dough begins to form. Gather the dough into a ball, flatten into a disk, wrap in plastic, and refrigerate for at least 30 minutes.

2. Preheat the oven to 400°F. and place the rack in the center of the oven. Butter an 11-inch-diameter false-bottom fluted tart pan. Let the dough soften slightly, then pat the crust into the pan with your hands to a relatively even thickness of ⅛ inch. Trim the edges even with the pan's rim. Refrigerate the pastry for 30 minutes or overnight.

3. **Prebake the tart shell:** Line the tart shell with foil. Fill with dried beans or pie weights. Bake for 10 minutes. Remove the foil and beans. Bake for 10 minutes longer, or until the tart shell is golden brown. Cool completely on a rack.

4. **Make the filling:** Reduce the heat to 350°F. Place the tart shell on a heavy, large baking sheet. In a heavy 2-quart saucepan, combine the butter, brown sugar, honey, and granulated sugar. Cook over low heat, stirring for 3 minutes, or until the sugars dissolve. Raise the heat and whisk until the mixture comes to a boil.

5. Continue boiling for about 1 minute, or until large bubbles form. Remove the pan from the heat. Stir in the cashews, macadamia nuts, almonds, pistachios, pine nuts, and cream. Immediately pour the filling into the tart shell. Bake for about 20 minutes, or until the filling bubbles (the filling may overflow slightly onto the baking sheet).

6. Cool the tart in the pan on a rack until the filling just begins to set. Gently remove the pan bottom and cool the tart completely, 4 to 5 hours. Sprinkle with salt to taste. Cut into wedges and serve.

WINE The richness of the caramel and the meatiness of the nuts make an aged tawny port sing with this tart. If you can spring for it, a twenty-year-old tawny from Portugal would be the best choice. That said, most Portuguese ten-year-old tawnies are terrific as well.

Steve Jenkins's
CHEESE EVENING

How about challenging the beloved French tradition of
cheese courses as dessert? Instead, make the cheese course the
main event. Now you have instant no-cook, work night dinner parties
for the holidays, or the solution to what to eat on a summer evening
when you're too lazy to move.

The genius is in the details and the
simplicity. Here is where pioneer cheesemonger Steve
Jenkins comes in. Back in the dark ages when cheese
counters sold mostly mummified industrial "cheese
product," Steve was tracking handmade
artisan cheeses. But as skilled a cheesemonger as Steve
Jenkins is, he has a strong streak of the chef in him,
as this cheese dinner plan proves.

For a cheese evening, Steve suggests you set out
three composed plates of three cheeses each, with
accompaniments: a cow cheese plate, a goat cheese plate, and a sheep
cheese plate. With this unusual approach to feeding friends, good
talk is nearly guaranteed. Some suggestions from Steve:

Cheese Primer (Workman,
1996) and *The Fairway Market
Cookbook* by **Steve Jenkins**
(Ecco/HarperCollins, 2008)

COW CHEESE PLATE

Consider an Epoisses from Burgundy; a blue from the United States or Italy, such as Gorgonzola Dolce (young) or Gorgonzola Stagionato (aged); and a Farmhouse English Somerset Cheddar like Keen's or Montgomery's.

Cow cheeses should be served with sweets, according to Steve. Think cantaloupe; Persian melon; dried figs, apricots, and cherries; and warmed almonds and hazelnuts. Drink a dry cider from France like the DuPont Brut apple cider, or a pear cider from Normandy or Alsace's Maeyaert cider.

GOAT CHEESE PLATE

Try a French chèvre like Le Chevrot; something American that's bolder, like Humboldt Fog; choose from Spain's Garrotxa from Catalonia, or Pata de Mulo or Queso Tietan from Castile-León. For balance, add a young Toma del Paglia from Italy.

Steve believes in pairing goat cheeses with savories—olives washed and dressed with chiles in hot oil, roasted tomatoes, and salted Spanish Marcona almonds.

SHEEP CHEESE PLATE

Go for the Corsican sheep cheese called Brindamour (also called Fleur du Maquis); an Italian Pecorino such as Rossillino and Corsignano; Azeitao or the custardy Serpa from Portugal; Spain's Roncal (Navarre) or Idiazábal (Pais Vasco—Basque region); and a French Basque Pyrenees sheep cheese such as Moulis, Ossau-Iraty, Erhaki, Prince de Claverolles, or Etorki.

Steve wants us to accompany these with both savories and sweets—a bitter Catalan honey, chunked chorizo sausage, and a cranberry-walnut bread. Pour a rough red, like a Rhône or a Syrah.

Fresh Ricotta Tart

Serves 8 to 10 | *1 hour 20 minutes prep time; 1½ hours oven time* | *Best served slightly warm or at room temperature, dusted with powdered sugar and set on a pool of puréed fruit*

Look to this tart when you need a quiet repose after a meal of bossy and domineering flavors. The tender, cookie-look crust holds together a lemon-perfumed ricotta custard that trembles as you put fork to mouth.

PASTRY

1 cup unbleached **all-purpose flour**, dipped and leveled (see page 304)

½ cup **cake flour**, dipped and leveled (see page 304)

3 tablespoons **sugar**

¼ teaspoon **salt**

1 stick (4 ounces) cold **unsalted butter**, cut into chunks

1 large **egg**, beaten

FILLING

1 pound 5 ounces **Homemade Ricotta** (page 119), or good-quality store-bought ricotta (2¼ cups)

½ cup **sugar**

Grated zest of 1 large **lemon**

5 large **egg yolks**

Pinch of **salt**

⅔ cup **heavy cream**, whipped

{ **COOK** *to* **Cook** }

This recipe calls for a 9 x 3-inch false-bottom quiche pan. If not available, you could substitute a 10-inch metal pie plate or an 11-inch standard tart pan and adjust the baking time as needed.

This piecrust and other sweet ones make very good sugar cookies as well.

1. Make the pastry: In a food processor, blend the all-purpose flour, cake flour, sugar, and salt, then pulse in the butter until the mixture looks like coarse meal. Add the egg and pulse only until the dough barely gathers together. Wrap and chill for 30 minutes to 2 days.

2. Prebake the tart shell: Preheat the oven to 400°F. and place the rack in the center of the oven. Grease a 9 × 3-inch false-bottom quiche pan. Roll out the crust to about ⅛ inch thick. Fit it into the pan, fluting the top edge of the crust. Chill the crust for 30 minutes, then line it with foil and weights. Bake for 10 minutes. Carefully remove the foil liner and bake for 5 minutes. Remove the crust from the oven and cool completely on a rack.

3. Make the filling: Reduce the heat to 300°F. In a large bowl, blend the ricotta, sugar, lemon zest, egg yolks, and salt. Gently fold in the whipped cream. Pour the filling into the prebaked tart crust. Bake it for 75 minutes, or until the filling firms and a knife inserted about 2 inches from the tart's edge comes out clean. Cool the tart on a rack and serve at room temperature.

As for butter versus margarine, I trust cows more than chemists.

—JOAN GUSSOW

Venetian Iced Raspberry Cream

| *Serves 6 to 8* | *45 minutes prep time; 8 hours to 2 months freezer time* | *Transfer the cream from the freezer to the refrigerator 2 hours before serving.* |

Blurring the lines between ice cream and mousse, simplicity and finesse, nostalgia and novelty, this is the kind of dessert that's hard to categorize but easy to love. Billows of softly whipped cream and meringue give it loft. Raspberries, puréed and whole, give it rosy tang. Brandy, black pepper, and a puréed whole vanilla bean—tricks from a Venetian cook—give it depth and brawn. This dessert needs a commitment, though once it's safely stashed in the freezer you can forget about it completely for up to 2 months.

Any fruit can stand in for the raspberries, and do play with the presentation. Try freezing this in a ring mold, lining the bottom with the extra berries so they glisten like a crown of rubies when turned out.

You will need a candy thermometer and a stand mixer—or if using a handheld mixer, another pair of hands.

The key here is the Italian meringue, a mixture of beaten egg whites cooked with hot sugar syrup (think airy, whipped marshmallows) that gives frozen desserts exceptional texture and stability. It's a little fussy but not difficult; just follow the instructions carefully and you'll be home free.

BERRIES

5½ cups fresh **raspberries**
7 tablespoons **sugar**, plus more to taste
1 plump **vanilla bean**, split lengthwise and cut into ½-inch lengths
Generous pinch of **salt**
¼ teaspoon freshly ground **black pepper**
2 teaspoons **rum** or **brandy**

(recipe continues)

ITALIAN MERINGUE

4 large **egg whites**, at room temperature
½ teaspoon **cream of tartar**
Generous pinch of **salt**
1⅓ cups **sugar**
2 tablespoons **light corn syrup**
1 cup cold **heavy cream**, whipped and chilled

GARNISH

2 cups fresh **raspberries**

1. Prepare the berries: In a medium bowl, toss 1 cup of the berries with
2 tablespoons of the sugar and set aside. Purée the remaining 4½ cups berries in
a food processor along with the remaining 5 tablespoons sugar and the vanilla
bean, salt, pepper, and rum. The vanilla bean should nearly disappear into the
purée. Taste for sugar, adding more if necessary. You want to taste the tang of the
berries, so don't oversweeten.

2. Pass the berry purée through a fine strainer to get rid of seeds and bits of
bean. Cover and chill.

3. Make the Italian meringue: Put the egg whites, cream of tartar, and salt in
the large bowl of a stand mixer, or, if using a handheld electric beater, put them in
a deep heatproof large bowl and have someone operate the beater. Put the sugar
and corn syrup and ¼ cup water in a small saucepan. Stir to blend. Attach a candy
thermometer to the side of the pan and set over medium-high heat. Do not stir
again as you bring the mix to a boil, and keep boiling it until the syrup reaches
245°F. (Check the temperature by carefully tipping the pan so the end of the
thermometer is immersed in syrup.) Occasionally wash down the sides of the pan
with a pastry brush dipped in cold water. Immediately turn the mixer to high
speed and start beating the egg whites.

4. The thermometer will hover around 245°F. for a few moments, and then it
will go up to 248°F. to 250°F. The beating whites should be near firm peaks.
Immediately pull the syrup from the stove, detaching the thermometer. Stand
back while you pour the hot syrup down the side of the bowl of the beating whites.
Keep beating at high speed for 4 minutes, then reduce the speed to medium and
beat for 5 minutes, or until the whites are at room temperature.

5. Assemble the dessert: With a big spatula, fold the berry purée and whipped cream into the whites until blended but still puffy and light. Pour half of the mixture into a 3-quart glass serving bowl. Cover with the reserved cup of sugared berries and their juices. Spread the remaining meringue mixture over the berries, cover, and freeze for at least 8 hours.

6. To serve, thaw the meringue in the refrigerator 2 hours before serving. Just before serving, scatter the fresh berries over the top. Spoon the cream into martini or coupe glasses or small bowls.

I am not interested in dishes that take three minutes and have no cholesterol.

—JULIA CHILD

Triple Chocolate Brownie Cake

| *Makes one 8-inch cake; serves 6 to 8* | *30 minutes prep time; 35 minutes oven time; 15 minutes cooling time* | *The cake keeps beautifully for 3 days, and in fact gets better as it sits.* |

Usually danger lurks in improvising cake recipes. Most cakes succeed because they're intricately calibrated mathematical formulas that don't invite fooling around, except in the case of the brownie—which is more pudding than cake, meaning it can take on nearly anything you want to try. This version is three chocolates (really a fourth if you count the cocoa nibs), spices, coffee, and a topping of coarse salt. Why not?

Unsalted butter
6 ounces **bittersweet** (about 70% cocoa solids) **chocolate** (Valrhona, Vosges, or Lindt Excellence)
2 ounces **unsweetened chocolate**
1 stick (4 ounces) **unsalted butter**, plus more for the pan
3 tablespoons **instant espresso** dissolved in 4 tablespoons boiling water
1 tablespoon **vanilla extract**
2 teaspoons ground **cinnamon**
2 teaspoons ground **allspice**
4 large **eggs**
1⅓ cups **sugar**
¼ cup **unsweetened cocoa powder**, sifted
¼ teaspoon **salt**
½ cup **cocoa nibs** or **toasted blanched whole almonds**, coarsely chopped
¼ cup unbleached **all-purpose flour**, dipped and leveled (see page 304)
2 teaspoons **coarse salt**
1 cup **heavy cream**, whipped (optional)

1. Preheat the oven to 375°F. Butter the bottom and sides of a shiny 8-inch springform pan and butter the

Cocoa nibs are the broken pieces of cocoa bean that remain after beans are roasted and crushed. They are crunchy and taste of bitter chocolate. Add them to cookies, cakes, scones, and savory sauces.

An 8-inch square pan can be used here instead of a round one, but the cake will need about 5 minutes additional baking time. And you want a shiny cake pan; a dark one changes cooking times and sometimes baking temperatures.

top of an 8-inch round of parchment paper and place it in the bottom of the pan.

2. Melt the chocolate: In a medium microwave-safe bowl, melt the bittersweet and unsweetened chocolates and the butter in the microwave at medium-low power for 2 to 3 minutes, or in a small stainless steel bowl set over a small saucepan of simmering water. Stir in the coffee, vanilla, cinnamon, and allspice and cool to room temperature.

3. Make the cake: In a large mixing bowl, whisk the eggs, sugar, cocoa powder, and salt until creamy. Stir in the cocoa nibs and flour and the melted chocolate mixture until smooth. Don't beat; just stir until everything is blended. Pour the batter into the pan and sprinkle with the coarse salt. Bake for 35 minutes, or until a knife inserted in the center comes out with a few streaks.

4. Cool on a cake rack for 15 minutes, then release the sides of the springform pan and set the cake on a cake plate. Cut the cake into small slivers and serve on its own or with a dollop of whipped cream.

WINE The ultimate wine for this chocolate cake is Banyuls, a relatively obscure but utterly delicious red dessert wine from the Mediterranean coast of France. But don't fret if you can't land one, as an aged tawny port from Portugal will be easy to find and nearly as delightful.

Decaffeinated coffee is kind of like kissing your sister.

—BOB IRWIN

Butternut "Pumpkin" Pie

Serves 10 to 12 | *45 minutes prep time; 1 hour chilling time for the pastry; 2½ hours oven time* | *Pies peak on their first day out of the oven, but this prebaked crust and roasted squash can easily wait 24 hours. Bake the pie hours before serving so it can cool.*

The touchstone for our Thanksgivings, this recipe has crossed oceans and crisscrossed the country, traveling with us wherever we've lived. We nixed pumpkin long ago in favor of butternut squash for its brighter flavor. The heartily spiced squash custard keeps evolving with our changing tastes. The latest touch is vanilla to point up the caramel edge of roasted squash. Black pepper entered the pie several years ago because it's so good with cinnamon and allspice.

PASTRY

Unsalted butter
1 recipe **pie pastry** (crust from Fresh Ricotta Tart, page 310)

FILLING

Olive oil
2 small to medium **butternut squash**, halved lengthwise and seeded
¾ cup **sugar**, or to taste
Generous ¼ teaspoon **salt**
Generous ½ teaspoon ground **ginger**
1½ teaspoons ground **cinnamon**
⅛ to ¼ teaspoon ground **cloves**
½ to 1 teaspoon ground **allspice**
1 tablespoon **vanilla extract**
⅛ teaspoon **black pepper**
½ cup **sour cream** (not low-fat)
½ cup **milk**
3 large **eggs**, beaten
1 cup **heavy cream**, whipped

{ COOK *to* Cook }

Adding eggs to a pie filling as the last ingredient allows you to taste the filling for flavor and balance with no danger of eating raw eggs.

There will be about a cup of extra filling that you can bake in a ramekin along with the pie. The squash can be roasted up to 2 days in advance.

1. Assemble the crust: Butter the inside and rim of a 10-inch shiny metal pie plate. Make the pie pastry, wrap, and chill for 30 minutes or up to 2 days. Roll it out to ⅛ inch thick and fit it into the pie plate. Leave a 1-inch overhang. Tuck that under so you have a standing border on the rim of the plate. Flute with your fingers and chill for 1 to 24 hours.

2. Prebake the crust: Preheat the oven to 400°F. Prebake the crust by lining it with foil, weight it with dried beans or rice, and bake for 10 minutes, or until firm. Carefully tease away the foil and weights, pierce the crust with a fork in several places, and bake for another 5 minutes, or until golden. Cool and keep at room temperature for up to 24 hours.

3. Roast the squash: Preheat the oven to 400°F. Oil a large cookie sheet. Arrange the squash pieces on the sheet flesh side down. Bake them for 1 hour, or until a knife slips easily into the thickest part of the squash. They should be extremely tender. Cool, then scoop out the squash and purée it completely in a food processor. You should end up with 3½ to 3¾ cups of purée.

4. Make the filling: Preheat the oven to 400°F. In a large bowl, whisk the squash purée, sugar, salt, ginger, cinnamon, cloves, allspice, vanilla, pepper, sour cream, and milk. Taste for sweetness and spiciness, adding more sugar and/or spices if needed. Then blend in the eggs completely.

5. Pour the filling into the baked pie shell. Set the shell on a cookie sheet to catch any spills. Bake for 15 minutes, then reduce the heat to 325°F. Bake for another 45 minutes to 1 hour, or until a knife inserted 1 inch or more in from the edge comes out nearly clean (the center will still be soft). Cool the pie on a rack. Chill if you are holding it more than a couple of hours. Serve the pie at room temperature and either top it with the whipped cream or just pass the cream at the table.

FALLEN Fruit

Fallen Fruit is one of the most inspiring artistic collaborations we've come across. This group of Los Angeles artists looks at how we humans relate to our public spaces. In the process they started mapping fruit trees growing on or over public spaces in Los Angeles— free food literally waiting to be gathered. It's turned into a fruit-advocacy group linking people and neighborhoods together with fallen-fruit harvests. At the same time the artists encourage people to plant trees and vegetables at the edges of their properties so passersby can share them. The maps and ideas are spreading to other cities. The takeaway here could run from "now you know what to do with those extra tomato plants" to walking your town with a new purpose.

Ginger Syrup for All Seasons

Makes 1¾ cups;	*5 minutes prep time;*	*Keeps refrigerated, covered, up to 3 months.*
doubles easily	*5 minutes stove time*	*Pear wedges warmed in the syrup become a*
		light dessert with an appealing edge of spice.

There is not much this syrup wouldn't improve. Fragrant with ginger, it's exquisite poured over fresh fruit, or used to steep dried apricots for a compote, or brushed over grilled chicken or yams, or mixed with seltzer or iced tea for a cool summer drink, or . . . you get the idea.

2 cups **sugar**
Generous ½ cup peeled, coarsely chopped fresh
   ginger
¼ teaspoon **salt**

1. Combine 1 cup water and the sugar, ginger, and salt in a 1½-quart saucepan set over medium-high heat. Bring the mixture to a boil, reduce the heat, and continue cooking for about 5 minutes, or until the syrup is slightly thickened. Do not stir, but do brush down the sides of the pan once or twice with a heatproof brush dipped in cold water.

2. Remove from the heat and let the ginger steep. The longer you let it steep, the more bite the syrup will have. After 45 minutes, taste the syrup and strain when it is to your taste. Store in a covered jar in the refrigerator.

Please remember, melted sugar is *hot*! So keep kids away and do not taste until completely cooled. This is not something to make while wearing flip-flops.

Frozen Lemon Soufflé with Candied Lemon Peel

Serves 8 to 10

1½ hours prep time; 1½ hours cooling time for the almond brittle; 12 hours freezer time

Prepare this dessert up to 2 months ahead. Serve frozen or partially defrosted in the refrigerator for 1 hour, but no longer. The components can be made a day ahead. Once the Italian meringue is finished, you need to fold everything together right away.

A lightbulb went off with the idea that this soufflé should be in the book when at a party everyone had not two, but three helpings. Billowy, creamy, and packed with lemon, this is one outrageously luxurious dessert. Though somewhat complicated to make, all frozen soufflés and mousses break down into three parts: the flavorings, the whipped cream, and the Italian or cooked meringue. It's a basic formula we can riff on without limit.

You will need a candy thermometer and a stand mixer—or, if using a handheld mixer, another pair of hands.

ALMOND BRITTLE

Canola oil
3 cups **sugar**
2 cups **roasted salted whole almonds**

LEMON PURÉE

Pulp of 5 medium **lemons**, trimmed of white pith and seeded (grate their zest first)
2 tablespoons **sugar**

{ **COOK** *to* **Cook** }

In this soufflé, there's an extra, a favorite French trick for frozen dessert: praline, which is essentially ground-up nut brittle. It's easy to make, and having a stash of the brittle around gives you instant house gifts, a good adjunct to a cup of strong coffee, and that crunch and sweet you crave around 10:00 p.m.

WHIPPED CREAM

2 cups very cold **heavy cream**

2 teaspoons **vanilla extract**

ITALIAN MERINGUE

6 large **egg whites**, at room temperature

1 teaspoon **cream of tartar**

Pinch of **salt**

2 cups **sugar**

2 tablespoons **light corn syrup**

Grated zest of 3 medium **lemons**

½ cup **Candied Lemon Peel** (page 102), all but
2 tablespoons cut into ¼-inch bits

WINE Fresh, light, and strikingly flavorful, this frozen soufflé calls for a wine of the same description. Nothing fits the bill like Moscato d'Asti, which is low in alcohol but full of fruity, foamy flavors that match this dessert beautifully.

1. Make the almond brittle: Spread a sheet of foil over a cookie sheet or large shallow pan and oil.

2. Combine the sugar and ¾ cup water in a heavy 4-quart saucepan. Have a heatproof brush and a cup of water handy. Cook the syrup over medium-high heat for 1 to 2 minutes, or until it is clear. Brush down the sides of the saucepan with the water as the syrup cooks; do not stir it. Boil the syrup for another minute, or until it is a rich golden brown.

3. Immediately remove the pan from the heat, stir in the almonds, and pour the mixture onto the oiled foil, spreading it into a single layer with a wooden spatula. Do not touch it.

4. Let the brittle sit for 90 minutes or even overnight until it is completely cool and hard. Break it up and grind it to a coarse powder in a food processor. Store the brittle in an airtight container for up to 1 week, or freeze it.

5. Make the lemon purée: In a blender or food processor, combine the lemon pulp and sugar; purée. Set aside. If making it ahead, cover and refrigerate for up to 3 days.

6. Whip the cream with the vanilla until soft peaks form. Chill.

7. Make the Italian meringue: Put the egg whites, cream of tartar, and salt in the large bowl of a stand mixer, or, if using a handheld electric beater, put them in a deep heatproof large bowl and have someone operate the beater. Put the sugar and corn syrup and ⅓ cup water in a 3-cup saucepan. Stir to blend. Attach a candy thermometer to the side of the pan and set over medium-high heat. Do not

(recipe continues)

stir again as you bring the mix to a boil, and keep boiling it until the syrup reaches 245°F. (Check the temperature by carefully tipping the pan so the end of the thermometer is immersed in syrup.) Occasionally wash down the sides of the pan with a pastry brush dipped in cold water. Immediately turn the mixer to high speed and start beating the egg whites.

8. The thermometer will hover around 245°F. for a few moments, and then it will go up to 248°F. to 250°F. The beating whites should be near firm peaks. Immediately pull the syrup from the stove, detaching the thermometer. Stand back while you pour the hot syrup down the side of the bowl of the beating whites. Keep beating at high speed for 4 minutes, then reduce the speed to medium and beat for 5 minutes, or until the whites are at room temperature. Fold in the lemon zest.

9. **Assemble the soufflé:** Have a 10-cup serving bowl handy. Scoop about 3 cups of the meringue into a very large mixing bowl along with the lemon purée. With a large plastic spatula, fold gently until blended. Fold in the remaining meringue, keeping it light and airy.

10. Fold in the whipped cream along with the cut-up candied lemon peel until only a very few streaks of white remain.

11. Transfer half of the mixture to the serving bowl. Top with ½ cup of the ground almond brittle, then the remaining half of the soufflé mixture. Top with another ½ cup brittle. Scatter the remaining pieces of candied peel over the soufflé. Cover the bowl and freeze until solid, a minimum of 12 hours.

12. Serve the soufflé frozen or partially defrosted and scooped into wineglasses.

Lord, fill my mouth with worthwhile stuff, and nudge me when I've said enough.

—ANONYMOUS

Acknowledgments

People sometimes say to us, "I don't know how you do this." Well, this is how. We get a lot of support from friends, colleagues, and families. We offer heartfelt thanks to the following, most of whom simply held their tongues when we swore that never again would we take on another book after surviving the first. We know it's no surprise to you that we are here again. Thanks for not gloating.

The World Champion Tongue Holders—Jennifer Luebke and Jennifer Russell—our partners of fifteen-plus years. It is the two of them who keep the heart of the program strong and vibrant and meet that deadline every single week, despite the chaos we keep throwing their way. We couldn't do it without you. Really. A special thanks to our original co-creator of the show, Tom Voegeli, without whom this ship would never have sailed. Judy Budreau and Brett Baldwin have helped put out fires and maintain our public face, on the Web and in the world at large. Judy Graham, who not only writes and edits our weekly newsletter, *Weeknight Kitchen*, but is a world-class editor in her own right. Thank you for the care you put into these pages, always with tight deadlines looming. Thanks, too, to our tester, Lynn Kelly, for her exacting work and endless patience as new ideas kept adding to the test lists.

Thanks to American Public Media for being real partners and continuing to believe in and fight for excellent radio, and to our many colleagues who support and feed us in ways they may never know: Mark Alfuth, Justin Barrett, Peter Clowney, Norma Cox, Dave Eden, Sheri Ettinger, Mitzi Gramling, Chris Heagle, Nick Kereokas, Chris Kohtz, Tricia Kostichka, Mary Pat Ladner, Jon McTaggart, Kate Moos, Bryan Munsell, John Nicholson, Twyla Olson, Rachel Riensche, Tim Roesler, John Ryan, Steven Smith, and Dave Sonderegger, and especially to Judy McAlpine, who never fails to remind us to ask for help.

We have endless appreciation for our friends at Clarkson Potter. Our editor, Emily Takoudes, helped us wrap our arms around this at times unwieldy book. This book would not be what it is without Emily, and without the skills of Peggy Paul, Doris Cooper, Jane Treuhaft, and Marysarah Quinn.

Thanks to Donna Passannante and Kate Tyler for their marketing and publicity finesse.

Thanks to Melissa Kronenthal, who streamlined this very cumbrous process with her sharp eyes, curious mind, and capable pen, and a message to our agent, Jane Dystel. We are happy you are on our side.

Thanks to Wayne Wolf of Blue Cup Creative—you are our treasure.

The beautiful photos in this book were captured by the graceful and talented Ellen Silverman and styled by Susie Theodorou with help from Rebecca Jurkevich and Rachel Fiedler. Thanks, too, to cover stylists Cyd McDowell and Paige Hicks. The author photos are by Ann Marsden, and thanks to Tom and Kathy Awe for the use of their lovely kitchen.

To our radio family, who make our work so joyful and frankly, easy: Jane and Michael Stern, Joshua Wesson, Melissa Clark, Steve Jenkins, Sally Schneider, Dorie Greenspan, Ray Isle, Francis Lam, John T. Edge, and John Willoughby. Thank you.

From Lynne: Truth be known, I built a career on one man's palate. His name is Frank Kasper and I've been lucky enough to eat, play, cook, and adventure with him for lo these many years. This book and so much more wouldn't have happened without him. To Judy Budreau, my assistant who readily took on extra work, and to the singular Judy Graham, who's been through three books now and still speaks to me and never fails to pitch in, my immense thanks. Special appreciation to Jeannine Myrvik for her support. Endless thanks to the dear friends who resisted saying "I told you so" when I had to have driven them nuts—Nan Bailey and Sam Hazlett, Marjorie Cater, Cara De Silva, Susan Erlich, Les and Eileen Meltzer, Bonnie and Al Porte, and Alice Sperling. And special gratitude to Tim and Ann Paradise, great cooks, generous souls, and our neighbors, who are always there with an open door, a plate of pasta, and a glass of wine. Finally, thanks to Sally Swift, gifted friend and partner in crime.

From Sally: My love and devotion, as always, to Patty Waters, Julie Hartley, Marie Dwyer, Kathleen Day-Coen, Dorothy Deetz, Tod Dresher, Karl Benson, Rick Nelson, Robert Davidian, Tom Adair, Stacia Rivers, Nanine Swift, Hans Sohlen, Sherry Guenther, and Susette Swift. My sturdy stable. I am forever grateful.

Washington, D.C., is now my home, and all the more so thanks to Pati Jinich and Michaele Weissman. Thank you for your generous spirits and wicked senses of humor. You've made me feel right at home. When I met my husband, Michael Franz, he told me quite charmingly and clearly that he had really good luck and if I stuck with him it would rub off on me, too. It worked—almost instantly—because not only did I get my love with my move to D.C., I inherited Rick Boothby, Rebecca Nichols, Paul Lukacs, and Marguerite "Velvet" Thomas in one fell swoop. How lucky is that? Thanks to Joe Yonan, Joan Nathan, Domenica Marchetti, and Dalya Luttwak for making me feel a little less at sea here as well. Henry . . . you are dearly missed.

I am most grateful of all for my singular friend Lynne Rossetto Kasper, the first person you want to invite to your party.

Index

Chicken
    chicken rice noodle soup, 44
    in Chinese master sauce,
        183–86
    cider-glazed, 189–91
    meatballs, sweet-sour, with
        candied lemon peel, 206–7
    pine-smoked, 193–94
    Sichuan chicken salad, 191
    in tart and savory rice, 191
    tomatillo chicken, 53
    wings, mahogany glazed,
        48–49
Chicken broths. *See* Broth
Chile(s)
    ancho cider-glazed hens,
        198–99
    brown sugar–chile flank
        steak, 252–53
    brown sugar–chile roast
        lamb, 244
    charred ginger-chile corn,
        286
    charred ginger-chile corn
        pudding, 163
    chile-spiked Mexican
        wedding cakes, 302–3
    farmer's market pasta,
        113–14
    lemon ice cream with, 293
    and lime, jicama and mango
        sticks in, 40
    roasted chile-coconut
        dressing, pineapple,
        greens, and tofu with,
        97–98
Chinese broccoli and garlic
    pork long-life noodles,
    126–27
Chinese celebration, 26–29
Chinese chicken and pork
    master broth, 61
Chinese hot and sour soup,
    68–69
Chinese master sauce, chicken
    in, 183–86
Chinese mushrooms, ginger
    shrimp stir-fry with snow
    peas, baby corn, and,
    209–11
Chocolate
    iced fudge lollies, 294
    triple chocolate brownie
        cake, 316–17

Cider
    ancho cider-glazed hens,
        198–99
    cider-glazed chicken, 189–91
Cinnamon pastry, 171
    golden pie of winter
        vegetables in, 168–71
Cinnamon-pomegranate
    tabbouleh, 104–5
Clark, Melissa, 179
Cochinita pibil, 223–26
Coconut-roasted chile
    dressing, pineapple,
    greens, and tofu with,
    97–98
Collards, timbale of sweet
    peppers, hominy, and,
    172–75
Cookies: chile-spiked Mexican
    wedding cakes, 302–3
Coriander oil, warmed, orange
    onion salad with, 77
Corn. *See also* Hominy
    baby, ginger shrimp stir-fry
        with snow peas, Chinese
        mushrooms, and, 209–11
    barley risotto with saffron,
        chives, and, 108–9
    charred ginger-chile corn,
        286
    charred ginger-chile corn
        pudding, 163
    slow rolled sweet corn in
        master sauce, 186
Cornbread
    butter-roasted, 136
    herb and garlic, 135–36
    pudding, with rough country
        greens, 134–38
Cornish game hens, ancho
    cider-glazed, 198–99
Croutons, fennel-herbed, 88
Cucumber(s)
    and melon salad, with mint,
        80–81
    yogurt raita, 250
Curried mussels, Karl's,
    213–14
Curry, sweet yam-tamarind,
    with basil and lime,
    165–67

Desserts. *See* Cake; Sweets;
    Tart

Dumplings, scallop–smoked
    salmon, Scandinavian
    broth with, 65–66

Egg pasta, hand-rolled,
    148–49
Eggplant: moussaka of lamb
    and red wine ragù, 153–56
Eggs, 161
    creamy scrambled, with
        tomatillo salsa, 53
    farmer's market pasta
        omelet, 114
    the 65° egg, 89; grilled
        lettuces with pine nut-
        Parmigiano cream and,
        86–87
    summer tomato pudding,
        161–63
El Cardenal, 52

Farmer's market pasta, 113–14
Farmhouse roasted potatoes,
    272–73
Fennel-herbed croutons, 88
Feta-stuffed phyllo torte,
    crispy, 179–80
Fish, 219. *See also* Salmon
    caramelized catfish sand
    pot, 141–43
Five-nut caramel tart, 305–7
Flank steak, brown sugar–
    chile, 252–53
French radish sauté, 270
Fresh pasta, Tim's, 124–25
Fudge lollies, iced, 294

Garlic
    buttermilk-garlic slaw with
        smoky paprika, 78–79
    crisp roast turkey with
        apple, basil, and, 200–204
    flash-sautéed squid with
        peppers and, 216–17
    garlic-oregano pickled
        onions, 225
    and herb cornbread, 135–36
    pintos and red wine soup
        with twenty cloves of, 72–73
Ginger
    charred ginger-chile corn,
        286
    charred ginger-chile corn
        pudding, 163

Seafood, 208–20. *See also*
   Salmon; Shrimp
   caramelized catfish sand
      pot, 141–43
   flash-sautéed squid with
      peppers and garlic,
      216–17
   Karl's curried mussels,
      213–14
Shallot-thyme green beans,
   277
Sherry dressing, warmed,
   smoked trout and
   watercress salad with,
   90–91
Shrimp
   ginger shrimp stir-fry with
      snow peas, Chinese
      mushrooms, and baby
      corn, 209–11
   rice paper rolls of herbs and,
      42–44
   tomatillo shrimp, 53
Sichuan chicken salad, 191
Sichuan dipping sauce, 185
Sichuan-inspired pickled
   vegetables, 55
Sichuan pepper and salt,
   roasted, 186
Sides, 269–89
   recipe list, 269
Slaw, buttermilk-garlic, with
   smoky paprika, 78–79
Smoked salmon. *See* Salmon
Smoked trout and watercress
   salad with warmed sherry
   dressing, 90–91
Smoke-roasted salmon,
   219–20
Snow peas, ginger shrimp
   stir-fry with Chinese
   mushrooms, baby corn,
   and, 209–11
Soufflé, frozen lemon, with
   candied lemon peel, 322–24
Soup(s), 57–75. *See also* Broth
   chicken rice noodle, 44
   Chinese hot and sour, 68–69
   Moroccan harira red lentil,
      70–71
   New England autumn, 59
   pintos and red wine, with
      twenty cloves of garlic,
      72–73

sweet yam-tamarind, with
   noodles and tofu, 167
tomato-melon, high summer,
   74–75
winter Sunday, 60
Spanish paprika, 177, 240
   buttermilk-garlic slaw with,
      78–79
   smoked romesco sauce,
      238–39
   tart Spanish broth, 60
Spiced pork, Malaysian,
   230–31
Spices, 227, 278
   biriyani spice blend, 249
   Moroccan, leg of lamb with
      honey and, 241–44
   West Indies spice blend, 175
Spring rolls
   rice paper rolls of herbs and
      shrimp, 42–44
   supper spring rolls with
      roasted chile dressing, 98
Squid, flash-sautéed, with
   peppers and garlic, 216–17
Starters, snacks, and small
   plates, 39–55
   recipe list, 39
Steak. *See* Beef
Stew, beef, 254–55
   quintessential, 256–59
Stir-fry, ginger shrimp, with
   snow peas, Chinese
   mushrooms, and baby
   corn, 209–11
Summer tomato pudding,
   161–63
Sweets, 291–324. *See also*
   Cake; Tart
   bread and butter jam
      pudding, 163
   butternut "pumpkin" pie,
      318–19
   chile-spiked Mexican
      wedding cakes, 302–3
   frozen lemon soufflé with
      candied lemon peel,
      322–24
   ginger syrup, 321
   iced fudge lollies, 294
   stirred old-fashioned lemon
      ice cream, 292–93
   Venetian iced raspberry
      cream, 313–15

Sweet-sour chicken meatballs
   with candied lemon peel,
   206–7
Syrup
   ginger, 321
   vinegar syrups, 103, 188

Tabbouleh, pomegranate-
   cinnamon, 104–5
Tamarind-sweet yam curry
   with basil and lime,
   165–67
Tart
   five-nut caramel, 305–7
   fresh ricotta, 310–11
Thanksgiving menus, 34–37
This, Hervé, 89
Thyme-shallot green beans,
   277
Timbale of sweet peppers,
   greens, and hominy, 172–75
Tofu
   sweet yam-tamarind soup
      with noodles and, 167
   tofu, pineapple, and greens
      with roasted chile-coconut
      dressing, 97–98
Tomatillo(s)
   salsa, with fresh cheese,
      52–53
   tortilla-tomatillo broth, 59
Tomato(es), 84
   high summer tomato-melon
      soup, 74–75
   midnight pasta with
      prosciutto, 110–11
   oven-roasted or broiled, 84
   and roasted peppers salad,
      83
   saffron tomato sauce, ricotta
      gnocchi with, 117–20
   smoked romesco sauce,
      238–39
   summer tomato pudding,
      161–63
   timbale of sweet peppers,
      greens, and hominy,
      172–75
Tortilla-tomatillo broth, 59
Triple chocolate brownie cake,
   316–17
Trout, smoked, and watercress
   salad with warmed sherry
   dressing, 90–91

Turkey
crisp roast, with garlic, apple and basil, 200–204
master broth, 58–60

Valenti, Tom, 284
Vegan Thanksgiving, 36–37
Vegetarian and vegan main dishes, 159–80
crispy feta-stuffed phyllo torte, 179–80
golden pie of winter vegetables in cinnamon pastry, 168–71
summer tomato pudding, 161–63
sweet yam-tamarind curry with basil and lime, 165–67
timbale of sweet peppers, greens, and hominy, 172–75
Venetian iced raspberry cream, 313–15

Viedstadt, Andreas, 232
Vietnamese green mango noodle salad with grilled pork, 128–30
Vietnamese Sunday lunch, 12–17
Vinegar, 188–89
balsamic syrup, 103

Walnut(s)
walnut-mortadella green beans, 277
and wild mushroom pâté, 50–51
Watercress and smoked trout salad with warmed sherry dressing, 90–91
Watermelon. *See also* Melon
watermelon water, 229
Wedding lamb biriyani, 245–50
West Indies green beans, 276–77
West Indies spice blend, 175

Wild mushroom and walnut pâté, 50–51
Winter holiday dinner, 32–33
Winter vegetables. *See also specific types*
gingered purée of winter roots, 274
golden pie of, in cinnamon pastry, 168–71
roasted grapes and, 282
winter Sunday soup, 60

Yams. *See also* Winter vegetables
yam-tamarind curry with basil and lime, 165–67
Yogurt raita, 250
Young, Grace, 93
Yu, Su-Mei, 97
Yucatán pork in banana leaves, 223–26

Zucchini, farmer's market pasta with, 113–14

If you aren't up for
a little magic now
and then, you
shouldn't waste your
time cooking.

—COLETTE